SCHUBERT
The Final Years

Gmunden, where Schubert spent several weeks in June, 1825

SCHUBERT
THE FINAL YEARS

by

John Reed

St. Martin's Press
New York

Copyright © 1972 by John Reed
All rights reserved
For information, write:
St. Martin's Press Inc., 175 Fifth Ave., New York,
N. Y. 10010
Printed in Great Britain
Library of Congress Catalog Card Number: 72–85509
First published in the United States of America in 1972

AFFILIATED PUBLISHERS: Macmillan & Company,
Limited, London - also at Bombay, Calcutta, Madras
and Melbourne - The Macmillan Company of Canada,
Limited, Toronto

For Jane and Kate,
who played their part

CONTENTS

⌘

ILLUSTRATIONS

❦

PREFACE

What is there new to be said about Schubert? To answer that question, and to relate it circumstantially to what this book attempts to do, I have to go back to the early months of the year 1959, shortly after the publication of O. E. Deutsch's *Schubert: Memoirs by his Friends*. Turning the pages of this fascinating, if somewhat curiously arranged, collection of Schubertiana, my attention was caught by a passage from Leopold von Sonnleithner's letter of 1858 to Luib. 'His great symphony he composed (uninvited) for the *Gesellschaft der Musikfreunde*, to whom he presented the autograph. He received a gift of a hundred florins for it, which was very welcome to him.' I had been interesting myself for some time in the supposedly missing symphony written at Gmunden and Gastein in 1825. I knew that Sonnleithner had been an official of the Vienna Music Society in Schubert's day, so he was not likely to be wrong thirty years after the event. I knew also that the financial transaction referred to took place, without a shadow of doubt, in October 1826, for it is fully documented. I was also convinced that the symphony referred to could only be the Great C Major. Only three of the symphonies had by then been performed in public, the Great C Major, the 'little' C major of 1818, and number five in B flat; and the two last seemed to be expressly excluded by the phrase 'his great symphony'. Besides, the Great was the only symphony then in print, and that only because of Schumann's and Mendelssohn's enthusiastic sponsorship twenty years earlier. The statement admitted only one interpretation. It meant that the symphony written in 1825 and presented to the Music Society in 1826 was the Great C Major. The more I thought about it the clearer the case became.

Impressed by the importance of this discovery, which seemed to put the story of Schubert's development in a quite different perspective, I made a thorough review of the evidence for the missing symphony of 1825, only to discover that there was none! There was plenty of evidence, certainly, that a symphony was begun at Gmunden in 1825, but none that it had disappeared. It was taken for granted, by all contemporary writers, that the 1825 work and the Great C Major were identical. The link between the two had already been remarked upon, notably by Maurice J. E. Brown in his *Critical Biography*; but the evidence seemed to me to justify the firm conclusion that there is only one symphony of Schubert's mature years, and that it is not a work of 1828 at all, but the 1825 work revised and updated. This version of events I set out in some detail in an article in *Music and Letters* for October 1959. It solved at least one critical problem, how to fit into the last six months of the composer's life, already overcrowded with major works, a symphony on the grandest scale and, after an interval, a full-scale revision of the same. It threw light also on an otherwise insoluble stylistic problem; on the difficulty of explaining how an exuberantly dynamic and optimistic work like the symphony came to be written cheek-by-jowl, so to speak, with works like the string quintet and the last piano sonatas, which seem to belong to a quite different, more reflective and sophisticated, emotional world. But the implications to my mind were even more far-reaching. If Sonnleithner's statement meant what it said, it called for a re-assessment of Schubert's development as man and artist during the last years of his life; and since nobody

else seemed disposed to take the matter sufficiently seriously
to make such a re-assessment, I have felt obliged to
attempt it myself. Perhaps because this is after all an
old controversy re-opened; perhaps because our notion
of Schubert's development is so shadowy anyway that not
even the re-dating of his most ambitious orchestral work is
felt to alter matters much; whatever the reason, there seemed
to be a fairly general disposition to believe that it did not
make much difference whether the Great C Major was written in 1825 or 1828. True, my article did appear in translation, through the good offices of the late Gerard Mackworth
Young, in the pages of the *Gasteiner Badeblatt*, but this doubtless owed something to local loyalty. More influential critical
journals survived the shock of its appearance with no trouble
at all. Programme notes continued to describe the Great C
Major as 'begun in March 1828' just as before. And I continued, over the next ten years, to devote what leisure time I
could to the study of Schubert's later years, and in particular
to the history of the Great C Major. The result is a book
which attempts, within a fairly strict chronological frame-
work, to give a critical account of the composer's last years,
on the assumption that the symphony (and, I would add, the
B flat piano trio) are much earlier works than is commonly
supposed.

The first answer therefore to the question: What is there
new to be said about Schubert?—must be that we are still a
long way from reaching agreed conclusions about the provenance even of his major works; and until that is done we
are in no position, as Sonnleithner long ago pointed out, to
present a convincing picture of the development of his art.
There is however another answer to the question, which
takes us to the heart of what might be called the Schubert

mystery, the relationship between the man and the artist. The perennial fascination of his personality lies in the contrast between the universality of his genius and what he seemed to be. 'One thing I ought to add for the sake of truth,' wrote Vogl's widow to her daughter, 'although I do not like doing it. Schubert was as undistinguished as a person as he was distinguished as a composer.' One might write this off as a purely personal and idiosyncratic judgment, were it not that there is ample confirmation from other contemporary observers that this is how it appeared, at least to the casual acquaintance. It is the source of the Schubert myth, the take-off point for all those stories of clairvoyant powers, masterpieces scribbled on the backs of menu cards, which are scattered so liberally about nineteenth-century criticism. Modern critics have tended to discount the whole literature of Schubert mythology, on the assumption, as Einstein puts it, that 'great composers must also be great men'. There can be no question, nearly 150 years after his death, that Schubert was a great composer; and if he sometimes appeared to his contemporaries as a rather uncouth little man of no particular distinction or presence with semi-magical powers, this can only be due to their blindness or malevolence. This view is itself, of course, an expression of the romantic belief in the hero as artist. From the point of view of the biographer, it has two disadvantages. It leaves him with a further problem on his hands, of trying to understand how it came about that this great man/artist made so little impression on his age that when he died his name was hardly known outside a few German cities. And it also, by implication, obliges us to believe that Schubert's friends and acquaintances were a set of imperceptive ninnies, unreliable as witnesses and incapable of recognising genius when they saw it. This, clearly, is not true.

A copperplate engraving of Franz Schubert by J. N. Passini, from the watercolour by W. A. Rieder; *below*, the title and opening bars of Schubert's Symphony in C Major, the Great C Major

A lithograph by Jakob Alt of Gmunden, where Schubert worked at his Symphony c. 1825

It seems to be the very opposite of the truth. Vogl, Schober, Spaun, Bauernfeld, Schwind, Jenger, Witteczek, Kupelwieser, Sonnleithner, Pinterics, Schönstein – these, and many others, were men of culture and refinement. Was any composer better served by his friends?

I have tried therefore to look afresh at the relationship of man and artist in the last years of his life, to reconcile the universal genius with the man of his age. Of course this is an impossible task, never completed; but the biographer can do no less than attempt it. Schubert is in modern times the most striking case of genius unrecognised, and in some respects the most puzzling. The clue somewhere lies in the tension between the springs of his personal ambition and the standards of public taste of his time. The problem is to show how the individual vision took shape against 'the very age and body of the time his form and pressure'. The historical Schubert is there, amply documented in the pages of O. E. Deutsch's monumental works of reference. It will not do to disregard him, or to set up in his place a more impressive figure of our own invention, more in keeping with our own notion of what a great composer ought to be. We have to accept him as he was, because only in that way can we also fairly assess the greatness of his achievement.

This book lays no claim to original research, nor have I attempted to make it a comprehensive survey of the compositions of these final years. I have been unashamedly selective, dealing at some length with the more important works, touching on others where they seem relevant to my purpose, and ignoring some altogether. If the book succeeds in its main purpose of presenting a credible portrait of the composer these limitations will not matter.

My debt to O. E. Deutsch will be everywhere apparent,

and I acknowledge it all the most gratefully because I have dared to question his judgment on the crucial question of the Gmunden/Gastein symphony. Deutsch himself, in the preface to his *Documentary Biography*, disclaimed the gift of analysis, and any ambition to 'link the whole together in a literary or scientific way', so I take heart from the thought that he would have welcomed the attempt here made to do just that, even though he would have dissented from some of the conclusions. Every true Schubertian should pay an annual tribute to his memory for providing in such an easily accessible form the indispensable tools of his trade. Maurice J. E. Brown has with characteristic generosity shown me much kindness and given valuable help both with the text and with the illustrations. My thanks are due to him for much help and encouragement over the years, and for the stimulus of his own work, especially the *Critical Biography* and *Essays on Schubert*, which I have consulted closely. I am also most grateful to Dr. Roger Fiske, who brought his judgment and scholarship to bear on the Ms. to my great advantage. Other friends, including Michael Kennedy and Eric Sams, have read the book in proof and made valuable suggestions. Needless to say, the responsibility for any surviving inaccuracies, mistakes, and misjudgments is entirely mine.

I am grateful to J. M. Dent and Sons for permission to quote freely from the indispensable *Schubert: a Documentary Biography*, and similarly to A. and C. Black Ltd. for permission to quote from *Schubert: Memoirs by his Friends*, both edited by Otto Erich Deutsch; also to Secker and Warburg for permission to quote a passage from *Buddenbrooks* by Thomas Mann on page 211 and to Universal Edition (Alfred A. Kalmus Ltd.) for permission to quote the first three bars of *Die Nacht*, by Richard Strauss.

Many people have given generously of their time and special knowledge to help in the selection of illustrations. I am grateful to them all, and especially to Frau Hilde Kosler and Herr Heinrich Zimburg of Badgastein, Frau Elfriede Prillinger of Gmunden, Mr. Douglas Matthews of the London Library, and Dr. Albert Mitringer and Dr. Hedwig Mitringer of Vienna.

Finally my thanks are due to my wife and family, who have made their own sacrifices on Schubert's behalf, and especially to my daughters Jane and Kate, who shared with me in the exploration of the songs and the piano duets. It seems only right that this book should be dedicated, with my love and gratitude, to them.

For permission to reproduce various manuscripts, sketches, and pictures as illustrations in this book I am indebted to the following, and tender my grateful thanks:
Views of Gmunden, *Museum der Stadt Gmunden*
Passini engraving of Schubert, *Historisches Museum, Wien*
Autograph of the Symphony in C major, called the Great, *Gesellschaft der Musikfreunde in Wien*
View of Badgastein, *The London Library*
View of Badgastein, *Bibliothèque Nationale, Paris*
Ms. of *Gesang* ('Who is Sylvia?'), *Wiener Stadtbibliothek*
Facsimile of first edition of *Winterreise, Trustees of the British Museum*
'Promenade at the City Gate', *The Courtauld Institute*
Ms. of *Das Lied im Grünen, Stanford University, California*
Sketch of Fantasia in F minor, *Louis Koch Collection*

Rusholme January 1972   John Reed

I

OCTOBER 1825–MARCH 1826

The composer of genius, sufficiently well-known to the musical world. . . .

There is something faintly provocative about the idea of beginning a book on Schubert in the twenty-ninth year of his life. Unlike Beethoven, for whose work Lenz's analysis into three periods has at least provided generally accepted terms of reference, the uneventful pattern of Schubert's life, coupled with the seeming homogeneity of his style, has made it extremely difficult to draw the threads of his life and art together in any convincing pattern of development. He worked, moreover, with a compulsive industry, but with a shy reserve that often left his closest friends in the dark about the progress of his artistic projects. Only rarely, in those voluminous documentary records, does he reveal directly his inner thoughts and ambitions. For the most part the work goes on, quietly, relentlessly, like a secret addiction. When he died, not only were his contemporaries completely unaware of the size and variety of his creative legacy; they had little idea of the relationship between the man they had known and the artist, and no means of assessing the development of the artist, because they had no sure chronological basis for making a judgment.

One school of thought, indeed, is prepared to solve the problem by dismissing the idea of development itself. 'Chez Schubert,' says Paul Landormy, 'point de renouvellement, point d'évolution. Du premier jour il est tout lui-même, et il restera, *jusqu'a sa dernière heure ce qu'il fut a 17 ans.*[1] It is true that a song like *Die Taubenpost*, which is one of the last he wrote, might belong to any year; psychological insight and purity of style are as remarkable in his first masterpiece, *Gretchen am Spinnrade*, as in, say, *Atlas*, one of his last. But even if we restrict ourselves to Schubert the songwriter the generalisation will not quite do. There may be, indeed there are, legitimate differences of opinion as to when the Heine songs were written, but their inward-looking intensity of feeling precludes an early date for them, not to mention the atmospheric expressiveness of the keyboard writing. Nor would we have any doubt in judging, say, the four Rückert songs of 1823 to belong to the middle years. *Winterreise* is of course a landmark, and a turning-point, as Schubert's friends fully realised. Outside the field of song there is even less truth in this assertion. Schubert's piano sonatas fall as readily into three periods as Beethoven's, and their formal characteristics are as readily discernible. One does not need to insist on the differences between the 'Trout' quintet of 1819 and the string quintet of 1828, or between the little C Major symphony of 1818 and the Great C Major, to see that it is patently untrue to say that Schubert was always himself, and always the same.

None the less, the detachment with which he followed the promptings of his own genius, and the resulting uncertainty about the chronology of many of his greatest compositions, make it difficult for the biographer to bring his life and work into satisfactory focus, and to evolve any sort of pattern. A second school of thought, preferring to stress the detachment of the artist, has adopted a kind of dual stance, suggesting that man and artist developed along different, even divergent lines, the artist advancing steadily towards the sublimity of

[1] Paul Landormy: *Schubert* (1928).

the Great C Major, the string quintet and the last songs, while the spirit of the man was gradually broken by the insensitivity of the age in which he lived. But this theory will not do either, and not only because there is every reason to believe (as will be made plain in Chapter III) that the Great C Major was written, not in 1828, but three years earlier. The compositions of 1828 vary in quality from the sublime to the jejune. Schubert's contemporaries believed that his genius was at its peak in the middle years, and that the later years represented a decline. However this may be, the biographer cannot escape the responsibility of attempting to relate the experience of the man to the work of the artist, for however complex the relationship, it affects everything else. Least of all can he escape the responsibility in the case of Schubert, whose creative powers, co-existing with that amiable, unimpressive, slightly grotesque physical presence, mystified his friends, and continue to puzzle his biographers.

There is therefore no alternative but to get to grips with such chronological problems as still remain to be solved, and to go back to the original sources so fully and conscientiously set out in the *Documentary Biography* by O. E. Deutsch. In fact, Schubert's working lifetime can be divided fairly obviously and satisfactorily into three. The unknown years ended in 1821. With pardonable over-simplification one can say that they finally ended on 7 March 1821 when Vogl sang *Erlkonig* at the grand charity concert in the Kärntnertor Theatre, for from that time Schubert was assured of local fame at least. And from the events of that time flowed not only publication of his songs, not only the prospect of success in the opera house, but a new current of creative energy which in the course of the next two years was to reveal itself in a series of works of unprecedented imaginative power—the quartet movement of December 1820, the cantata *Lazarus*, the Unfinished Symphony and the Wanderer Fantasia.

The year 1825 is also a climactic one. In October 1825 Schubert returned to Vienna after an absence of five months, the longest, happiest and most productive holiday of his life. This holiday in Upper Austria with his friend and patron Michael Vogl marks the climax of two years of enormous creativity, in which he had been preoccupied with chamber music and with 'grand symphony'; and since this brings us face to face with the central problem of Schubert criticism, it seems a good place to start. For during those five months among the mountains he wrote a symphony whose connection (or identification) with the Great C Major symphony has always been a matter of controversy.

October 1825 sees not merely a change of scene, but a change of mood and a reconstruction of the Schubert circle. It marks the end of his close association with Michael Vogl, the craggy, serious-minded opera singer, to whose generous patronage he owed so much. Vogl went off to spend the winter in Italy and returned to astonish his friends with the announcement of his engagement. He and Schober represent, so to speak, the two poles of Schubert's nature, the one serious and disciplined, the other sensual and impulsive. Towards Vogl, the older man, Schubert felt gratitude and a kind of ironic respect (which Bohm's caricature of the two 'setting off to fight and conquer' exactly touches off); towards Schober, affection and loyalty, tinged with admiration for his social assurance and arrogant disdain for the Philistines. Vogl was, however, a serious man and a serious artist, while Schober was a dilettante; it is not without significance that October 1825 marks the renewal of the latter's leadership of the Schubert circle.

The circle itself was greatly changed from the great days of 1822, when Schubert, Schober and Leopold Kupelwieser had formed a 'poetic-musical-painting triumvirate', as Spaun called it (Schober representing, a little improbably, literature in this grand alliance). True, Kupelwieser also returned to Vienna about this time, after two years' study in Rome. But he was too absorbed in his own work, and in the prospect of marriage with the incomparable Johanna Lutz to spend much time with his old friends, and he rarely appears on the scene. The new triumvirate, consisting of Schubert, Schwind and Bauernfeld, with Schober as a kind of constitutional monarch, strikes a new note. The reading parties had long ago been discontinued; they petered out in 1824 soon after the departure of Schober and Kupelweiser in a crescendo of discord between the aesthetes and the hearties. Instead, an air of conscientious gaiety seems to invade the Schubert circle, and of growing hostility to the ideals and standards of *Biedermeier* Vienna. The spirit of the Davidsbund is born.

The new mood finds expression in the diaries of Eduard von Bauernfeld, a young lawyer with literary ambitions, who now takes his place for the first time in the circle of Schubert's intimate friends, and whose writings provide us with much of the detailed background to these final years of the composer's life.

When we turn to consider the artistic output of these years, it is clear that October 1825 represents the end of the most creative period of Schubert's life. In the twenty months that separate January 1824 and October 1825 he had written two of the three great string quartets, the octet, four major works for piano duet—the Grand Duo sonata, the opus 35 variations in A flat major, the Divertissement à la Hongroise, and his best set of marches (op. 40)—three great piano sonatas, the B flat major piano trio, and the Great C Major symphony.[1] By comparison, there seems to be a dampening down of the creative fire over the next few months; only two major works – the G major string quartet and the G major piano sonata – make their appearance in 1826; between October 1825 and the next great turning-point, the composition of the first part of the *Winterreise* in January 1827, Schubert, preoccupied with the need to find the means of social and financial security, seems concerned to keep the publishers happy.

There is thus a *prima facie* case at least for dividing Schubert's working life into three parts, each with its special characteristics, and for regarding October 1825 as the beginning of the final phase. But the thesis raises a number of crucial questions, which concern the provenance of the one great symphony of his mature years, of the B flat piano trio, and of the great lyrical compositions of his maturity. Without at least provisional answers to these questions no convincing picture of his artistic development can be given. This must be our justification for beginning on 4 October 1825, when Schubert took farewell of his friends in Linz and set off for Vienna with his old friend and duet partner, Josef von Gahy[2] at the end of the longest and happiest summer of his life.

Arriving in the capital on October 6, Schubert re-established himself in his old lodgings in the Wieden suburb, next door to Schwind, and prepared to take up the old life with his friends. Bauernfeld noted in his diary: 'Schubert is

---

[1] I am aware that this statement begs a number of critical questions, and must ask the reader to suspend judgment of them until a later stage.

[2] For whom Schubert reputedly wrote the duet Rondo in D major of 1818 ('Notre amitié est invariable').

back. Inn and coffee-house gathering with friends, often until two or three in the morning.

> Shamefully, we confess
> Every night
> Drinking and laziness
> Give us delight.

Schober is the worst in this. True, he has nothing to do, and actually does nothing, for which he is often reproached by Moritz.'[1]

The comment is a little unfair perhaps to Schober, who had returned from Breslau after a two-year flirtation with the acting profession, having decided that life *à la Wilhelm Meister*, as Bauernfeld put it, was not going to provide the right medium for his talents. He was soon, however, to turn his attention to a more commercial field, when in the following spring he took over the management of a printing business. Moritz (von Schwind) was an ambitious painter, full of romantic sentiment, whose intimacy with Schubert dated from 1823. There had been a coolness between the two earlier in the year, when Schubert's casual unconcern for the social proprieties had managed to offend Netti Hönig, Schwind's girl-friend: but all was now forgotten and forgiven. There is a rather undergraduate brashness about Bauernfeld's note, a sort of complacent bohemianism, which could give a false impression. (O. E. Deutsch reassuringly reminds us that Schubert rarely stayed up after midnight.) But the contrast between the sophistication of the capital and the unassuming gaiety of Linz, where Schubert had so recently basked in the admiration and affection of his friends, has also to be taken

---

[1] *Schubert: a Documentary Biography* by O. E. Deutsch, translated by Eric Blom, London 1946.

into account. We catch a glimpse of it in a letter of Anton Ottenwalt, Spaun's brother-in-law, who visited the capital on business in November with his wife Marie. They found Schubert's involvement with his own circle puzzling, hurtful even. 'About Schubert I am bound to complain,' wrote Marie, 'for he did not once come to see me . . . and yet he had seemed so much at home with us at Linz: yet when I saw him again at Schober's, and so friendly, I could not be angry with him after all: one must make allowances for such a genius.'[1] Anton is more explicit. He clearly regards Schober as Schubert's evil genius, and does not conceal his disapproval. 'Schober has no following; Schwind is attached to him with absolute devotion, and Schubert too still likes his company; a certain Bauernfeld shares his lodgings.' In the eyes of Anton Ottenwalt (and many others) it was Schober who was responsible for encouraging Schubert's sexual adventures, and thus for his long and damaging illness; and clearly his suspicions are not allayed, for he goes on to speak of Schubert's 'genius for divine creation, unimpaired by the passions of an eagerly burning sensuality'.

The moral permissiveness of the Schubert circle provides the theme for an amusing pantomime which Bauernfeld wrote for the party held at Schober's on New Year's Eve. Schober appears in it as a kind of philosophical Pantaloon, dedicated to a life of vegetable idleness on the highest grounds of principle, and all the other members of the circle–plus a crowd of hearties–pay him ironic and exaggerated respect. Harlequin (Moritz von Schwind) protests his undying love for Columbine (Anna Hönig), but seems willing at Schober's command to renounce her in the sacred name of art. There is no need to lose one's head, declares Pantaloon/Schober. 'Visit her, talk

[1] *Documentary Biography* (No. 605), *op. cit.*

to her, live with her; but do not make her the centre of your being.'

As a kind of sub-plot, Bauernfeld's friend Mayerhofer and his girl-friend Jeannette von Mitis are portrayed as a pair of infatuated lovers, not to be distracted from the serious business of making love. They finally expire exhausted in each other's arms, and are borne off-stage in a triumphal procession Hamlet-fashion.

The star part, however, is Schober's. Bauernfeld does not spare his affectations. He is made to display a Falstaffian capacity for self-indulgence masquerading as high principle; the centre of the play is a set piece in which he lectures his disciples on the sacred duty of complete idleness. Anticipating the doctrines of some twentieth-century flower-people, Schober declares: 'This, my friends, shall henceforth be my life. I disdain position, occupation, industry. On this bed I shall remain lying, on my flower-bed—nothing shall disturb me—I shall receive mankind purely spiritually and thus react upon it. Business, however spiritual, is unworthy of me—only the eternal substance of man and of woman shall I keep ever before me, and so lead life back to its pure primeval condition.'[1] Amid the general applause which greets this proclamation, Harlequin ventures to hope that the great tragedy Pantaloon has promised to write for their manager will now soon be finished. 'What are you thinking of?' replies Schober, 'writing a tragedy too is an action, and therefore below my dignity.' So the friends disperse, promising to mould their ideas upon Schober's 'great thoughts'. The *reductio ad absurdum* of Schober's theory of total inertia is reached when he finds it inconsistent with his beliefs to go to the lavatory; for here at least principle has in the end to give way to

[1] *Documentary Biography* (No. 614), *op. cit.*

practical necessity. The pantomime ends with the apotheosis of Pantaloon/Schober, who lies on a sofa surrounded by a silent throng of pipe-smoking acolytes.

Schubert (Pierrot) plays only a minor part in all this, and it would be foolish to treat a light-hearted extravaganza too seriously. Bauernfeld, who had been living with his mistress for several years, was pleased to contrast the liberal attitudes of his new friends with what he regarded as the moral prudery of more conventional people – like Anton Ottenwalt and his provincial circle. The skit throws an interesting light, however, both on the internal relations of the circle, particularly on the personal ascendancy which Schober seems to have re-established since his return to the fold, and on the conflict between conventional social and moral standards and the attitudes of what might be called the Schober protest movement, in an age when all forms of political protest were forbidden.

The compositions of this autumn and winter are slight, consisting entirely of songs and piano duet works, for which there was an assured demand. The constantly recurring theme of these years is the search for financial security, and the incentive to concentrate on marketable compositions was obvious enough. But there is surely another reason for the slender output of these months. Some time between October 1825 and October 1826 Schubert must have completed and scored the symphony drafted at Gmunden and Gastein; and since in the summer of 1826 he was busy with the G major string quartet and the G major piano sonata the obvious inference is that the work was done in the months following his return to Vienna. (Unlike Beethoven, Schubert seems not to have worked on more than one major work at a time.) The economic pressures are not hard to discern. Schubert had recently taken up with the new publishing house of Anton Pennauer, whose manager Hüther, writing to the composer in July, had expressed interest in a new duet work—'should you feel inclined to write a fairly brilliant work of not too large dimensions, such as a grand polonaise, or rondo, with an introduction, or a fantasy'.[1] We shall find the same brief repeatedly in letters from Probst, Schott, and others. The new piano-playing public demanded something 'brilliant', 'showy', but 'not too difficult'. Schubert responded with two *pièces d'occasion*, the Grand Funeral March on the death of the Emperor Alexander, written in December, and the Grand Coronation March for his successor Nicholas I. They serve their purpose as salon pieces for amateur pianists admirably, but neither has the stamp of greatness. (Schubert had already written his best funeral music, number 5 of the six marches of opus 40, written at Zseliz in 1824.) It is possible also that the six polonaises for piano duet (opus 61) were the result of Hüther's prompting, but if so something went wrong, for they were published by Cappi and Czerny.

A much more interesting work is the three-movement duet sonata probably written in the autumn of 1825. It consists of a first movement in sonata form in E minor, a theme and variations (Andantino) in B minor, and a Rondo allegretto in E minor. It does not have quite the freshness of the B flat duet sonata of 1818, but it is a delightful work to play. The taste of the time and the presumption of the publisher (Thaddäus Weigl) are reflected in the deliberate splitting up of the work to provide attractive offerings. The first movement appeared in June 1826 as a 'Divertissement en forme d'une Marche brillante et raisonnée', and the other two a year later as op. 84 nos. 1 and 2 with even more spurious French dressing.

[1] *Documentary Biography* (No. 573), *op. cit.*

29

Everything about this procedure, even the passing salute to sonata form implied in the word 'raisonnée', smells of sales promotion, and clearly indicates the widening gap between Schubert's creative ambitions and the trend of public taste.

Writing to his father in July 1825, Schubert explained his intention of publishing the 'Lady of the Lake' songs (op. 52) with English and German words, in the hope of making his name known in England. Enthusiasm for the works of Sir Walter Scott had spread rapidly, and it seemed a good idea to take advantage of the fashion; moreover these songs had proved immensely popular when sung by Vogl during their summer tour. Their success encouraged Schubert to enlist the help of Jakob Craigher (author of *Die junge Nonne*) in preparing translations of classic authors 'in the metre of the originals, which he will then set to music and have published with the original text'.[1] The formula had already been used for Colley Cibber's 'The Blind Boy', which Schubert set earlier in the year. Craigher was enthusiastic when the project was discussed in October, and one result was probably the three Metastasio poems later published as op. 83. For the time being, however, we hear no more of it.

Of the songs of this autumn and winter, two groups are of particular interest, those by Ernst Schulze and the last Goethe settings. Schulze's verses are in the same tradition as those of Wilhelm Müller, bitter-sweet songs in which the pain and bewilderment of love find symbolic expression and consolation in nature. The first one Schubert set, *Im Walde* (March 1825) sets the tone for them all. The verses, one feels, would not seem out of place in *Winterreise*; the wanderer's broken heart seeks rest, and finds none, in forest, mountain and sea. Schubert sets the scene with eight bars of

[1] *Documentary Biography* (No. 596), *op. cit.*

driving triplets, and maintains the pace relentlessly through six verses. It is not easy to bring off without monotony, and the same applies to *Auf der Bruck* (a galloping song which Schubert sets to a steady eight quavers in a bar) and *Über Wildemann*. It is as though the torrent of energy that rushes through the finale of the Great C major symphony overflows into the songs of the period; once Schubert's imagination is seized by a pianistic figure it dominates the song. The variety and originality of these figures is a source of constant delight to the pianist, and certainly the initial inspiration seems often to come from them, not from a lyrical phrase.

In the best songs of the period the accompaniments have an orchestral fluency that gives a special intimacy to the partnership between singer and pianist. One of these is *Im Frühling*, the best of the Schulze songs, written in March 1826. The lover's joy in spring is heightened by the remembrance of past happiness and present loss. Schubert finds a reflective little tune that exactly catches the mood, and writes a dazzling set of piano variations on it. In this song and in *Fischerweise* (the other incontrovertibly great song of these months) the note of innocence and joy seems to sound again after an interval of many months.

In January Schubert bade farewell to Goethe with his last settings of the *Wilhelm Meister* songs. The four songs, which had all been set before, were published as op. 62 in March 1827. The third and best known of these, *So lasst mich scheinen*, is a much lovelier setting than that of April 1821, with the B major section of which it has close affinities; and if the music seems to us perhaps over-sensuous for the little waif Mignon's pathetic salute to eternity, we have to remember that the composer of *Death and the Maiden* had long ago come to terms with death. Had he not only a few months earlier written to chide his brother Ferdinand for worrying about the future 'as though death were the worst that can happen to a man'?

The group includes two settings of *Nur wer die Sehnsucht kennt*, a song which Schubert set again and again, and never with complete and definitive success. The first is a duet version for Mignon and the Harper, as Goethe suggests it should be. Though effective in an operatic kind of way, it misses the simple pathos of Mignon's plight. The fourth is yet another solo setting, for which Schubert returned to A minor (the key of desolation, of *Der Leiermann*) and to a tune he had written many years earlier for *In's stille Land* (D.403). It is an unaffectedly moving little tune, to which the sharpened fourth in the second bar gives a characteristically Schubertian poignancy:

Example 1

At the words 'Es schwindelt mir, es brennt mein Einge-weide'[1] Schubert breaks off. Rapid triplets in the accompaniment seem to signal a little too clearly the child's agitation, so that the passage has almost the effect of an interruption, and the song falls short of complete unity of mood and form. In this, as in other settings, the violence of the girl's cry seems to have been a stumbling-block, an example of too

[1] My senses reel, my vitals burn.

close attention to the words; for the version which seems most successful is the first (D. 310) of October 1815, where the cry from the heart is none the less moving for being contained within a musical form of classical directness and restraint. It is a curious fact that the growing technical mastery and intensity of feeling that Schubert displayed in the songs of his last years are not to be found in his last Goethe settings. Perhaps the poet no longer exercised the same fascination over his mind; perhaps the motives which underlay the composition of this last group were partly economic, an attempt to build on past success. At all events, the best Goethe songs are those of 1814 and 1815, and a rather smaller group from the boom years of 1821 and 1822. We cannot say that the Goethe songs throw any light on Schubert's development as a composer, for the very first one he wrote, *Gretchen am Spinnrade*, is a perfect song, and perfection admits of no further development. The truth appears to be that his genius had a peculiarly literary bias in that only if a text or an author provided him with a certain kind of imaginative excitement could his creative processes work at full stretch. In the last years of his life Goethe ceased to sound for him; others took his place. We must compare the Goethe masterpieces not with the last Goethe settings, but with the best Heine, Müller and Schulze songs.

The events as well as the publications of the period suggest a restless search for status and financial security, which culminates in March 1826 in two new initiatives, the plan to make a further bid for operatic success in collaboration with Bauernfeld, and the decision to apply for a Vice-Kappellmeister post at court. Before we take up the story of these simultaneous but possibly inconsistent challenges to fortune, it is worth looking at Schubert's actual position at the beginning of his thirtieth year, in an attempt to answer two questions: What was his reputation as a composer? And how serious was his lack of money?

The latter question has been bedevilled by romantic mythology and by the misleading finality of the table of earnings included by O. E. Deutsch as Appendix III of the *Documentary Biography*. A combination of the two has resulted in extravagant statements by romantically minded biographers, of which Newman Flower's is an extreme example. In *Franz Schubert: the Man and his Circle*, he describes Schubert as the man who received, in return for 'more than a thousand works of extreme brilliance', '£75 as the sum total of his life's earnings'. This is pure nonsense. Not only does it take no account at all of the change in the value of money. Its impressive arithmetical precision is quite bogus. Schubert lived mainly on his fees from publishers, but also on fees for teaching and playing—sometimes at concerts, sometimes at houses of the well-to-do—on presents from dedicatees, special commissions for compositions, liturgical and other, and contributions to almanacs and anthologies. Much of this we have no accurate means of assessing, but his publishers' fees are at this time usually on record, and his income from this source alone can be fairly confidently estimated.

It has to be said at the outset that the table of earnings referred to above is quite out of date. The figures are invalidated by the fact that Deutsch got into a muddle over the value of the Viennese florin in relation to the old assimilated currency (he bravely drew attention to this himself in the April 1955 issue of *Music and Letters*); and by the fact that more evidence has come to light about, for instance, Schubert's employment as a coach at the Kärntnertor Theatre in 1821.[1]

[1] See Maurice Brown: *Essays on Schubert*, London 1966.

34

We have Spaun's word for it, and Bauernfeld's, that Schubert managed to extort better fees from his publishers as time went on. We know that, in this autumn of 1825, Artaria paid 200 florins for the seven 'Lady of the Lake' songs. This may have owed something to the author's international reputation, and certainly Schubert was delighted with it, so it was probably higher than usual. But Haslinger paid 290 florins for the thirteen songs of the so-called 'Swansong' cycle after the composer's death; and Schott of Mainz paid 30 florins for the part-song *Mondenschein*. These fully documented transactions make nonsense of Lachner's assertion that he went round selling Schubert songs for trifling sums.

There is reliable evidence, also, about his fees for instrumental works. Artaria gave 120 florins for the D major piano sonata written at Gastein and the *Divertissement à la Hongroise*. Schott gave 60 (though Schubert asked 100) for the E flat major piano trio, and Haslinger gave 70 each for the last three piano sonatas after the composer's death. The going rate in these later years appears therefore to have been 20–25 florins each for songs, major instrumental works 60 florins each, with piano duet pieces possibly coming in between. Armed with these figures, and with the list of Schubert's publications in the last three years of his life, we can arrive at a reasonable estimate of his income from fees (see overleaf).[1]

The figures, it should be noted, do not include fees for commissioned liturgical works, and there were several such in 1828 alone. The German mass, a comparatively slight work, brought in 40 florins in October 1827. Nor do they include performance fees (there were several in 1827), teaching fees,

---

[1] The knowledgeable reader will notice that, to avoid confusion, I have quoted all sums in Assimilated Currency. The florin A.C. was then worth about two shillings in old English money.

Florins

1826 'Lady of the Lake' songs Op. 52   200*

19 other songs at 20 florins each   380

Op. 53 D major Sonata ⎱
Op. 54 Divertissement à la Hongroise ⎰   120*

Op. 42 A minor sonata   60

5 other piano works at 30 florins each   150

4 works without op. nos., say,   100

Total   1010

1827 Op. 62 Four Goethe songs   100

Op. 74 *Die Advokaten*   30

24 other songs at 20 florins each   480

Op. 78 G major sonata   60

9 other instrumental works at 30 florins
each   270

5 other commissioned vocal works without
op. no.   150

Total   1090

Florins

1828 Op. 89 *Winterreise* 24 songs in 2 books   500

Op. 92 3 Goethe songs   75

Op. 85 and 86 3 Walter Scott songs   75

Op. 64 3 male-voice quartets   90

18 other songs at 20 florins each   360

Op. 100 E flat piano trio   60*

Op. 94 2 books Moments musicals   60

Op. 91 Graz waltzes   30

2 works without op. nos.   60

Total   1310

* Items asterisked are actual, others estimated.

presents from dedicatees or the proceeds of Schubert's concert in 1828—which amounted to 320 florins. So it looks as though his total income from various sources at this time must have been at least 1,500 florins a year.

This is worth £150 a year at contemporary rates, and possibly £1,800 at 1960 values. On this last point the best evidence is the level of wages and salaries at the time. Schubert's salary as an assistant in his father's school was 80 florins (£8) a year. The teaching post he applied for in 1816 offered 500 (£50) a year, with no restrictions on private teaching. These salaries were perhaps low even by contemporary English standards. But British evidence tells a similar story. Mrs. Rundell's *New System of Domestic Economy* (1825) gives the annual budget for 'a gentleman, his lady, three children, and a maid servant'—£250. When Thomas Carlyle set up house in London in 1834 with his wife his income was £150 a year. To convert these figures to modern standards we should need to multiply by twelve at least.

Two inferences can safely be drawn from this analysis. First, the romantic picture of a penniless genius, a Viennese Schaunard, carelessly spawning masterpieces while his friends make desperate efforts to raise the wind, is worthless fantasy. £150 a year in those days was not riches, but it was not poverty either.[1] The evidence of his close friends is clear.

[1] For those with a taste for the economics of genius it may be of interest to compare Schubert's fees with Beethoven's. In 1815 Beethoven asked 350 florins from Thomson of Edinburgh for six original songs, but the offer was not taken up. For folksong arrangements Thomson seems to have paid only 14 florins each. The standard fee list drawn up by Steiner and Haslinger for Beethoven in 1820 quoted (for exclusive rights) 135 fl. for a sonata and 180 for a grand sonata

There is of course a wealth of other evidence in the Schubert documents about the level of prices and salaries, which tends to support the conclusions reached here.

Schubert liked good living–'pheasants and punch' was Schwind's phrase–and spent freely when in funds. 'We alternated between want and plenty,' said Bauernfeld, 'Among the three of us, it was Schubert who played the part of a Croesus and who, off and on, used to be rolling in money.'[1] Those vividly atmospheric sketches of the Schubertians at play left us by Kupelwieser and Schwind evoke an elegant comfort-loving society far removed from a Bohemian garret.

But there is another side to the picture. Schubert had raised himself by the power of his own genius, and with the help of well-to-do friends, from modest circumstances to the fashionable artistic circle of Viennese society. He lived at a level which seemed extravagant to his family and sometimes to his friends. But, totally dependent on fees and other unpredictable earnings, there was no security in his life and no prospect of it. The road to success lay through the opera house or through the church, for he had neither the skill nor the temperament for the life of a virtuoso performer. And once his bid for operatic success failed, as it did in 1822 and 1823, he was never free of that nagging pre-occupation with money matters which runs like a ground-bass of complaint through the story of these final years. To make matters worse, the trend of public taste moved sharply away from his own conservative standards just when he needed a steady and increasing income from his fees. The situation led to growing bitterness and disillusion.

'11 January 1826. . . . Teltscher brought Schubert lithographed,' noted Sophie Müller, the star of the Court Theatre, at whose house Schubert was a regular visitor at this time. The new portrait engraving of the composer had been an-

---

[1] *Schubert: Memoirs by his Friends*, collected and edited by O. E. Deutsch, London 1958.

nounced by Cappi in December as an 'extremely good likeness of the composer Franz Schubert,' engraved by Passini,
and Teltscher's lithograph followed a month later. Cappi's
blurb goes on: 'the composer of genius, sufficiently well-
known to the musical world, who has so often enchanted his
hearers with his vocal compositions in particular, appears
here as a speaking likeness'.[1] This is fame, of a sort; and
there is other evidence to prove that Schubert was by no
means an unknown genius working away in obscurity. In this
same month, January 1826, the publisher of a waltz-collec-
tion singles out as his star contributors Beethoven, Karl
Czerny, Hummel, and Schubert, a nice juxtaposition, it
might be thought, of the journeymen and the immortals.
More significant perhaps is the fact that Schubert's name is
beginning to be known outside Vienna, not only in provincial
capitals like Linz and Graz, but in Prague and Pesth, Mainz
and even further afield. His work begins to be noticed in
periodicals throughout Germany, and even the Vienna correspondent of the recently established London *Harmonicon* gives
him an occasional mention. The profession of musical journal-
ism hardly existed, and these notices are usually brief and
insensitive, reflecting the conventional attitudes of the time.
In 1826, however, the Weimar *Musical Post* gave an enthusiastic welcome to the A minor string quartet, published
two years earlier, and the A minor piano sonata (op. 42),
which had been a great success with Schubert's provincial
admirers during his 1825 tour, was given thoughtful and
sympathetic notices in various periodicals. In Zurich it made
a deep impression on Georg Nägeli, composer, critic, and
publisher of anthologies of keyboard music. He thought it a
'capital piece' and wrote to ask Schubert to contribute a

[1] *Documentary Biography* (No. 607), *op. cit.*

39

sonata to his new anthology. When, in April 1826, Schubert came to apply for a Kapellmeister post at court, he could claim without undue exaggeration that his name was favourably known 'not only in Vienna, but throughout Germany'.

This picture, also, needs qualification. He is still, even in Vienna, the composer of 'vocal compositions in particular'. As an instrumental composer he was, except for the discerning minority of critics mentioned above, virtually unknown. The reputation as a composer of instrumental and orchestral forms which he had set out to build at the end of 1823, when his operatic hopes collapsed, was still unmade. Of the projected group of three string quartets, one was published, and another written: but there was little prospect of further publication, and the third had still to be written. Of the piano sonatas, the first 'grand sonata'–op. 42 in A minor had already appeared, and the second–op. 53 in D major was in preparation. The first had had a *succès d'estime*, but the piano sonata had an old-fashioned air about it. Public performance of a piano sonata was a very rare event (only one of Beethoven's sonatas, it is said, was performed publicly in his lifetime); and in the domestic market the demand was all for fantasias, dances, duet pieces ('brilliant but not too difficult') and trivial salon pieces. As for the long projected grand symphony, it was now written, or at least drafted, but there was little hope of performance, and still less of publication. Small wonder that the decadence of public taste, the demand for 'wretched fashionable stuff' becomes a recurrent complaint with Schubert. His gods were Mozart and Beethoven. There was, as Sonnleithner said, nothing of the musician of the future about him. He wanted to emulate Beethoven in the great classical forms of sonata and sym-

Badgastein, an aquatint by Johann Jakob Strüdt, 1800

Gesang ('Who is Sylvia?') written in July 1826 (See page 48)

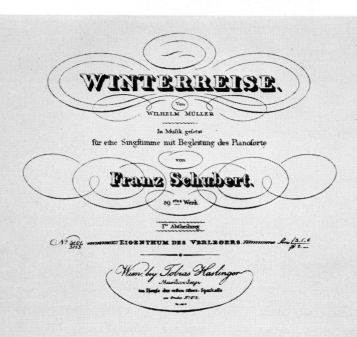

Above, the title page of the first edition, January 1828, of *Winterreise* (Part 1) published by Tobias Haslinger, Vienna; *below*, *Wasserufluth* from the same edition of *Winterreise* (See page 137)

phony, at a time when Beethoven himself was regarded as a kind of licensed eccentric.

Meanwhile lesser men did well. Anselm Hüttenbrenner wrote a set of *Erlkönig* waltzes as early as 1821. In 1829 Diabelli published a set of *Erlkönig* galops, and in 1834 the exploitation of Schubert's song reached a grand climax with the production by Adolf Müller of a grand romantic drama, the Erl King musical, complete with moveable scenery, chorus, and orchestra.

One event which catches the attention, the first performance of the D minor string quartet in February, was doubtless intended as a step towards publication. In fact there seem to have been two performances, one at the house of the singer Josef Barth and one later in the month at Franz Lachner's, led by Ignaz Schuppanzigh. There seems no reason to doubt that Lachner, now a coach at the Kärntnertor Theatre, took the initiative in the matter in order to help his friend, though he later embroidered the story misleadingly. The D minor quartet had been written two years earlier, in the early months of 1824, and Schuppanzigh's reservations about its difficulty may just possibly have had something to do with its failure to appear in print. Within a few months Schubert, nothing daunted, was to set to work on the third and last quartet of the group.

It is not really surprising, therefore, to find that his star was regarded as being on the wane. According to the correspondent of the Berlin *Musical Times* his public 'seems to be gradually diminishing'. The cause of German opera, with which he had been associated in the heady days of long ago, seemed lost beyond recall. He had not fulfilled the hopes held out for him, and even his songs, still appearing regularly, no longer made the stir they had done in 1821.

It is against this background that we have to consider a series of events, in the spring of 1826, which seemed to hold out brighter hopes. The first was Schubert's decision, encouraged by his friends, to apply for the vacant Vice-Kapellmeister post in Vienna. There was also a renewal of Barbaja's lease of the Court theatres on condition that something was done to help German opera, which was sufficient to revive Schubert's operatic ambitions.

On April 7th he wrote out, in appropriately obsequious jargon, his application for Vice-Kapellmeister. He summarised his career and qualifications, enclosing the testimonial Salieri had written for him in 1819 when he first worked for the Court theatres. Claiming to be well-known as a vocal and instrumental composer throughout Germany, he adds with a touching dignity that 'I have not the advantage of employment, and hope by means of an assured career to attain fully to my intended goal.'[1] An assured career; the opportunity to write the music he wanted to write undistracted by financial worry or the demands of a professional routine: when one considers the work that already lay behind him it does not seem much to ask. But it was to elude him to the end.

[1] *Documentary Biography* (No. 646), *op. cit.*

II

APRIL—SEPTEMBER 1826

> In the hope that my name may be not
> wholly unknown to you, I venture to en-
> quire whether you would not be disinclined
> to acquire some of my compositions at
> reasonable terms, being very desirous of
> becoming as well known as possible in
> Germany.
>
> Schubert to Probst of Leipzig:
> August 1826

It was inevitable that Bauernfeld, with his passion for the theatre, and Schubert, who had so nearly made his mark as an opera composer, should plan an opera in collaboration. The idea had been mooted early in 1825, when their acquaintance first grew into friendship. But at that time Schubert's mind was set on a poem by Ernst Schulze, a version of the story of the enchanted rose. He had already tried, and discarded, one libretto on this text by his artistically minded doctor Bernhardt. He took this version to Zseliz with him in 1824, but finding it unusable, instead dedicated the six marches of op. 40 written that summer to Bernhardt, possibly as a compensation for hurt feelings. Now he tried to persuade Bauernfeld of the merits of this subject, without success. Bauernfeld's idea was an opera based on the legend of the Count of Gleichen, a rather daring story by contemporary standards about a man who returns from his travels in the east with a new wife, and succeeds in establishing a viable *ménage à trois* with the first. It seemed to Bauern-feld to offer scope for 'dramatic and musical contrasts, orient and occident, janissaries and knighthood, romantic wooing and wedded love', for all the fun of the operative fair in fact. In the end, Schubert allowed himself to be persuaded. The story was likely to fall foul of the censor, but there were other opera houses in the world beside the Kärntnertor.[1] Besides, he could not afford, in present circumstances, to surrender all hope of success in the theatre.

In the spring of 1825, however, any such plan seemed academic, for the fortunes of German opera were at their lowest ebb. Schubert's contracts were with the Kärntnertor Theatre (where he had worked briefly as a coach in 1820–1), and with the Theater an der Wien (where *Rosamunde* had been staged in 1823), both under the management of the Italian impresario Domenico Barbaja. His lease expired in March 1825. Visiting companies kept things going for a few months, but by the autumn both theatres were closed. 'German opera is dead,' wrote Franz Hüther to Schubert in July. 'I am told there is to be only ballet and *opera italiana*.' As it turned out, however, this forecast was unduly pessimistic. After pro-tracted negotiation, Barbaja emerged in the following April with a new lease, to run for two years from May 1st. More-over, the decision was taken to open with *Der Freischütz*, and Louis Duport, Barbaja's manager, made it known that he was in the market for new German operas. Prospects beginning to look a good deal brighter, it was agreed in April that Bauernfeld should set to work on *The Count of Gleichen*.

No sooner was this settled, however, than an opportunity cropped up for Bauernfeld to go on an extended tour of Carinthia and Upper Austria with his friend Mayerhofer, who

---

[1] *Documentary Biography* (Nos. 540, 652), *op. cit.*

was to make a survey of those provinces for his military superiors. This was too good an opportunity to miss, especially as it opened up the possibility of a reunion for the Schubertians in the summer at Linz. After a farewell party on April 14th, Bauernfeld and Mayerhofer set off on a glorious spring morning for their journey into the blue, as Bauernfeld described it in his diary. 'Greetings to thee, boredom, mother of the Muses!' he noted. 'Thus I thought of the libretto for Schubert and set to work on *The Count of Gleichen*.'[1]

Within a few days of their departure the circle was reinforced by the return of two old friends, Michael Vogl and Josef von Spaun, the latter after an absence from Vienna of nearly five years. The news of Vogl's engagement—at 58—to Kunigunde Rosa created no small stir among the Schubertians, and it cannot have improved Schubert's spirits much. Whether his holiday plans were dependent this year, as often before, on Vogl's generous companionship, we do not know, but it seems likely. There were to be no more triumphal tours like that of 1825, though Vogl continues to appear at occasional Schubertiads in Vienna. Spaun returned to take up a post in the public lottery office. Schubert's oldest and most faithful friend had kept in touch with him in the intervening years; he no longer occupies the central place in the composer's circle, for the centre of gravity has moved towards a more aggressive and sophisticated artistic creed than was consistent with Spaun's background and professional integrity; but once again his home becomes the centre for the most memorable Schubertiads. Years later he wrote: 'Back in Vienna again from Lemberg, I found Schubert in the full flowering of his talent. At last he was finding more recognition and he was receiving payment for his works, even

[1] *Documentary Biography* (No. 625), *op. cit.*

though this was miserable in comparison with their value. His condition had improved, though it continued to be unsatisfactory.'[1] Whatever the causes of the malaise that settles like a cloud on Schubert's affairs in 1826, it does not seem to be due to his being worse off financially than he had been.

The opera libretto made rapid progress. Bauernfeld wrote that the first act was finished in a week–'and most of the numbers I have composed and sung as well'. Life in Carinthia seemed to offer compensations for the two bachelors, for they had left their girl-friends behind them in Vienna. Early in May they write a joint letter from Villach, urging Schubert to join them. Bauernfeld, in high spirits, breaks into doggerel verse:

> 'Drinks and games, good friends and dames,
> They go to our head like wine.
> Leave the Viennese their Prater,
> Villach, Villach–there it's fine!'

Schubert's reply, which is a tale of woe, strikes a very different note.

'Please don't stay away so long. It is very sad and miserable here–boredom has taken the upper hand too much already. Of Schober and Schwind one hears nothing but lamentations, far more heart-rending than those we heard during Passion Week. . . . I am not working at all. The weather here is truly appalling, the Almighty seems to have forsaken us altogether, for the sun simply refuses to shine. It is May, and we cannot sit in any garden yet. Awful! appalling!! ghastly!!! and the most cruel thing on earth for me.'[2] Certainly the Schubertians seemed to have struck a bad patch; Schober was ill, and

---

[1] *Memoirs* (p. 136), *op. cit.*, p. 136.
[2] *Documentary Biography* (Nos. 653, 656), *op. cit.*

Schwind's affair with Netti Hönig was not progressing at all smoothly. But it cannot have been literally true that Schubert was doing no work, for some time during this inclement spring he wrote the two Characteristic Marches for piano duet (op. 121), which are lively and energetic enough, and the G major quartet must have begun to take shape in his mind about this time. Moreover, his hopes are firmly set on the new opera. 'Your having done the opera is a clever move; only I could wish to see it before me already,' he writes to Bauernfeld. 'They have asked for my libretti here, to see what they can do with them. If your book were ready now I could submit that to them . . . or send it to Madame Milder in Berlin.' If this proved a little dampening to Bauernfeld's enthusiasm, it did not prevent his pressing on with the libretto. At this date, towards the end of May, it still seems to be Schubert's intention to join up with the other friends at Linz in June. This part of the plan was to founder for lack of money, however. Schubert soldiered on in Vienna, and at Währing with Schober, while Bauernfeld retraced the route of Schubert's 1825 tour through the mountains of Upper Austria.

This was a serious disappointment, but in some way or other, even in the darkest years, Schubert never fails to respond to spring's magical power of renewal. The year 1826 is no exception. It is clear that things were going badly. But among the compositions of the time are *Im Frühling*, and *Fischerweise*, and the three lovely Shakespeare songs written at Währing in July. He stayed for several weeks with Schober and his mother at Währing, a village with early associations for him, partly because his mother was buried there, partly because it was a favourite spot for a country walk.[1] Now it

[1] *Documentary Biography* (No. 87), *op. cit.*

provides a relief from the capital, a setting in which his creative energies are released, not only in the Shakespeare songs, but in the G major string quartet.

The songs were to follow the new plan of setting German translations side by side with the original text, but in this case he used not Craigher, but Bauernfeld, who was engaged in a translation of the plays for Trentsensky's Vienna edition, and possibly drew Schubert's attention to them. The manuscript survives, a small notebook with hand-drawn staves, consistent with the idea that they were a holiday inspiration, but not really with picturesque stories of notes on the back of pub menus. More important, it shows clearly that the echo-phrases in the accompaniment to *An Sylvia*—surely one of the loveliest uses of this device—were afterthoughts, for they are crowded in above the stave. It is one of Schubert's greatest songs, deceptively simple in its appeal, never losing its freshness, and profoundly subtle in its exploitation of the contrapuntal effect of voice-line against the accompanist's marching left hand. The *Trinklied* (from 'Antony and Cleopatra') does not reach the same standard as *An Sylvia* and 'Hark hark the lark'; yet it seems strange that these songs did not achieve publication in his lifetime as a group. Only *An Sylvia* at last appeared, in 1828, in a group dedicated to Marie Pachler of Graz—and then only as a replacement for the rather unsatisfactory setting of 'Edward'.

In June Nägeli of Zurich approached Schubert by way of Karl Czerny with a request for a contribution to his projected anthology of piano sonatas. Schubert acknowledged the proposal on 4 July with a friendly note accepting the commission, but asking for 120 florins in advance. This seems to have frightened off Nägeli, for nothing more is heard of it; and when, in the autumn, the G major piano sonata was written it went to Haslinger. But by this time Schubert was also in touch with two Leipzig publishers, who, he may well have thought, were in a better position to promote his interests than Nägeli. It is one of those occasions when one feels that matters might have been more tactfully handled; on the other hand, Schubert's need of money was becoming acute. Only a few days later, on 10 July, he has finally to call off the summer holiday in Linz.

The weeks spent at Währing left an even greater legacy than the Shakespeare songs, for there, in the ten last days of June, he wrote out the fair copy of the G major string quartet. It is sometimes assumed, from the fact that the manuscript is dated 20–30 June, that the whole process of composition occupied only ten days, but this seems unlikely. The work was the fulfilment of a long-cherished plan, to complete as a substantial *oeuvre* three string quartets; it is also, of all Schubert's work, the most concentrated, the most highly organised, and the most consciously designed. Though no sketches have survived, they must surely have existed. Moreover, it was Schubert's practice throughout his life to date the final version of a work regardless of any preparatory sketches; examples range from the early piano sonata in E major (D. 157) in 1815 to the fair copy of the F minor piano duet Fantasia in April 1828. What the manuscript represents is probably the final phase of composition of a work which had been in his mind for two years, and which may have been sketched a month or two earlier. For the stimulus to start work on it may have come from the private performances of the D minor quartet already mentioned, or possibly from the Beethoven concert of 21 March, which we know Schubert attended, and at which the B flat major quartet op. 130, with the Grosse Fuge as finale, was first performed. It was

Beethoven's example which inspired and permeated him – the words are Sonnleithner's; and it does not seem fanciful to suppose that this evidence of the master's preoccupation with the quartet medium renewed his ambition to complete his own work.

Schubert's shyness of the key of G major is noteworthy. He never used it for a major orchestral work, reserving it for lyrical second subjects like those of the Great C Major. Nor, until this year, had he chosen it for a major instrumental work. His natural feeling for flat-side harmonies, and for modulating via the mediant, seems to leave G major off the main road, so to speak, of his harmonic excursions. All the more remarkable then, that the two major works of 1826, written one after the other, should both explore in subtle detail the tonality of G major. The contrast in form and texture between these two works, the quartet and the piano sonata opus 78, is as striking as the identity of key; so that it is difficult not to feel that Schubert was consciously experimenting.

The G major quartet is an essay on the instability of the third: and since the third is the key interval in Schubert's world of tonal ambiguity, it presents a picture of that world almost in summary form, and in a key which in equal temperament emphasises the contrast between the brightness of the major and the poignance of the minor. The contrast had been exploited often enough, in songs like *An die Nachtigall* (D.497), and in the variations of the D minor quartet (Death and the Maiden). Indeed, there are grounds for asking whether it may not have had some special symbolic association for Schubert with death, as friend to life. However, this may be, the opening statement is an epigrammatic sequence of moving semitones, which emphasise the instability of the tonic before finally re-asserting it. On these foundations Schubert builds a long complex movement, which needs to be taken at the *molto moderato* marking if the quivering strings are to avoid an effect of restlessness, even of monotony. The assertion that major implies minor and vice-versa recurs like a point of reference before the recapitulation and again at the end, so that the movement has a logical coherence and tautness which seems a little uncharacteristic. One can agree with those critics who hold this to be Schubert's best quartet movement, much as one might agree that *Othello* is Shakespeare's best, that is best-made, play. But it seems a little too cerebral to rank as quintessential Schubert.

These reservations do not, however, apply to the slow movement, which explores the tonal possibilities to be found in a series of descending thirds anchored to the mediant, with the help of a lovely tune first heard from the 'cello.

Example 2

The middle section of this movement is a kind of tonal battle reminiscent of the slow movement of Beethoven's G major concerto, in which first violin and viola insistently sound a minor third in bare octaves against the centrifugal tendencies of tremolando chords exploring remoter harmonic regions. The effect is violently disturbing. Only after a quicksilver scherzo, also based on the minor third, do we reach, in the Trio, the still centre of the work, with a heart-easing *Ländler* tune which stays happily in G major.

Example 3

And only then, with the violins' answer, does Schubert allow us to hear at long last the key of B major, the mediant itself. It sounds like a glimpse of paradise after the storm and stress of the first two movements.

Example 4

The finale, as is the way with Schubert's last movements, steps down from these exalted regions. One of his non-stop six-eight galloping movements, and not perhaps the best, it sums up the major-minor argument without adding very much to it.

In its structural unity and architectural quality the G major quartet comes nearest perhaps of all Schubert's instrumental works to the Beethovenian ideal of music as the expression of a pre-conceived idea; and for this very reason the internal thematic relationships are more explicit than they are, for instance, in the Unfinished Symphony, or the string quintet, or the F minor Fantasy. Each movement seems to be carefully signposted, as though the composer were engaged in a systematic analysis of the tonal relationships of the triad. The first movement's emphatic reiteration of major/minor implications has already been noted. Both the slow movement and the trio are prefaced by a unison B natural. In the slow movement this is revealed (ultimately) as a dominant to E major/minor; in the trio however it leads gently into the reassurance of G major (Example 3). Meanwhile the scherzo has explored the tonality of B minor with the help of neapolitan relationships. These subtleties, it need hardly be said, do not need to be consciously apprehended, but they give the quartet a special place in the affections of musicians. It is in the technical sense perhaps Schubert's most considerable—and most carefully considered—chamber work, and it is a sad commentary on the times that no publisher could be found to take an interest in it until twenty-five years after it was written.

The G major piano sonata, completed four months later, offers such an illuminating contrast that, even if it means looking ahead a little, it must be considered next. The sonata is lyrical and expansive where the quartet is concentrated; homophonic where the quartet is contrapuntal; and it has a relaxed open-air quality which seems almost naïve beside the sophistication of the quartet. In place of the five-note fragment that serves the quartet for first subject, we have a flowing paragraph sixteen bars long, marked *cantabile*, which stays securely within reach of the tonic and repeats itself before leading gently into a second-subject itself twelve bars long (thus anticipating a method which was to yield interesting results in the B flat major sonata of 1828).[1] Throughout the sonata our attention is focussed not on the tonal relationships, which are strikingly simple and direct, but on Schubert's power of melodic extension and decoration. As

[1] In his monumental *History of Sonata Form* William Newman identifies two basic and contrasted techniques of musical construction, the method of 'motivic play', with which a whole movement is built, by sequence and imitation, upon a fragmentary idea, and the method of 'phrase-grouping', in which longer melodic phrases, juxtaposed and related, form the basis of the movement. Schubert might almost have set out to illustrate this distinction in composing these two opening movements.

though to remind us, however, that he is still the master of the sudden and illuminating modulation, Schubert in the Trio first charms us with a delicate little dance tune in B major and then dazzles us by slipping enharmonically into A flat major and back again in the space of a few bars. The slow movement, over which, to judge from the sketches, Schubert took a great deal of trouble, has a hauntingly beautiful middle section in B minor/B major, a splendid example of melodic extension.[1]

It might almost be said that these two works present two quite different sides of the composer's musical personality, the inner Schubert, whom his contemporaries called *mystisch*, lyrical, contemplative, expansive, the poet of the keyboard; and the extrovert Schubert, the plastic artist. And if the quartet was a kind of experiment in a mode of writing not entirely natural to him, the sonata looks like a reversion to a more characteristic manner. Schubert dedicated it to Josef von Spaun, who happened to visit him one morning while he was at work on it, and called it Sonata IV, for reasons which are now undiscoverable, for the D major sonata had appeared only in April as the second grand sonata. Possibly he was leaving room for the work Nägeli had asked for. We do not know, but it is of interest that when the work appeared in April 1827, Haslinger gave it the more fashionable title of fantasia. Fantasia and sonata, it has to be admitted, were widely interchangeable terms; and of all Schubert's sonatas, the G major sonata suffers least outrage from the new title.

Meanwhile Bauernfeld, whom we left exploring Carinthia, had moved on to Upper Austria on his own, in the expectation of joining forces with Schubert at Gmunden. Instead, he found a depressing letter awaiting him there.

[1] See *Critical Biography* (p. 276), by Maurice Brown, London 1958.

'Vienna, 10 July. I cannot possibly get to Gmunden or any where else, for I have no money at all, and altogether things go very badly with me. I do not trouble about it, and am cheerful. For the rest, come to Vienna as soon as possible. . . . It would be splendid if your libretto were favourably received. Then at least there would be money, if not reputation as well! Schwind is quite in the dumps about Nettel! Schober is a privileged business man. *Vogl is married*!!!

Please do come as soon as possible! Because of your opera.

Your   Schubert.

At Linz you need only mention my name to be well received.'[1]

Responsibility seemed to be lying in wait for the Schubertians. Schober, repressing his conscientious objections to purposeful employment, had taken over the management of a printing business, and left Währing at half-past eight every morning for the city just like any ordinary man of business. Schwind's affair with Netti Hönig had come near to breaking point. (Netti read him a lecture on his irreligious way of life and Schwind told her to 'go and fall in love with the Pope', which Bauernfeld thought capital.) Vogl had gone off to Steyr, lapped in domesticity, to show off his new wife. Kupelwieser held aloof from the circle. Spaun set off for his summer holiday, alone, on 7 July, and arrived at Linz in time to welcome Bauernfeld later that month. At Linz Bauernfeld lingered for two more weeks before returning to Vienna by river-boat. At last, at the end of July, the Schubertians were reunited at the landing-stage of Nussdorf. 'Schwind and Schubert ran to meet me out of the coffee-house,' says Bauernfeld, 'great rejoicing! "Where is the opera?" asked

[1] *Documentary Biography* (No. 673), *op. cit.*

Schubert. "Here!" I solemnly handed him *The Count of Gleichen*.' From Nussdorf the friends went on to join Schober at Währing, and the talk went on far into the night. But with all the rejoicing, the shades of the prison house were not quite dispelled, for Bauernfeld adds, as a footnote in his diary, in his self-conscious way: 'Poetry is over, the prose of life begins anew.'[1] He was to take up his official appointment in the lottery office in September.

In August the fortunes of the group seemed to be at their lowest ebb. Schubert was unwell. There was no news of the Vice-Kapellmeister post; the papers were to languish for several months yet in the office of the Court Chamberlain. Schwind was unhappy about his lack of recognition as an artist, suffering from the after-effects of his row with Netti, and at odds with Schober, whose business affairs were going none too well. The three military marches of op. 51 appeared in piano duet form and the four Rückert songs of 1823 were also published this month. Two notices in July, one from Leipzig and the other from Frankfort, temper discreet praise with a warning that Schubert's work 'is not likely to appeal to a large public'. Money and fame seemed equally elusive.

To make matters worse, a move to get Schubert a job as coach at the opera house ended, if Schindler, Beethoven's friend and biographer,[2] is to be believed, in disaster.

Schindler's reliability as a witness has often been called in question, and the story he tells with such a wealth of circumstantial detail has been given short shrift by O. E. Deutsch. Yet there is nothing inherently improbable in it; it was recounted only thirty years after the event and never denied;

---

[1] *Documentary Biography* (No. 684), *op. cit.*
[2] *Beethoven As I Knew Him* by Anton Felix Schindler, London 1966.

and it is much more difficult to believe that Schindler maliciously invented the whole thing than that he is relating, with some straining after dramatic effect, a story based on fact. According to Schindler Michael Vogl, in an attempt to put his friend's affairs on a sounder footing, persuaded Duport, Barbaja's manager, to consider Schubert for the vacant post. At his request, Schubert submitted a trial score based on a short libretto by Georg Hofmann and this work, having done well in rehearsal, was given at a full audition with orchestra and principals under the composer's direction. All this seems easily credible. Schubert had worked with Hofmann before on the productions of *The Twin Brothers* and *The Magic Harp*; it seems likely enough also that Vogl, whose influence must still have counted for something with the Kärntnertor management, would put in a word for his friend. But at this point, according to the story, everything began to go wrong. The leading lady was the young star Nanette Schechner, then the toast of Vienna, and a singer whose performance in German opera had evoked the enthusiasm of the public and of Schubert himself. At the audition she complained that the orchestra was too heavy in the climaxes, asking for modifications and cuts which Schubert stubbornly refused. Things went from bad to worse; the more his friends appealed for a little diplomacy, the more obstinate he became, until, when Duport himself pleaded in vain for Schubert to be conciliatory, the conductor on trial stormed out with the score under his arm shouting 'I will alter nothing!' Collapse of Schubert's hopes of a career as an operatic conductor.

In the last resort judgment of the matter must depend upon our estimate of Schindler's character and Schubert's temperament. As for the latter, he was never at his best on public occasions. His consciousness of his own genius, combined with social diffidence, tended to set him apart, and his embarrassment at being cast in the role of apprentice conductor would not be lessened by finding himself face to face with the glamorous Schechner. As for Schindler, he has often been found guilty of inaccuracy,[1] but never, surely, of the malicious dishonesty he must have shown if we suppose him to have invented the episode, complete with incidental inaccuracies intended presumably to give dramatic verisimilitude to the whole. Leopold Sonnleithner, whose trustworthiness in such matters one learns to respect, says that Schindler's story 'may not be without foundation, though I heard nothing about it at the time'. He adds that the real reason why Schubert lost his job at the Kärntnertor was his lack of punctuality, but in saying this he must have been thinking of the earlier period, in 1821, when Schubert was for a short time employed at the theatre as a coach. If it happened, the episode would help to explain not only the gloom which settled over Schubert's affairs at this time, but also the way his enthusiasm for *The Count of Gleichen* seems to evaporate between Bauernfeld's return at the end of July, when he was obviously eager to get to work on it, and October, when the Viennese censorship banned the libretto. According to Bauernfeld, Schubert decided to compose it all the same, presumably in the hope of getting it performed in Berlin or in Prague, but the earliest sketches in fact date from June 1827.

A happier event occurred in September when Schubert's old friend Leopold Kupelwieser married Johanna Lutz.

[1] Though the major charge against him in regard to this story, that he made Schechner out to be already past her prime when she was in fact at the beginning of her career, turns out not to be true. It was Zierer, an eye-witness to the scene, who made this mistake, not Schindler.

Schubert played for dancing and Schwind made a speech. In the records of the Schubertians Johanna's letters to her Leopold, during his absence in Italy, shine like a beacon of commonsense and goodwill. She was evidently a woman of rare charm and intelligence, and it is entirely in keeping with her affectionate nature that she should preserve, as a treasured memory of her wedding day, one of the tunes that Schubert improvised as he sat at the piano. In December 1942 this tune came to light, when Richard Strauss happened to meet one of the descendants of Leopold and Johanna, heard the story, copied down the tune preserved orally by more than a century of family tradition, and orchestrated it.

Example 5

Although this is a charming tune, truth to tell its charm is not entirely Schubertian; the mood and phrasing seem more reminiscent of a later waltz-king than Schubert.[1] This is only to be expected, for a hundred years of oral tradition are unlikely to have left the tune as it was first played. The modulations in the second section, and particularly the sudden swing into the minor for two bars ring true, however, so that we can without difficulty feel ourselves for one

[1] Brown, *Critical Biography* (pp. 244–5), *op. cit.*

moment to be in the presence of the master, and of a young bride who was proud to be his friend.

Before this event took place, Schubert decided to take the initiative in trying to get his instrumental music published. On 12 August he writes in almost identical terms to the two most reputable Leipzig publishers, Probst and Breitkopf und Härtel.

'Sir, In the hope that my name may not be wholly unknown to you, I most politely enquire whether you would not be disinclined to require some of my compositions at reasonable terms, being desirous of becoming as well known as possible in Germany.'[1] He goes on to mention as immediately available songs, string quartets–presumably the ones in D minor and G major–pianoforte sonatas–including no doubt the G major–four-handed piano pieces, and the octet. The inclusion of this last piece is interesting as a confirmation that its presentation to Count Troyer, who had commissioned and presumably paid for the work, was not thought of as including the publication rights; a point not without its relevance to the case of the Great C major Symphony.

To this approach Breitkopf and Härtel responded with an offer to publish a work on a trial basis, in return for a number of free copies, and suggesting a keyboard work for this purpose. To sugar this pill, the writer, counting perhaps on the ability of the firm's reputation to attract a young composer, holds out the bait of a 'lasting relationship'; and points out, disingenuously one feels sure, that Schubert is an unknown quantity commercially.[2]

To this offer Schubert did not bother to reply. Probst was more forthcoming, however. As the German agent for

[1] *Documentary Biography* (Nos. 688–9), *op. cit.*
[2] *Idem* (No. 695), *op. cit.*

Artaria, who had during the last year published a number of important Schubert works, he could hardly claim to be completely unaware of the composer's existence. His letter urges that reasonable concessions have to be made to popular taste. 'I must frankly confess to you that our public does not yet sufficiently and generally understand the peculiar, often ingenious, but perhaps now and then somewhat curious procedures of your mind's creations';[1] and he goes on to ask for songs (still the first choice it seems) and 'not too difficult pianoforte compositions for 2 and 4 hands, agreeable and easily comprehensible'. Thus began an association which was to end only with the publication of the E flat major piano trio in the month of Schubert's death, the final, and only, success in Schubert's campaign to get his work published outside Austria. Later that autumn Schubert sent Probst three manuscripts. We have no means of telling what they were, but since he asked eighty florins each for them they were probably substantial works.[2] The publisher temporised, explaining that he was fully occupied for the time being with the collected edition of the works of Friedrich Kalkbrenner—where are they now, one wonders—and that he thought the fee asked must be a mistake. In the summer of 1827 the two men met in Vienna, but little progress seems to have been made, for there the matter rested until February 1828, when Probst himself reopened it. As for Schubert's hope of making his name in Germany as an instrumental composer, it must have seemed more remote in the autumn, after the abortive correspondence with the two Leipzig publishers, than at the beginning of the year.

[1] *Documentary Biography* (No. 694), *op. cit.*
[2] A phrase in a later letter of Probst suggests that they may have been early piano works.

A notable absentee from Schubert's list of works sent to Probst as available for publication in August 1826, and one about which we are sadly short of information, is the B flat major piano trio opus 99. The provenance of this work is a mystery. The manuscript has not survived; there is no record of performance, no direct reference in the contemporary documents. The one certainty is that it was written before the E flat major trio, since Schubert himself gave it an earlier opus number, and it appears in Diabelli's list of 1831 as 'premier grand trio'. Beyond that we are in the realm of subjective judgment, though not of pure conjecture. For the question is not beyond the reach of argument, and since it is crucial to the story of Schubert's development as a composer, the obligation to form a critical judgment on it is not to be evaded. Fortunately some evidence, of a mainly negative kind, does exist.

The first point is that the manuscript cannot have been in Schubert's possession at the time of his death. All the surviving chamber music was taken over by Diabelli from Ferdinand Schubert soon after the composer's death, and an itemised list prepared. If the B flat piano trio had been among it, it would certainly have been listed in Ferdinand's receipt, as in fact the earlier string trio in the same key (D.581) was.[1] For the commercial importance of Schubert's enormous musical heritage was already beginning to dawn on Diabelli, and it is clear that the transaction was carefully negotiated. Kreissle, Schubert's first biographer, quotes a complementary document drawn up by Diabelli himself, in which he lays claim to all the opus numbers up to and including number 153, with certain itemised exceptions.[2]

[1] *Documentary Biography* (No. XXXVIII, p. 901), *op. cit.*
[2] See *The Life of Franz Schubert* (vol. II, p. 245) by Kreissle von Hellborn, translated by Arthur Duke Coleridge, London 1869.

Now it is true that the B flat piano trio occurs neither in Ferdinand's list, as one of the works included in the deal, nor in Diabelli's list of opus numbers specifically excluded. For this, however, there may be a simple explanation; what we can be sure of is that the piano trio was not among the works Schubert left behind at Schober's at his death.

It is a safe assumption also, when we consider the importance Schubert attached to the publication of his chamber music in these final years of his life, that had opus 99 been available for publication in August 1826, or in 1828, it would have been offered to Probst, as indeed the E flat piano trio was, or to Schott. In fact, it is never mentioned in his correspondence with those publishers, and this is all the more remarkable in view of the anxiety he shows to see the E flat trio in print. Indeed, the note of desperation which reveals itself in his correspondence with Probst over the E flat trio – 'I request that the edition should be faultless, and look forward to it longingly' – looks like the sequel to an earlier disappointment over the B flat trio. Probst, who accepted opus 100 reluctantly, did not fail to point out that such a work 'is rarely capable of bringing in anything'; and for this reason, if for no other, it seems extremely unlikely that the B flat trio could have been written and disposed of to a publisher in 1827 without some record surviving of the transaction.

The customary attribution of the B flat piano trio to the year 1827 rests on nothing more substantial than that the two piano trios carry adjacent opus numbers; and since the E flat trio is known to have been written in November 1827, the earlier trio is assumed to belong to that year also. Schubert's opus numbers, however, are a notoriously unreliable guide to the order in which his works were written; the contiguity of the two piano trios means nothing more than that, in giving Probst the opus number, in August 1828, for the E flat trio, he reserved the preceding number for the unpublished earlier work. The conclusion we face, if the above line of argument is accepted, is that the B flat trio cannot have been in Schubert's hands in August 1826, in February 1828, or at the time of his death: and that it is extremely improbable that it could have been written and sold, without documentary evidence surviving, between August 1826 and November 1827, when he wrote opus 100. (Why, one wonders, if it was disposed of to a publisher with such totally unexpected ease, was it not also published?) The inescapable inference is that the B flat trio was completed and sold before 1826, that it was a work not of his final but of his middle years. Sold, but not published, so that Schubert was powerless either to insist on its publication or to dispose of it elsewhere. If that was the fate of this splendid work, would it not help to explain Schubert's desperate anxiety to see the later piano trio in print before his death?

As a hypothesis this rests mainly on negative evidence, but taken in conjunction with the internal evidence it gathers strength. It is not simply that a passage like the following, from the finale, betrays unmistakeably its affinity with the 1825 piano sonatas and the Great C Major:

Example 6

The gaiety and exuberance, the almost swaggering assurance

of the work present a strong contrast with the more reflective character of the E flat trio; the scherzo reminds us much
more of the Trout quintet of 1819 than of the corresponding
movement from opus 100; and if one has to choose between
two over-lengthy movements, the cheeky prolixity of the
opus 99 rondo finale seems to have more in common with the
corresponding movements of the three piano sonatas of 1825
than it does with the somewhat mawkish prolixity of the
opus 100 finale, and for that reason perhaps to wear better.[1]

Two slender scraps of circumstantial evidence do indeed
exist to support the hypothesis that the B flat piano trio
belongs to 1825. According to a long-established tradition,
the trio movement called *Notturno* (D.897) used in its middle
section a rhythm Schubert picked up from a gang of navvies
during his stay there in August 1825, the characteristic of
which is a stress on the second beat of a three-beat bar,
where the workmen bring their hammers down in unison.[2]
(Schubert was to use the same rhythm, with infinitely more
subtlety and effect, in the slow movement of the B flat major
piano sonata, written in the last months of his life.) Now the
Notturno has always been thought to be a rejected slow movement of the B flat piano trio. In the absence of any other
evidence as to its date, it seems reasonable to suppose that
Schubert was also at work on the trio during that eventful
summer, and that the *Notturno* was intended as one movement of it.

[1] There is also a noteworthy affinity between the first movement of
opus 99 and the song *Des Sängers Habe* of February 1825, as Einstein
noted, and Richard Capell also some years earlier. See *Schubert* (p. 317)
by Alfred Einstein, London 1951, and *Schubert's Songs* (p. 214) by
Richard Capell, London 1928.
[2] The point was elaborated by Karl Klier in 1952. See Brown,
Critical Biography, p. 168.

The second point relates to the generally accepted fact that the genesis of the work must have owed something to Schubert's friendship with Schuppanzigh, Linke, and Bocklet, the professional musicians who are associated with Schubert's emergence as a composer of chamber music in 1824. It is the pianist Karl Maria von Bocklet who, it seems likely, must have taken a special interest in the piano trio. Schubert became acquainted with Bocklet in about 1823 (he was a violinist at the Theater an der Wien before becoming a virtuoso pianist), and was clearly on friendly terms with him in 1825, for he dedicated the D major piano sonata (also written at Gastein) to him; and writing from Carinthia in the following spring, Bauernfeld suddenly says: 'How is Bocklet? I can never forget his playing, and I long for him,' a remark which suggests that by this time Bocklet was among the inner circle of Schubert's friends.[1] So far as Bocklet's interest in the work is concerned, therefore, 1825 is clearly an acceptable date.

The conclusion we come to is that opus 99 must join the growing tally of important works which are much earlier than they are commonly supposed to be; that it was completed and sold long before Schubert made his overtures to Probst and to Breitkopf and Härtel in August 1826. Why, then, was it not published until 1836? And why, if the trio's existence was well known—it had indeed been performed, if Spaun's evidence is to be accepted—did it not appear in Diabelli's list of 1830, in which the opus numbers excluded from his bargain with Ferdinand were individually mentioned?

[1] In his *Essays on Schubert*, Maurice Brown says that Schubert's association with these players was not confirmed until 1827; but as far as Schuppanzigh and Bocklet are concerned, the friendship seems to have developed much earlier.

To answer these questions we have to look at the tangled skein of relations between the various Viennese publishing houses at that time, and particularly at the process of commercial expansion by which Diabelli established his supremacy in the music publishing world in the 1830s. Between 1829 and 1835 Diabelli bought out Pennauer, Weigl, Artaria, Cappi and Czerny, and Leidesdorf, the successor of Sauer and Liedesdorf. All these firms had issued Schubert works, and presumably still held Schubert manuscripts in 1830. If, in 1830, Diabelli was in negotiation for their Schubert interests as part of a package deal, it is understandable that he would not have specifically excluded them from the deal with Ferdinand, for he would regard them as covered by the separate negotiations. That this is what happened is confirmed by the fact that he failed to list among the excluded items any of the works belonging to Sauer and Leidesdorf, Pennauer, Weigl, and Matthias Artaria. Somewhere among them was the unpublished B flat piano trio; where, it is at present impossible to say. But speculation can go a little further, if it be accepted that Diabelli would not have delayed the publication of the Trio once it came into his hands, particularly in view of the respectable success already achieved by the companion piece opus 100. Weigl and Matthias Artaria were taken over in 1833, Pennauer and Leidesdorf in 1835; the B flat piano trio was published in 1836. It looks therefore as though either Leidesdorf or Pennauer must bear the responsibility for keeping the work hidden from a not very expectant public for ten long years.

One other possible explanation of the disappearance of the B flat piano trio may be worth mentioning, though it is based on pure conjecture. Readers of Louis Spohr's autobiography will remember the strange case of Herr Johann von Tost, a mysterious stranger who presented himself to the composer soon after the latter's arrival in Vienna and put a financial proposition to him. In return for substantial fees, not to mention the furnishing of Spohr's new house in suitably elegant style, Tost was to have sole rights to, and personal possession of, all his new compositions for a period of three years, after which they would revert to the composer to dispose of as he wished. It transpired that Tost was an early exponent of the doctrine that sponsorship of the arts is good for business. As he explained the matter to Spohr, his motives were twofold. 'First, I want to be invited to the *musicales* where your pieces will be played, and therefore I must have them in my possession. Secondly, I hope that on my business trips the possession of such treasures will bring me the acquaintance-ship of music lovers who, in turn, may be useful to me in my business.' It seems likely that, in an age when the ownership of new works was still an important status symbol (and when 'passing off' was by no means unknown) such an arrangement was fairly common. Haydn had made a similar bargain with Tost many years earlier, and in the increasingly commercial atmosphere of Vienna in the 1820s others may well have followed his example. Such a transaction could conceivably have kept the trio out of circulation from 1825 to 1828 when, according to Nottebohm, it was given a performance by Schuppanzigh, Bocklet and Linke, but if so no record has survived.

His operatic hopes dashed, and with little hope of publication for his string quartets, Schubert turned his attention to the symphony he had begun at Gmunden and Gastein, which now, completed and scored, awaited performance. This work, the grand symphony which he had conceived as the chief object of his ambition two years earlier, had come to occupy a position of crucial concern in his mind. How to get it performed? The only hope lay in the Vienna Music Society with which Schubert had long and close links. Leopold von Sonnleithner, one of the officials of the Society, had been his friend for many years and had taken an active part in getting his songs first performed and then published in 1821. Since then, his work had been regularly included in the Society's concerts. Early in October[1] therefore he writes to the Committee:

'Convinced of the Austrian Musical Society's noble intention to support any artistic endeavour as far as possible, I venture, as a native artist, to dedicate to them this, my Symphony, and to commend it most politely to their protection.'

The wording of this is singular. 'This, my Symphony'—as though content to rest his reputation as a composer on this one work; the appeal to patriotic feeling; and the hint of resignation in the final words. Schubert's action seems to have caused the Committee some surprise and embarrassment, not least because a dedication carried certain financial obligations to the composer which the Society was not in a position to meet. According to Pohl, the Society's official historian, the Vice-President reported the position to the Committee at a meeting on 9 October, when it was resolved to send Schubert 100 florins, not as a fee for the symphony, (possibly because that might have been taken as a promise of performance) but as a token of goodwill and encouragement.

[1] C. F. Pohl, the historian of the Philharmonic Society, dates this letter between October 9 and 12, i.e. after the committee meeting of October 9. It is true, as Maurice Brown has pointed out, that the letter itself is undated; but as the corresponding documents are dated, and nobody has suggested that Schubert dedicated *two* symphonies to the Society, there seems little doubt that Pohl is right.

The secretary, Josef Sonnleithner (Leopold's uncle, and the author of the first libretto for *Fidelio*) agreed to find the money himself if the Society could not raise it. Accordingly on 12 October the Society's Treasurer was instructed to send Schubert 100 florins, with a letter from Vice-President Kiesewetter asking him 'to accept the enclosed, not as a fee, but as a token of the Society's sense of obligation towards you, and of the thanks with which it acknowledges the interest you have shown it'.[1] Though the letter makes no direct reference to the symphony, there is a clear allusion to it in the words 'not as a fee'; and indeed, a contemporary document from the Society's archives assigns a library catalogue number to the piece.

The transaction of October 1826 is thus fully documented. But did Schubert actually pass over to the Society a symphonic score in return for that 100 florins? If so, what was it? The Great C Major symphony, or some other work, since lost? No satisfactory view of Schubert's development as a composer can be found unless at least provisional answers to these questions can be found. It is to the analysis of this problem that we turn in the next chapter.

[1] *Documentary Biography* (No. 713), *op. cit.* See also Nos. 709, 710, 711, 712, 714, 715.

II

'THIS, MY SYMPHONY . . .'

His great Symphony he composed (unin-
vited) for the Music Society, to whom he
presented the autograph. . . .
Leopold von Sonnleithner

Schubert had made no secret of his intention to write a grand symphony. He mapped out his plan of campaign to Kupelwieser in March 1824 with more than his customary deliberation, and doubtless to other close friends too; for Schwind twice mentions, as an important item of news in letters of that year, his friend's resolve to write a symphony.[1] At Zseliz in the summer of 1824, though he did not write a symphony as Schwind expected, he put his genius to school with two keyboard works of such clearly symphonic dimensions, and of so orchestral a texture, that those critics may be forgiven who have mistakenly assumed one of them, the Grand Duo sonata, to be *the* symphony in disguise. In a sense it was, for it is the first complete Schubert work to achieve the scale and stature of 'grand symphony'. The influence of Beethoven is plain enough, and so it is in the splendid set of variations in A flat major opus 35, also written at Zseliz, a work more characteristically Schubertian in its harmonic adventuring and one that reminds us subtly and insistently of Beethoven's A major symphony. But neither piece success-fully realised Schubert's ambition to write a work which would marry his own lyrical and harmonic genius to the

[1] *Documentary Biography* (Nos. 475 and 492), *op. cit.*

71

proportions of grand symphony. The Grand Duo is certainly symphonic, but it is not, as the Great C Major is, a summing-up of the essential Schubert; the opus 35 variations explore remote tonal regions in a splendidly Schubertian manner, but a theme and variations do not make a symphony. He was content to leave them both as classics of the keyboard duet literature.

It is equally well established that the projected grand symphony was written, or at any rate started, at Gmunden and Gastein in the summer of 1825. Anton Ottenwalt, in a letter to his brother-in-law Josef von Spaun of July 1825, makes a special point of it, and clearly refers to Schubert's hope of a Vienna performance in the coming winter.[1] Schubert seems to have expressed the same hope in a letter to Schwind, for we find Schwind replying on 14 August: 'About your symphony we may be quite hopeful. Old Hönig is dean of the faculty of jurisprudence, and as such is to give a concert. That will afford a better opportunity of having it performed; indeed we count upon it.'[2] These references suggest that the symphony was already well advanced, or that Schubert was being unduly optimistic in looking for a per-formance that winter; or perhaps that both statements are true. In the event, as we have seen, no performance followed, and it was with a certain feeling of resignation to an unrelent-ing destiny that Schubert commended 'this, my symphony' to the protection of the Philharmonic Society in October 1826.

Scattered among the Schubert documents are various references to the 'symphony written at Gastein', all in terms

[1] *Documentary Biography* (No. 569), *op. cit.*
[2] *Idem* (No. 581). 'Old Hönig' was Netti's father, and it is doubtful if his willingness to promote Schubert's interests was ever more than a pious hope on Schwind's part.

which identify it implicitly or explicitly with the Great C
Major. They range from the obituary tributes of 1828 to the
flurry of Schubert reminiscences which followed the publication of Kreissle's biography in the 1860s. For fifty years
after the composer's death, a period of growing concern to
bring his unpublished work to light, it was taken for granted
that the Great C Major was the only symphony of his mature
years, and that it is the symphony begun in 1825 at Gmunden
and Gastein and presented to the Philharmonic Society in
1826. The witnesses include Bauernfeld, Spaun, Sonnleithner, and Ferdinand Schubert, all those who were close
enough to Schubert to know something of the course of
events. It was not till 1881 that Grove rediscovered some of
the references to the 'symphony written at Gastein' and,
resting his case on the proposition: The Great C Major is
dated March 1828, therefore it cannot be the symphony
written in 1825 and presented to the Vienna Society in 1826,
launched upon an unsuspecting world the theory of a missing
'Gastein symphony'. The contention in these pages is that
Grove was misled by his incomplete knowledge of the facts,
and by his understandable predisposition to add to the growing tally of unknown Schubert masterpieces; that in suggesting that a major work of Schubert's last years had been written and lost without trace he implied that the friends and
contemporaries of the composer were either fools or liars;
and that, on any objective review of the evidence, the 'missing Gastein symphony' is one of the great non-events of
musical history. In support of this thesis, two propositions
need to be established: first, that Schubert's friends knew
what they were talking about, and that their evidence admits
of only one conclusion; and second, that the date on the
manuscript of the Great C Major can be explained without

recourse to the hypothesis of an earlier missing symphony.[1]
The first of these propositions involves us in an examination
of the contemporary, and near-contemporary, evidence, and
of the credentials of the witnesses, the first being Josef von
Spaun, the composer's oldest friend and the author of the
first biographical account of his life and work.

Spaun's article, written immediately after Schubert's death
and expanded and edited by his brother-in-law Anton Ottenwalt, was published in a Linz newspaper in March 1829. In
the main it tends to play down Schubert's achievements as an
instrumental and orchestral composer, for Spaun believed, as
he explained himself in a letter to Bauernfeld, that 'Schubert
should be treated as a song composer by his biographers', and
that other things 'should be dealt with as being subordinate'.[2]
Yet he does include: 'In 1825, at Gastein, a grand Symphony
for which the composer himself had a vast preference', a
curious form of words which invites the suspicion that Spaun
found this preference difficult to understand, and failed to
share it. There is no suggestion that the work is missing,
though the article elsewhere comments on the loss of some
early works, and it seems inconceivable that Spaun could
have failed to refer to the fact had it been lost. Many years
later, when he wrote down (in 1864) some notes on
Schubert for his family, he added: 'In Gastein he composed
his greatest and most beautiful symphony', a remark which can
have had no meaning unless it referred to the Great C Major,

[1] The argument of this chapter is set out in a rather different form in
my article 'The Gastein Symphony Reconsidered', *Music and Letters*,
October 1959.

[2] In the same letter he says: 'For all the admiration I have given the
dear departed for years, I still feel that we shall never make a Mozart or
a Haydn out of him in instrumental and church composition, whereas in
song he is unsurpassed . . .' See *Documentary Biography* (No. 33 and
notes), *op. cit.*

then slowly establishing itself in the orchestral repertoire.

Spaun's article was passed on to Bauernfeld, together with some notes prepared by Ferdinand Schubert, and used by him as the basis of an obituary published in a Vienna periodical in June 1829. It is not surprising, therefore, to find him referring to the 1825 symphony in terms very similar to Spaun's: 'To the larger works of his last years belongs further a Symphony written at Gastein in 1825, for which its author had a special liking.'

Much more weight must be attached to the statements of Ferdinand Schubert, because he had a strong financial interest in the disposal of his brother's unpublished works, and, as his correspondence with Pachler and with Schober over the projected performance of *Alfonso und Estrella* shows,[1] was capable of pursuing that interest with some ruthlessness. Now the bargain between Ferdinand and Diabelli, by which the publisher in 1830 took over the remaining songs and chamber music, expressly excluded the symphonies; so that had there been any question of a missing symphony Ferdinand would have had the strongest possible motives for advertising the fact. Let us see what steps he did take between 1830 and 1859, when he died (in debt), to advertise the existence of the symphonies, and what light they throw on the problem of the relationship between the 'symphony written at Gastein' and the Great C Major.

[1] The ownership of the score of this opera proved quite a bone of contention. On Schubert's death the score was in Graz and Ferdinand did not discover its whereabouts until 1842, when he asked for its return. In 1841, Schober, who wrote the libretto, asked Ferdinand to send it to Weimar so that Liszt could consider a production there. Ferdinand, who had recently opened negotiations with Breitkopf and Härtel for the purchase of all the operas, sent a temporising reply which drew an angry response from Schober. Echoes of the affair rumbled on into the 1860s. See *Memoirs* (pp. 402, 405 *et seq*, 412, 419 *et seq*, and 433), *op. cit.*

The story is closely linked with Robert Schumann's pro-
selytising zeal on behalf of Schubert's music. In April 1835
Ferdinand, counting on Schumann's expressed enthusiasm,
sent to Leipzig a summarised statement of the works still
available, with an invitation to any interested publisher to
get into touch with him. The appeal, which was published
both in Schumann's *Neue Zeitschrift für Musik* and in the Paris
Gazette Musicale, seems to have had no effect. Under the title
Symphonies, the following are listed: in D (1813), in D
(1815), in B flat (1815), in C minor (1816), in B flat (1816),
in C major (1818), in C minor (his last). Predictably, this
list omits the Unfinished, as it was hidden away in Anselm
Huttenbrenner's desk, and the incomplete E minor sketch of
1821; its vagueness over the last item, and the inaccuracy in
the key, is due to the fact that Ferdinand had not at this time
seen the manuscript of the Great C Major, and was writing on
hearsay.[1] There the matter rested until the beginning of
1839, when Schumann visited Ferdinand in Vienna and was
astonished and delighted to find a great hoard of Schubert
masterpieces awaiting publication. The story is well-known,
how he immediately wrote to Breitkopf and Härtel to urge
the importance of the manuscripts and Ferdinand's need of
money; and how, at the publishers' instigation, he encouraged Ferdinand to forward information and scores to
Leipzig. On 31 January 1839, his brother's birthday, Ferdinand wrote:

'I have learnt through Herr Schumann that you might not

[1] It is not true, as was once thought, that the manuscript of the Great
C Major did not come into the possession of the Philharmonic Society
until late in the 1830s. Ferdinand himself, as we shall see, makes it plain
that the original had all along been in the Society's possession, and C. F.
Pohl many years later confirmed the fact. See *Documentary Biography*
(No. 45), *op. cit.*, and *Memoirs*, *op. cit.*, p. 459.

be averse to purchasing some of the compositions of my late brother (Franz Schubert) especially symphonies, but that you would first like to see the manuscripts. I hasten, therefore, to inform you that I shall have the honour of sending you immediately two of my brother's *seven* existing symphonies, through Messrs. Diabelli and Co. with the next consignment of their publications. Of the symphony no. 6, you will receive not only the score, but also the transcribed parts, because this work has already been performed once with great success in Vienna (in 1829) by the Philharmonic Society in the Imperial *Redouten-Saal*). . . . Of the Symphony no. 7 you will receive only an accurate Transcript (copied by myself), because the manuscript itself is preserved as an autograph memorial in the archives of the Austrian Philharmonic Society.'[1]

Ferdinand goes on to ask 700 florins as a comprehensive fee for the seven symphonies, or individual fees ranging from 100 florins to 200 for the last, and begs for the favour of an answer as soon as possible.

This letter has been quoted at length, because it establishes the identity of the Great C Major and the work presented to the Society and preserved as a memorial in the Society's library. If, at this time, there had been two Schubert symphonies in the archives of the Society—as Grove's hypothesis would lead us to suppose—is it conceivable that Ferdinand would not have been aware of the fact, and have advertised it? Is it conceivable, alternatively, had an earlier symphony been written and presented to the Society in 1826, that it could have been lost at some time between that date and 1830 without this extraordinary event being noticed and remarked upon?

[1] *Documentary Biography* (No. 45), *op. cit.*

In the 1840s the Viennese singer and collector of music autographs Alois Fuchs set out to compile, with Ferdinand's help, a thematic catalogue of Schubert's works which was intended to serve as an appendix to a biography of the composer. Fuchs' plans were dogged by ill-health and the biographical project came to nothing. The thematic catalogue, however, was handed over to Ferdinand and seems to have been added to at various times by him. The symphonic section includes the same seven works as Ferdinand's letter to Breitkopf and Härtel, but with much more detail. For the seventh symphony, for instance, the incipits of the Great C Major are written out in Ferdinand's hand and the entry reads: '7 Symphony for orchestra in C (no. 7) March 1828 for the Vienna Music Society. . . . Autograph with the Music Society.' The symphonic sketch in E of August 1821 is included as number 8, and a space at the end is left for the Unfinished, an interesting indication that even at this time its existence was known.

These facts prove beyond doubt that the importance of establishing the sequence and dates of Schubert's symphonies was by no means unrecognised by Ferdinand; that the identity of the Great C Major with the symphony presented to the Vienna Music Society was never doubted by him; and that Ferdinand, who would have had the keenest personal and financial interest in the matter, never so much as hinted at the existence of a missing symphony. So far the evidence, however, is mainly negative. For a positive link between the events of 1825–6 and the Great C Major we must turn to Leopold von Sonnleithner, Schubert's friend and patron and then an official of the Society, of which his uncle, Josef, was founder and secretary.

Of all those in the composer's entourage, Sonnleithner

comes closest in his musicality and judgment to the standards
of twentieth-century criticism. A lawyer, with a lawyer's
concern for fact, he was the first to realise that any critical
assessment of Schubert's development must depend upon
first compiling a reliable chronological list of his works.[1] His
disinterested concern for his friend's welfare is attested by
the part he played in getting the first songs published in 1821,
by his attempts to recover missing works like the *Prometheus*
cantata, and by his scrupulous confession, late in life, that he
once, at Diabelli's instigation, tampered with the text of
Schiller's *Punschlied* (D.277). He left us the only authoritative contemporary account of Schubert's manner of performing his own songs, and the fullest description of the
musical life of Vienna in those days. He represents at its best
the musical tradition of upper-middle class Vienna which
provided the background for Schubert's emergence as a composer.

In the 1850s, Luib began to collect material for a Schubert
biography and turned to Sonnleithner for help. In response,
Sonnleithner wrote in 1857 a long account of his friend's life
and work, stressing the need for a chronological catalogue,
and giving invaluable detail about, among other things, the
Great C Major. 'Schubert composed,' he wrote, 'mostly as
the result of an inner urge or to please friends, without any
question of a fee. Only extremely seldom did he receive
(except from his publisher) a gift for a dedication. His great
symphony he composed (uninvited) for the Music Society, to
whom he presented the autograph. He received a gift of 100
florins for it, which was very welcome to him. The amount in
itself is not large, but in view of the Society's means it is not
inconsiderable.'[2] As we have seen, the gift of 100 florins is

[1] *Memoirs* (p. 117), *op. cit.*   [2] *Idem* (p. 113), *op. cit.*

fully documented; it took place in October 1826. 'His great symphony' can only refer to the Great C Major, for Sonnleithner, writing thirty years after the event, could not possibly have referred in these terms, in this context, to a lost work,[1] without further explanation. The passage admits of only one conclusion: that Sonnleithner, who was in the best position to know, identified the Great C Major as the work begun in 1825 and presented to the Society in October 1826.

Why then, it may be asked, has such an aura of confusion and mystery gathered about the question? For confusion there certainly is. It begins with Bauernfeld's biographical article, which lists two symphonies in an appendix, one in 1825, and one ('last symphony') in 1828, and reaches a peak of impenetrability in Schindler and Kreissle. Even Schubert's friends, however, knew comparatively little about his orchestral and instrumental compositions. He was still regarded primarily as a song writer, and—to anticipate for a moment the conclusion to which the argument leads—they must have been as puzzled as we are by his decision to head the score of the Great C Major with the date of the final recension. Moreover, there seem to have been two other elements in the situation. I have suggested elsewhere that Schubert's disappointment at the failure of the Music Society to give a performance of what he regarded as his greatest composition may have led to an estrangement between himself and the Society; a suggestion with which the faintly apologetic tone

[1] To suppose that he could (as O. E. Deutsch does) seems a curious failure of historical imagination. To attempt a modern analogy, it is rather as though Mr. Michael Kennedy, writing in the 1970s, should refer *tout court* to 'Elgar's unfinished symphony' without explaining that he meant, not the well-known work commissioned by the B.B.C., but a quite different work whose existence none of his readers suspected.

of Sonnleithner's reference in the letter to Luib is entirely consistent. If so, it would have been a case of least said soonest mended. To those unaware of the true story, what added to the confusion was the decision to include in the Society's concert of 14 December 1828, only a month after Schubert's death, not the Great C Major, but the 'little C major' of 1818 (D.589). Schindler, for instance, seems to have been misled by this into supposing that it was the little C major which was presented to the Society; for he evidently believes, in his biographical sketch of 1857, that it was the Great C Major that was written in 1817/18, noting that it was 'composed in his twentieth year'—i.e. in 1817—and including it under that year in his accompanying catalogue of works.[1] This confusion between the roles played by the two symphonies persisted well into the sixties. In January 1861 a Vienna music paper[2] carried the following letter, supposed to have been written by Gustav Nottebohm. 'In the programme of a Society concert on 14 December 1828, which we have before us, appears, among the works performed, a "Symphony in C by Franz Schubert". As the biographical information on Franz Schubert omits this early performance of a Symphony, which took place four weeks after his death, and reports only later ones, it would be interesting to discover which Symphony is referred to: whether the sixth or the well-known, and published, seventh, both of which are in C major. . . . Perhaps someone can give us precise information on the subject.' A few days later Leopold von Sonnleithner himself wrote to clear the matter up:

'Sir, With reference to an enquiry in No. 3 of your journal I can give the following information, and I can vouch for the truth of it, as an ear-witness and part-organiser.

[1] *Memoirs* (pp. 316 and 322), *op. cit.*   [2] *Deutsche Musik-Zeitung.*

'On 14 December 1828 at a concert of the Music Society of the Austrian Kingdom, it was not the great (seventh) but the smaller (sixth) C major symphony by Franz Schubert which was performed. The same one was repeated on 12 March 1829, in the *Concert Spirituel*. The programme of this last concert, which I have in front of me, only has the simple statement: Symphony by Fr. Schubert, without any indication of the key, and without the addition of "new" or "performed for the first time"—which was always the custom in such cases. . . .

'Soon after it had been composed, the great C major symphony was rehearsed by the Music Society in the practices at the Conservatoire, but it was provisionally put on one side because of its length and difficulty. It was only on 15 December 1839 that a performance of this symphony, and in its entirety, was planned for one of the Society's concerts; but at the very first orchestral rehearsal the paid "artists" refused to carry out the necessary number of rehearsals, as a result of which the Concert committee had to confine themselves, for this occasion, to the first two movements. On 1 December 1850 the whole symphony was given for the first time, at one of the Society's concerts, in Vienna.'[1]

This correspondence was sparked off, it seems, by a Society concert at which the scherzo of the little C major was billed as 'Scherzo of the 6th Symphony, composed in 1825', an indication that Schindler's error in transposing the two works had been fairly generally accepted.

It is doubtful, however, whether the uncertainty over the provenance of the great C major symphony would ever have led to the extravagant hypothesis of a missing symphony if Grove had not lent the weight of his great authority to it. And since the origin of the theory is as interesting a story in

[1] *Memoirs* (pp. 430–1), *op. cit.*

its way as the origin of the symphony, it deserves closer examination.

Though George Grove had been acquainted with the Great C Major since 1856, when Manns gave the first public performance in England at the Crystal Palace, it was not until 1866 that his enthusiasm for Schubert's orchestral work was really fired. Alerted by Kreissle's biography, published in 1865, to the existence of a vast literature of unpublished Schubert works, he wrote to Spina, Diabelli's successor in Vienna, to enquire in particular about the *Rosamunde* music. As a result three of the numbers were played with great success in November. Grove wrote eagerly for more. That year saw also the first great performance of the Great C Major (so Grove himself called it); and this may well mean the first complete performance. In the following spring the Unfinished Symphony was published, and immediately included in the Crystal Palace programme for 6 April 1867. By this time the quest for new Schubert masterpieces had taken on almost the character of a crusade in Grove's mind. When, in the autumn of 1867 he set out for Vienna with Sullivan, it was with the declared intention of bringing to light not only the missing parts of the *Rosemunde* music, but also if possible the whole corpus of Schubert's symphonies, of which only the Great C Major and the Unfinished had so far appeared.

The story of their success was told by Grove in dramatic detail in the appendix to the English translation of Kreissle's biography[1] and is well-known. His elation is understandable; it helps to explain, against the background of the comparative coolness of the Viennese public at that time towards Schubert, his later confidence in his own judgment over the question of the 'Gastein symphony'. What is of more importance, in the

[1] Kreissle von Hellborn (Appendix to Vol. II), *op. cit.*

present context, is the full and precise account he gives of the
various symphonic manuscripts he examined and copied, and
in particular his comments on the manuscript of the last one,
which he and Sullivan examined in the library of the Music
Society. 'It differs from the MSS of all Schubert's other
Symphonies that I have had the privilege of examining, in
containing very many and very important alterations and
afterthoughts.' And noting the original and the revised form
of the main themes in the first and second movements, he
goes on: 'The first theme of the Allegro . . . was evidently
altered much later, since it appears in its original form all
through the first movement, and has been at every recurrence
scratched through with the pen.'[1] Grove was thus the first to
draw attention to the fact that some considerable time must
have elapsed between the completion of the score and the
revision, though he seems completely to have missed the
significance of this in the later controversy with Pohl.

Even at this time, if we may judge from a footnote, he was
aware of Schwind's reference to a symphony in 1825, but it
was not till 1881, when he got to work on his Schubert
biography for the Dictionary, that the theory of a missing
'Gastein symphony' took shape in his mind. In the *Life and
Letters of Sir George Grove* his biographer Charles Graves
describes the 'untiring importunity which he displayed in
seeking for corroborative evidence'. A series of letters
between Grove and Stanford, then on a visit to Vienna,
appears[2] to have been concerned almost exclusively with
Schubert matters in general, and with the theory of the missing symphony in particular. Grove's industry as a corre-

[1] Kreissle von Hellborn (Vol. II, p. 320), *op. cit.*

[2] 'appears', because the letters themselves seem to have been destroyed by Graves on completion of the biography. Various attempts to
trace them have all failed.

spondent was impressive. He sent off a string of queries to Stanford on 13 September and another two days later:

'A third letter broaches the theory of the missing Gastein symphony of 1826. Stanford replied on the 17th adducing evidence that conflicted with Grove's view, and the latter begins his rejoinder dated September 20th, "Yours of the 17th at first gave me profound disappointment. I nearly wept at having to give up the 10th. symphony. But on looking again at the entry in Pohl's book I have a little revived", and he forthwith gives reasons for adhering to his original view as to the independent existence of the Gastein symphony. A second letter, written the same night at 11 p.m., adds further arguments drawn from Ferdinand Schubert's article in the *Neue Zeitschrift für Musik* of April 30th 1839. Lastly, a final questionnaire on a postcard followed on the 21st prefaced with the words "What a *horrible* bore you must think me, but Schubert is *my existence*".'[1]

It is a pity this correspondence has not survived in full, for it would be interesting to read Stanford's report of the 'conflicting evidence' which so nearly persuaded Grove that he was wrong. On the other hand, it is not likely that it would add anything to the case Pohl convincingly puts in the public correspondence which ensued. For Grove now determined, against Stanford's advice, to publish his cherished theory of 'Another Unknown Symphony by Schubert'. A few days later, on 28 September, under this title, he writes to *The Times* and to the *Daily News*, first recapitulating the transactions which took place in 1826 between Schubert and the Music Society of Vienna and which were described in the last chapter. He continues:

[1] *Life and Letters of Sir George Grove* (p. 274), by C. L. Graves, London 1903.

'There seems no doubt, therefore, that the transaction was completed, the money paid, and the symphony delivered, doubtless with the usual formal dedication to the society. This work, however, must surely be a different one from that referred to in the opening of my letter, of which the autograph is now in the library of the Music Society of Vienna which (according to Schubert's custom on commencing a composition) is dated at the head of the first page "March 1828", and which contains no dedication to the society or any trace of having been specially intended for them. This latter (the well-known "No. 9") appears to have been in the year 1838 in the keeping, not of the society, but of Ferdinand Schubert, by whom it was shown to Robert Schumann during his visit to the Austrian capital. . . . This symphony was at that time, then, clearly with the others in Ferdinand Schubert's custody. How or why it came from him into the safe keeping of the Musik-Verein is a question of minor interest. A far more important one is: where is the score which Schubert submitted to the society in October 1826? A confusion in date between 1826 and 1828 seems hardly possible, but it could be easily removed by inspecting the society's ledger, where the 100 florins would naturally be entered.

'It can hardly have been destroyed, and if it fortunately exists in some nook or corner of the society's collection or elsewhere its recovery will be a matter of extraordinary interest to the musical world.'[1]

It is evident here how far Grove's enthusiasm and the serendipitous events of 1867 had led him astray. He is quite wrong in supposing that the Great C Major only came into the Society's possession after 1838; it had been there at least

[1] *Memoirs* (pp. 456–8), *op. cit.*

since 1828. He is quite wrong in concluding that the Great C Major was not the symphony presented to the Society; Ferdinand Schubert and Alois Fuchs clearly annotated it 'for the Music Society'. And in suggesting that the real symphony Schubert presented to the Society might be lurking unknown and unnoticed 'in some nook or corner of the society's collection' he was being not merely tactless but defamatory. If *The Times* is read in heaven (which is open to question) Leopold Sonnleithner must have turned in his grave.

This K. F. Pohl, the librarian of the Music Society, was quick to point out. But it would be tedious to follow the ensuing correspondence in detail, especially as the protagonists are obviously at cross-purposes.[1] Grove is intent on proving the existence of a symphony of 1825/6, taking it for granted that if it exists it must be missing; Pohl insists that the theory of a missing symphony is an affront to Schubert's friends and an offence against common sense, taking it for granted that the 1825/6 work and the Great C Major must be one and the same. Pohl was clearly right, but in the romantic climate of the day Grove's authority carried the day; the myth of the missing Gastein symphony was born. What is more surprising is the respect paid to it by later scholars. At the time, Grove's theory was received with a good deal of scepticism. Stanford himself wrote: 'When he [Grove] pointed out the possibility of another Schubert symphony, which his own enthusiasm had exalted into a certainty, the insistence on his pet theory almost roused that most equable of librarians, C. F. Pohl of the *Gesellschaft der Musikfreunde* in Vienna, to active wrath. When I visited Vienna he complained to me bitterly that Grove's statements

[1] *Memoirs* (pp. 459–62), *op. cit.*

practically amounted to an accusation of carelessness in the administration of his library.'[1] And he goes on to express his own belief that Grove had 'strained his conclusions beyond the justification of his premises'. Nearly fifty years later O. E. Deutsch, without offering his readers the courtesy of discussing the pros and cons, declares flatly: 'Pohl was wrong in supposing that the Great C Major was written in 1826 and only revised in 1828.'[2] Maurice Brown, who in an appendix to his *Critical Biography* of Schubert leaves open the possibility that the symphony sketched at Gmunden and Gastein in 1825 was later worked up into the Great C Major, stops short of accepting Pohl's view and sums up inconclusively. The myth has shown remarkable vitality, and the reason is not far to seek.

The crux of the matter is of course the dated autograph. So long as one takes that 'March 1828' at the head of the Ms. at its face value, the conclusion seems inescapable that, even if there were not two symphonies, there must at least have been two manuscripts. But dates are not always to be taken at their face value, as Pohl pointed out; certainly not the date on the Ms. of Mozart's *Requiem* or (for different reasons) that of the Ms. of the first half of the Forty-Eight. Moreover there is clear evidence in the autograph itself that the date cannot possibly be that of the inception of the work. As we have seen, Grove himself was the first to draw attention to the fact that the manuscript had undergone extensive revision, and that there must have been a lapse of time between the completion of the original score and the alterations which feature so prominently in it. So the first subject of the first movement originally appeared throughout as:

[1] *Pages from an Unwritten Diary*, by Stanford, London 1914.
[2] *Memoirs* (p. 460), *op. cit.*

Example 7

And the oboe's counter theme at bar 24 of the Andante[1] appeared throughout the movement as:

Example 8

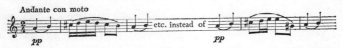

These and many other additions, excisions, and second thoughts were all carefully noted in Grove's appendix to Kreissle, and justify his conclusion that the first four movements (Grove seems to count the trio as a separate movement) are 'literally crowded with alterations; so much so that the work looks as if it were made up of afterthoughts'. It is a measure of the extent to which he later allowed his judgment to be clouded by his enthusiasm that in 1881 he could declare that 'the alterations in the Ms. of the symphony of 1828 are not serious, and are in very few cases more than would naturally arise during the progress of the work'.[2]

We have to postulate, therefore, that at least two quite distinct work-phases are represented in the autograph, and the problem of the date has to be re-stated. Does 'March 1828' refer to the original score or to the final recension? To this there can surely be only one answer, for there simply

[1] When Schubert did alter a melodic line he usually did so to great effect. These revisions may be compared with that of the beginning of the Andante of the 1823 piano sonata in A minor, and with the alteration in bar 4 of the Great C Major itself, where the original version had C for E.

[2] Letter to *The Athenaeum*, 19 November 1881. Quoted in *Memoirs, op. cit.*, p. 462.

was not time for Schubert to have begun the work in March 1828, completed it, and then later revised it before his death eight months later. To suppose that he could is to underestimate grossly the scale and stature of 'this, my symphony' and to ignore the already phenomenal output of those months, which included the three last piano sonatas, the string quintet in C major, the E flat major mass, two first-rate keyboard duet works, and many other smaller works.

Pohl was clearly right in concluding that the manuscript of the Great C Major is the manuscript which Schubert scored in 1826 and presented to the Music Society, which the Society failed to perform, and which Schubert revised and dated with a view to publication in March 1828. Grove's enthusiasm for his cause unwittingly led him to cling to a half-truth which has seriously distorted the whole corpus of Schubert criticism since his day.

There is a special purity and power about the romantic imagination at its first impulse, before it outgrows the classical forms which give it birth, which invest the art of the first three decades of the nineteenth century with a unique character. A sense of innocence and of joy, a certain intensity of vision, a serenity in the contemplation of nature as of a kind of incandescence; these elements are common to *Tintern Abbey*, to Girtin's *Rainbow over the Exe*, to Samuel Palmer's *The Bright Cloud*, to a Field *Nocturne* or a Schubert *Impromptu*: and so is a classical clarity of form. This should not surprise us, for the unity of the arts was no academic notion to the romantics, and least of all to Schubert, whose close friends were not musicians but writers, painters, and liberals (i.e. political radicals). The triumvirate of the arts which played so prominent a part in his life in 1822/3 (Schober, Kupelwieser, and Schubert) and again in 1824/6 (Schubert, Schwind, Bauernfeld) was no mere social convenience; it became a kind of slogan in the battle against the philistines. It is possible to deplore this extra-musical quality in Schubert's work as a kind of distraction from the serious business of composition. It is possible also, and perhaps more perceptive, to regard it as the mainspring of his genius, and the impulse which drew him to Goethe, Schiller, Wilhelm Müller and many others. To see a representative collection of early romantic painting is to be forcibly reminded that *Erlkönig, Die junge Nonne, Der Zwerg* (not to mention the Walter Scott songs) belong to the collective sub-consciousness, so to speak, of the romantic movement. One need not go far from home, either. In 1825, when Schubert was in Upper Austria sketching out the Great C Major, Samuel Palmer began the splendid series of paintings that mark off his visionary years from the rest. An interesting parallel can be drawn between the two men. Both entered fully into the romantic concern for the unity of the arts. Palmer wrote music, and verses about twilight that remind us of *Im Abendrot*; Schubert wrote verses and joined in the literary and artistic games of the Atzenbrugg company. Both were contemptuous of the taste and artistic standards of their day,[1] and followed their own genius in opposition to it. Just as Sonnleithner thought Schubert would have done better to seek out the guidance of a more mature composer, so Palmer's son thought his father lacked 'the healthy emulation of the schools when he might have profited by seeing the workmanship of those more experienced than himself'. And both,

[1] Palmer said that John Linnell had been sent by God 'to pluck me from the pit of modern art'. See Geoffrey Grigson, *Samuel Palmer: The Visionary Years*, London 1947.

neglected in their own day, have gained steadily in stature over the years, as the uniqueness and purity of their own romantic vision has come to be recognised. Those gibbous moons which so haunted Samuel Palmer's imagination find a kind of musical analogue in *Nacht und Träume* and in *Die Nebensonnen*.

The unifying element for these early romantics was the intuitive feeling for nature as the consoling metaphor of reality, the double vision, of which William Blake was perhaps the most consciously passionate exponent. Palmer said of Blake that 'to walk with him in the country was to perceive the soul of beauty through the forms of matter'. The relevance of these generalities to the understanding of Schubert's genius—and of the Great C Major symphony in particular—is not simply that many of his best songs, and both the great song-cycles, provide a kind of commentary upon them; it is clear that the idea of nature as the universal metaphor of human existence had taken a conscious hold on his imagination. The evidence lies in *An Schwager Kronos*, in *Die Allmacht* (written at Gastein in 1825), in *Im Abendrot*, in many other single songs, and in the trouble he took over a poem which seems to us to develop the idea with a naïve literalness—Goethe's *Gesang der Geister über den Wassern*:

'The soul of Man is like the water; from heaven it comes, to heaven it ascends. . . . Soul of mankind, how like the water, fate of mankind, how like the wind.'

Schubert set this poem first in September 1816, and again in March 1817. But in December 1820, when the patronage of the Sonnleithner family and others led to public recognition and acclaim, he began to work on a much more ambitious version for vocal octet with accompaniment for strings which received its first performance at the public concert at the Kärntnertor Theatre on 7 March 1821. For this Schubert wrote various sketches, and it is clear from the scale of the work, and of the forces used, that he planned a major work. In the event his plans miscarried, partly because the performance, according to Sonnleithner, was under-rehearsed; also because, truth to tell, the work promises more than it delivers, so that even a good performance leaves an impression of inflated eloquence. Its very failure, however, provides a pointer to the nature of that grand symphony round which Schubert's ambition crystallised in the years which followed, and the musical ideas on which its perhaps over-elaborate structure was built remained in his mind to find fuller expression later.

What is being suggested here is that the symphonic idea—and *a fortiori* the idea of 'grand symphony'—was consciously linked in Schubert's mind with the apprehension of natural beauty as the vesture of God; that the Great C Major symphony is the culmination and summation of this idea; and that its identity with the 'symphony written at Gastein' in the summer of 1825 is therefore a matter of crucial importance to his development as a composer. What light does the internal evidence throw on this assertion?

Most critics would probably admit that there is something wrong with March 1828 as the date of the symphony. By which, if invited, they would explain themselves to mean not simply that the date left Schubert no time in which to write it, but also that it does not sound like a work of 1828, not like the string quintet, for instance, or the F minor duet fantasia. One needs only the evidence of one's ears to agree that its energy and exuberance, Terpsichorean drive and generosity of scale all suggest a date pre-*Winterreise*, even if no account is taken of the many specific cross-references which link the symphony in style and idiom with other works of 1824 and 1825. Yet there is little disposition to reopen the question of the date, or to write off finally the possibility of a new mature Schubert symphony turning up in some cob-webbed attic, perhaps because to do so would be to give hostages to fortune; and also perhaps because to do so would mean taking a fresh look at the whole process of Schubert's development as a composer. For modern scholarship, which has been thorough in demolishing some of the romantic accretions to the Schubert story which nineteenth-century biographers took pleasure in, has been slow to question the essentially romantic concept of Schubert's career as a single meteoric rise which reached its apogee in the *annus mirabilis* of 1828, before plunging to its premature end. Does it matter whether the Great C Major symphony was written in 1825 or in 1828? The answer can only be that nothing can matter more to our idea of Schubert's development, indeed that no consistent account of his development can be given until the question is resolved. For on any critical showing the symphony represents Schubert's climacteric, the final and definitive expression of his symphonic idea. The musical con-cepts which there find their full and appropriate shape and context have grown up, so to speak, with the composer, so that listening to the early symphonies and chamber music—particularly symphonies number three, number six, and the unscored E minor symphony of 1821, and the B flat quartet of 1814—frequently seems to the listener like catching a glimpse of an old friend in disguise. It is not quite true to say that Schubert wrote not eight symphonies but eight versions of one symphony; for the Unfinished is *sui generis*, and num-ber four (the Tragic) and the light-hearted number five in B flat

are sharply and successfully differentiated. It is true, however, that from 1818 onwards, as the romantic conception of
grand symphony supplanted in his mind and imagination the
eighteenth-century conventions of *Spielmusik*, much of his
orchestral and instrumental music takes on the character of
sketches for the Great C Major.

This process has been documented in considerable detail,
notably by Mosco Carner[1] and by Maurice Brown,[2] and most
of the cross-references are sufficiently well-known not to
require illustration here. Attention should be drawn to one
of these recurrent ideas, however, both because it seems to
have escaped notice, and because it throws an interesting light
on the germ of the symphony itself and its association with
the transcendental view of nature.

As though to leave no doubt about the thematic unity of
his symphonic masterpiece, Schubert begins with a long
introduction in which a solemn hymn-like tune is played first
by two horns in unison, without benefit of key as it were,
then by the strings, then with brass and woodwind, and
finally in full orchestra with a kind of processional triplet
accompaniment on the violins. The tune is a Schubertian
summing up in itself, not only because of the rising third
which features so prominently in it—and which plays so big a
part in the symphony's subsequent development—but also
because it presents in outline the composer's favourite key
relationships at a third from the tonic.

Example 9

[1] In *Schubert: A Symposium* (ed.) Gerald Abraham, London 1947.
[2] In *The Genesis of the Great C Major Symphony* (*Essays on Schubert* 1966).

Where does this tune come from? The rising third is of
course a commonplace, and its association with a modulation
to the relative minor frequent in Schubert, often in a mood
of exaltation, as in *Verklärung* (D. 59). Significantly, when he
came to set Goethe's *Gesang der Geister über den Wassern*, he
set the opening words to an almost identical phrase:

Example 10

And at the words 'Wind ist der Welle lieblicher Buhle'
Schubert reminds us sharply of the modulation he was to use
in elliptical form at bar 27 of the symphony; the following
bars have an even more familiar ring about them:

Example 11

Even more to the point, perhaps, in that it belongs un-
questionably to August 1825, and was written in Gastein, is
Die Allmacht, Schubert's hymn of praise to the Creator, the
opening phrase of which repeats in augmented form that of
the symphony.

Example 12

These self-quotations only serve to confirm what is perhaps sufficiently obvious, that the primordial hymn which announces the theme of the Great C Major is a hymn to the glory of the natural world. And the many references in the symphony to the other compositions of 1825—the four-times rhythmically repeated notes, the 'run-up to the wicket' in triplet rhythm before a cadence back to the tonic, the ambiguous use of chromatically adjacent sevenths and sixths, these fingerprints of the years 1824 and 1825, and many others, leave no doubt where the internal evidence points on the question of the symphony's origin. The question is not whether it could have been written in 1825/6, but whether it could have been written at any other time; and the more one studies the evidence the more difficult it becomes to believe that it could.

According to Schindler, Schubert's meeting with Archbishop Pyrker (the author of *Die Allmacht*) in Gastein was treasured by the composer as one of the most inspiring moments of his life. But in truth we need no other evidence for the charismatic effect of the mountains upon Schubert than his own letters—especially those of his family—during those summer months of 1825 and the observations of his friends. 'I have never seen him like this,' wrote Ottenwalt to Spaun of the composer's stay with them, 'nor heard; serious, profound, and as though inspired.'[1] A few days earlier he reported: 'Schubert looks so well and strong, is so comfortably bright and so generally communicative that one cannot fail to be sincerely delighted about it. . . . By the way, he worked at a symphony at Gmunden, which is to be performed in Vienna this winter.'[2]

[1] *Documentary Biography* (No. 574), *op. cit.*
[2] *Idem* (No. 569), *op. cit.*

We do not need to look further for that symphony than the Great C Major, for its pages bear the imprint everywhere of Schubert's romantic feeling for natural beauty, both in its total conception and in detail. Nobody, for example, who has heard the notes of the traditional alpenhorn echoing round the mountain valleys can doubt where Schubert found the inspiration for the 'horns of Elfland faintly blowing' which so magically illumine the first movement of the symphony. The irony is that the provenance of Schubert's greatest symphonic work has been fatally obscured by Grove's injudicious enthusiasm for the notion of 'another unknown symphony' by his favourite composer. Grove's case was never made out. He persuaded himself of its validity against the evidence and against the advice of those best qualified to judge. As for the date on the manuscript of the symphony, that raises quite distinct problems which will need to be considered in their proper place.

IV

OCTOBER 1826–SEPTEMBER 1827

*There is no one who understands the pain
or the joy of others! We always imagine we
are coming together, and we always
merely go side by side. Oh what torture
for those who recognise this!*

Schubert's Journal

The year 1827 brings us face to face with the problem of
the relationship between man and artist in Schubert in
its most acute form. The general and philosophical aspect of
the matter—the difficulty of reconciling the portrait of the
modest little man who is revealed to us in the contemporary
records with the creative genius whose works compel our
love and admiration—is by no means peculiar to Schubert,
though he is perhaps the most striking example in musical
history of the inner-directed composer, working away in
obedience to his own imaginative vision and in contemptuous
disregard of the conventions of popular taste. After all, few
of us will recognise with conviction the author of *Hamlet* in
the Droeshout engraving, or find it easy to relate the trivi-
alities and mild obscenities of Mozart's letters with the profundity of his mature compositions. The mysterious nature of
the creative gift, and the oddity of its appearance in otherwise normally imperfect human beings, was something that
the contemporaries of Beethoven and Schubert did not fail to
remark upon, and it played its part in the evolution of the
romantic conception of the Hero as Artist. To do them

justice, however, Schubert's friends and acquaintances were less concerned with metaphysics than with the almost comical incongruity of the thing; so Albert Stadler recalls with affectionate glee how Schubert, the poetic interpreter of nature in all her magical moods, lay abed on a glorious October morning at Steyregg and refused to join him in a walk to see the view from a nearby hill; so Spaun tells of the self-effacing modesty of his friend when accompanying Schonstein in the drawing-rooms of socially superior persons like Karoline, Princess Kinsky, preferring to be overlooked, as he said, 'because that way he felt less embarrassed'. However one looks at it, this contrast between the personality of the man and the stature of the composer cannot fail to attract attention in the year 1827, because a number of events, some of concern only within the Schubert circle itself, and others, like the visit of Edward Holmes to Vienna, providing a glimpse from the outside, bring it sharply into focus.

There is, however, another aspect of the relation between man and artist which is of more immediate concern to the biographer, and it, too, cannot be evaded in the year which saw the composition of *Winterreise*. The twelve months which followed the presentation of the symphony to the Music Society in October 1826 are in quantitative terms the least productive of Schubert's working life. A handful of songs, of which perhaps only one, *Das Lied im Grünen*, is of the highest quality by Schubertian standards; a virtuoso piece for violin and piano, obviously designed as a vehicle for Slavik's technical fireworks, and a rather superficial set of variations for piano duet; a sentimental setting of Neumann's devotional hymns (the so-called German Mass) effective in a popular style, but seemingly quite unrelated to the Schubert of, say, the A flat major mass; a few sketches for the first act of

Bauernfeld's opera *Der Graf von Gleichen*; half a dozen part-songs; and one altogether delightful piano piece in his best *moment musical* manner,[1] given as a parting gift to his young friend Ferdinand Walcher, these are all that is known for certain of the output of those twelve months, these—and *Winterreise*, a work of unprecedented pessimism and power, which is known to have left the composer exhausted and which puzzled and shocked his friends. It is impossible not to find reflected in this the pressure of external circumstance, not to feel that the vision of the artist, even though following a natural line of development, has been sharpened and coloured by the disappointments of the man. On this point Schubert's friends all agree. Spaun, Mayrhofer, and Bauernfeld all testify to the depression which hung over their friend at this time, and Spaun and Mayrhofer both link it with *Winterreise*. Spaun goes so far as to suggest that the composition of the song cycle so exhausted the composer that it shortened his life, while Mayrhofer finds the contrast in tone between the *Müllerin* and *Winterreise* cycles reflected in Schubert's changed circumstances: 'Although gloomy in some details, and especially at the end, much is offered nevertheless [in *Die Schöne Müllerin*] that is fresh, tender, and pleasurable. Not so with the *Winterreise*, the very choice of which shows how much more serious the composer became. He had been long and seriously ill, had gone through disheartening experiences, and life for him had shed its rosy colour; winter had come for him. The poet's irony, rooted in despair, appealed to him; he expressed it in cutting tones. I was painfully moved.'[2]

[1] Allegretto in C Minor (D.915). It is possible, also, that work on the *Impromptus* of op. 90 may have started that summer, but in general they seem to belong to the autumn.

[2] *Memoirs* (p. 15), *op. cit.*

Modern critics have tended to follow Richard Capell in finding 'Spaun's sound sense more attractive than Mayrhofer's theory'. It is difficult to see why, for it is Spaun's view of course which is pure theory. It belongs to his later (1858) notes on Schubert, and is a piece of unverifiable speculation, at variance with the contemporary evidence, which suggests that Schubert, when typhoid fever unexpectedly carried him off, was in better health than he had been for some years.[1] Less than justice, on the other hand, has been done to Mayr-hofer, whose statement of the case, allowing for a little pardonable over-emphasis natural enough in the circum-stances, does not go beyond the known facts. It is important, however, that Mayrhofer's view should be fairly stated. He does not suggest (as Capell pretends) that the relationship between Schubert's state of mind and *Winterreise* is one of simple cause and effect. Schubert did not compose *Frühlings-traum* because of his own disenchantment; he found in the depth of his own disillusion and hopelessness the imaginative strength to make of Müller's lyric a masterpiece. 'What I produce,' he had written three years earlier, 'is due to my understanding of music and to my sorrows.' Man and artist inhabit one world, and nowhere is the truth of this more apparent than in *Winterreise*. *Frühlingstraum* itself echoes Schubert's own words, written to his brother Ferdinand from Zseliz in July 1824. 'True, it is no longer that happy time during which each object seems to us to be surrounded by a youthful glory, but a period of fateful recognition of a miserable reality, which I endeavour to beautify as far as possible by my imagination (thank God). We fancy that

[1] So Spaun's own first account (of 1829) suggests. See *Memoirs* (p. 28), 'Enjoying sound health, Schubert at first paid no attention to the indis-position which had been troubling him for some time.'

happiness lies in places where once we were happier, whereas actually it is only in ourselves. . . .'[1] But that was three years ago, and whereas then he could go on to claim that he was able to find happiness and peace in himself, that claim no longer seemed true. The truth of his words bit home, and made of Müller's songs a painful reality which only the imagination could transcend.

Thanks to Spaun's careful record of events, we have an account of the very moment in time when, so to speak, the private world of Schubert's creative imagination and the public world of February/March 1827 acknowledged their interdependence, and the account fully bears out Mayrhofer's view. 'For a time,' Spaun writes, 'Schubert's mood became more gloomy and he seemed upset. When I asked him what was the matter he merely said to me: 'Well, you will soon hear it and understand.' One day he said to me: 'Come to Schober's today, I will sing you a cycle of awe-inspiring songs. I am anxious to know what you will say about them. They have affected me more than has been the case with any other songs.' So, in a voice wrought with emotion, he sang the whole of the *Winterreise* through to us. We were quite dumbfounded by the gloomy mood of these songs and Schober said he had only liked one song, *Der Lindenbaum*. To which Schubert said, "I like these songs more than all the others, and you will get to like them too."'[2]

---

[1] *Documentary Biography* (No. 484), *op. cit.*

[2] *Memoirs* (pp. 137–8), *op. cit.* Incidentally, it must surely have been Part I, not the whole work, that Schubert sang. It seems most unlikely that Schubert kept the songs to himself until after the completion of Part II in October 1827. Besides, he probably thought Part I *was* the complete work in February, not then having seen the additional songs included in the complete work. Schober's judgment seems to confirm this. For had he heard Part II also, he might well have singled out *Die Post*, which is almost a Schubert love-song, for commendation.

In the face of this evidence, it will not do to point to the detachment of the artist and to say that there is nothing to explain in the pathos of the *Winterreise* music. Schubert's detachment was remarkable enough, not least in 1823 when he is thought to have worked at the *Müllerin* songs while in hospital suffering from venereal disease. What is new in the 1827 situation, if the evidence of his friends is to be believed, is a kind of attachment, a congruity of mood between man and artist which produced one masterpiece of despair and disillusion and a number of small compositions of altogether lesser stature. Underlying Capell's refusal to relate the biographical evidence and the evidence of the work itself, however, is another question. If Mayrhofer was right, how came there to be 'an array of compositions of 1827 and 1828 all glowing with the spirit of spring'?[1] What, one wonders, does he have in mind? The E flat major piano trio? Surely it strikes a more reflective and autumnal note than the earlier B flat trio? If one describes the string quintet of 1828 as 'glowing with the spirit of spring' how would one describe the 'Trout' quintet? Is there no difference in tone and level of sophistication between the A flat major mass of 1819/22 and the E flat mass of 1828? Would anyone be prepared to call the Heine songs of *Schwanengesang* springlike? There is, indeed, one work, normally attributed to 1828, which sorts oddly with its neighbours, and in its optimism and energy the Great C Major Symphony belongs to high summer, if not to spring. Not the least important reason for restoring it to its original date is that it does not fit in, stylistically that is, anywhere else. But in the main the compositions of 1828 strike a more mature sophisticated note. The cloud base lifted, but only to reveal a new landscape. The andante of the

[1] *Schubert's Songs* (p. 230), by Richard Capell, London 1928.

Great C Major takes delight in the here and now. God's in His heaven, but the feet of the happy wanderer are firmly on the ground, as those marching quavers in the andante declare. Three years later, the adagio of the string quintet belongs to a different, more spiritual, world; this, or something like this, must be the music of the spheres, fixed in timeless contemplation. The sublimity of this vision is not arrived at easily, however. It is important that we should recognise, between the optimism of the 'wanderer symphony' (the phrase is Mosco Carner's) and the contemplative splendour of the quintet, the pathetic alienated figure of *Der Leiermann*.

As it happens, we have a clearer picture of the social circle to which Schubert belonged at this period than ever before, thanks mainly to the diaries of Franz and Fritz von Hartmann, These two young men, both law students, were members of a well-known Linz family and friends of Spaun's, who introduced them to the Schubert circle. From November 1826, when they returned to the capital, they record in some detail at least the external movements of the Schubertians. We learn a good deal about the pubs[1] they frequented, and when they went to bed; something of their love affairs and rows; very little about Schubert as a man and a composer. None the less, the very scrappiness of these diaries, and the short-sighted glimpse they give us of great events seen through the eyes of a contemporary, guarantees their truth and their validity. Fritz goes to a concert and hears the 'grandiose' symphony—the Ninth—by Beethoven, but what seems to impress him most is a 'glorious symphony' by the Abbé

[1] The good English word seems to be the nearest equivalent one can find for the places which Schubert and his friends frequented; though it is only an approximation, it seems preferable to the anachronistic 'coffee-house', or the bucolic tone of 'ale-house'.

Vogler—actually the overture to his opera *Samori*, so O. E. Deutsch, the discoverer of the diaries, informs us. This is just what we should expect. (In England at that time the symphonies of Cipriani Potter were thought by some critics to rival Beethoven's in merit.) A few days later, however, brother Franz writes a long and moving account of his going to see the dead body of 'the divine Beethoven' lying-in-state, and of his begging a lock of the great man's hair from the old janitor. It is this inconsequent mixture of the trivial and the significant that gives the diaries their fascination.

Like artistic young men of any period, the Schubertians congregated every night at the particular pub they happened to favour at the moment. That winter the rendezvous was 'The Green Anchor', and the name recurs with monotonous regularity in Franz's diary, so that it is possible to build up a fairly complete picture of at least the social side of Schubert's life at this time. The evening would often begin with a visit to Bogner's coffee house; and frequently the group would go on to a party before ending the evening at the 'Anchor'. Occasionally also there would be a grander Schubertiad at the house of one of the more well-to-do of Schubert's friends and patrons—at Spaun's, or Schober's, or Witteczek's, or Hönig's, or even a reception at one of the more noble houses. Not to mention the regular concerts of the Music Society, which usually included at least one Schubert item; after which the younger and gayer members would again assemble at the 'Anchor'.

During the month of December 1826, for instance, Franz von Hartmann's diary gives us several fascinating glimpses of the complexities of Viennese society, rigidly stratified in certain respects, yet mingling diverse elements in the love of music and art. In addition to the routine visits to Bogner's and to the 'Anchor', there was a party at Spaun's on the 8th, at which Schubert 'played a magnificent but melancholy piece of his own composition', probably the slow movement of the recently completed G major sonata. A fairly typical entry for the 12th records a busy evening: 'I went to Bogner's coffee-house, where I saw Spax [Max von Spaun, Josef's brother], Schober, and Derffel, and fetched Fritz. We stayed there until 6.40. Then we called for Pepi [Josef] Spaun, who paid for us at the Burg Theatre, where "The Settlement of Succession", after Hoffmann's tale of the same name, was splendidly and staggeringly performed. . . . We then went to the "Anchor", where Enderes, Schober, and Schubert were too. Home at last toward midnight.'

On the 15th everybody went to Spaun's for what Franz calls a 'big, big, Schubertiad'. All the regular members of the circle were there, besides well-to-do government officials such as Kurzrock and his wife, Josef Pompe, and Witteczek, the collector of Schubert Mss., old friends of Schubert like Johan Mayrhofer and Leopold Kupelwieser (with his new wife), Vogl, Bauernfeld, Grillparzer, and many others.[1] Gahy played duets with Schubert, Vogl sang 'almost 30' splendid songs. After seeing his girl-friend home Franz returned to the 'Anchor' to find Schober, Schubert, Schwind, Derffel, and Bauernfeld still there. 'Merry. Then home. To bed at 1 o'clock.' The following day there was more music at the home of Netti Hönig, Schwind's sweetheart, to which the Hartmanns were not invited. On Sunday 17th the Linz group took Schubert and Gahy out to Nussdorf for the day to visit Spaun's relations the Wanderers. More duets. More

[1] This party may have been in Schwind's mind, as O. E. Deutsch suggests, when he sketched his famous 'Schubert evening at Josef von Spaun's'. But the picture is a kind of composite portrait of a period, rather than a reminiscence of one actual occasion.

songs. And back to the 'Anchor' at night. On the 18th the Schubertiad was held at Witteczek's, preceded by a visit to the coffee-house. On the 21st and the 28th there were Music Society concerts, and on the 31st a New Year's Eve party at Schober's, but with no repetition of the satirical goings-on which Bauernfeld had produced a year earlier.

Isolated and spotlighted in this way, the diarists may give a misleading impression of a continuous round of drinking and party-going. It was always Schubert's habit to work in the morning, to take a walk (if possible) in the afternoon, and to relax with his friends in the evening. The routine had not changed; and it is consistent not only with Schubert's astonishing productivity, but also with the occasional fits of depression which his friends remarked upon.

The diaries are invaluable in helping to build up the social background against which the 'composer of genius, sufficiently well-known to the musical world' lived and worked. It would be a great mistake, however, to assume that the tastes and values of the Schubert circle were typical of Vienna as a whole. How would it look to a well-informed visitor from England? Fortunately we know the answer.

In 1827 a group of London artists, hearing that Mozart's aged sister was living in poverty, decided at the suggestion of Vincent Novello to see what could be done to help. One of them, the young organist and critic Edward Holmes, agreed to go to Vienna to reconnoitre the situation and, perhaps with the example of the illustrious Dr. Charles Burney in mind, decided to make a leisurely tour of it, and record his impressions of the state of German music in the process. Holmes reached Vienna in March 1827. He makes no mention of the more confidential aspect of his visit, but his book, generously titled,[1] gives us a lively account of the state of musical taste and performance at that time as they appeared to a cultivated young man with high but conservative standards of musicianship. He is severe on the depravity of taste, especially in Munich and Vienna. Of the latter he writes: 'From the specimens of the musical performances I have met with, there is scarcely a corner of Europe in which the taste of the operatic community can be worse. It has been said that the people of Vienna are Rossini mad, but they are not only mad for him, but mad for his worst imitators; with good ears, they tolerate the worst of music. They out-herod Herod in their noisy and vociferous applause of their favourites: this is the system now employed towards a lady who is in the good graces of the audience; she receives a loud greeting on her entrance, is interrupted with bravos in the middle of her song; there is more applause when she has finished, and after quitting the stage she is regularly called back to make her obeisance, and to hear fresh acclamations. . . .' This is the world in which Schubert hoped for an operatic success. 'The German opera is not much patronised by the Viennese, who doat upon these things which are foreign and despise their own good writers. Both the Italian and German operas are played at the same house; but the latter is considered by the public as a mere foil to the former, and by the managers as a mere stop-gap.' Nor does instrumental music fare much better. 'The flippancy of taste displayed by the more fashionable concert-goers in Vienna may be imagined from an exhibition of instrumental playing with

[1] *A Ramble among the Musicians of Germany, giving some account of the operas of Munich, Dresden, Berlin, etc. with remarks upon the church music, singers, performers, and composers and a sample of the pleasures and inconveniences that await the lover of art on a similar excursion.* By a Musical Professor (1828).

which they were entertained on one occasion when I was present, the prominent parts of which were variations for the violin, performed by Madame Paeravicini, and the first movement of Hummel's pianoforte concerto in B minor played by Frederic Worlitzer of Berlin, a boy thirteen years old.' It was for this public that show pieces like the B minor Rondo Brilliant and the C major Fantasie for violin and piano were written—and, perhaps one might add, *The Shepherd on the Rock.*

Holmes' book gives invaluable information on contemporary trends, the Walter Scott craze, the modulatory excesses[1] of 'modern' composers like Boieldieu, Weber, and —one feels he would have added had he known—Schubert. Its particular relevance here is that it puts the comparatively small world of the Schubertians into perspective. As he says, 'the pleasure of the greater mass of listeners is always consulted . . . and it has caused the amateurs to withdraw themselves into private societies, where they may pursue their own tastes without interruption. Of these societies there exist all sorts, even to the humble style of popular songs. . . .' In one of those private societies of Vienna he might have found, had he been fortunate enough to meet him, or persistent enough to seek him out, one of the great creative geniuses of the age, struggling to keep afloat amid the cross-currents of contemporary taste by writing virtuoso pieces for the fashionable concert-goer, part-songs for the humble amateurs, and *Winterreise* for posterity. It is a pity, indeed, that they never met, for Schubert himself was always ready to hold forth about 'the idle and insignificant life that charac-

---

[1] 'The well-trained ear is little prepared for such a remorseless succession of harmonies as this – C, B flat, E flat, B natural – without preparation or management.' (Edward Holmes.)

terises our time'.[1] But the myopia which no contemporary observer can escape also inhibits Edward Holmes. Lamenting the sad losses sustained by German music, he recalls 'Beethoven, and Winter, Fesca, Danzi, Andreas Romberg, and Weber, all dead', but makes no mention of the living Schubert.

If Edward Holmes' account leaves us in no doubt that Schubert had not at this time established an international reputation, it is clear from that of another outside observer who visited Vienna that summer that his fame had spread well beyond the capital. Heinrich Hoffmann, the poet and folklorist, arrived in Vienna from Breslau with the singer Panofka at the end of June, while Schubert was staying at an inn in the suburb of Dornbach. Intent on meeting the composer, the two friends make several abortive trips to Dornbach in the hope of coming across him. Schubert proves elusive. Finally they send him an invitation to dinner, which is ignored. But some days later they are at Grinzing sampling the new wine when—'suddenly Panofka calls out "That's him!" and hurries over to Schubert who, surrounded by several young ladies, is just looking for a seat. Panofka brings him over to me. Overjoyed and surprised I greet him, mention in passing how much trouble we had gone to to find him, how very pleased I was to make his acquaintance personally, etc. Schubert stands before me embarrassed, does not quite know what he ought to answer, and after a few words, takes his leave and—does not appear again. "No," I say to Panofka, "that is really a bit too much! I would honestly much rather I had never seen him; then I could never have thought of the creator of such tender melodies as an ordinary, indifferent, or even ill-mannered person. As it is, apart

[1] See *Documentary Biography* (No. 498), *op. cit.*

from his behaviour today, the man is no different from any other Viennese; he speaks Viennese, like every Viennese he has fine linen, a clean coat, a shiny hat and in his face, in his whole bearing, nothing that resembles my Schubert."[1]

Not for the first time, the expectations of a hero-worshipping young man are shattered by a personal encounter with genius. One can make full allowances for Hoffmann's state of mind, however, and still feel that the episode sums up fairly enough the problem of the relationship between man and artist which we have identified as the heart of the Schubert mystery. For Hoffmann's reaction is by no means untypical; the comments on Schubert's personality which we have, even from his closest friends, all agree that it was unimpressive at first acquaintance. Sonnleithner said he might have been taken for a Bavarian peasant, and Anselm Hüttenbrenner thought his outward appearance 'anything but striking or prepossessing'. Unsympathetic observers such as Franz von Ardlau put it more brutally: 'One would never have suspected, in this wooden appearance, in this unprepossessing exterior, the greatly gifted creator of so many wonderful songs.' And sympathetic acquaintances like Vogl's wife Kunigunde, who must have got to know Schubert at about this time, agree: 'One thing I ought to add for the sake of truth,' she writes to her daughter, 'though I do not like doing it; Schubert was as undistinguished as a man as he was distinguished as a composer.'[2] Doubtless the visual paradox of the man was what Schwind had in mind many years later when, asked what the composer looked like by some in-

[1] *Memoirs* (pp. 284–5), *op. cit.*, quoting Hoffmann's *Autobiography*. Hoffmann's disappointment is echoed by the violinist Louis Schlosser, who first saw Schubert—on the platform—in or about 1822. (See *Memoirs*, p. 328.)

[2] *Memoirs* (p. 218), *op. cit.*

quisitive nonentity, he replied with calculated but exaggerated frankness, 'Like a drunken cabby!'

In Schubert's lifetime, and for many years after, the accepted solution to this problem was that Schubert was a natural composer, who wrote music as the silkworm secretes thread, and with as little knowledge of what he was doing. Vogl's distinction between somnambulistic composers (like Schubert) and those who compose 'through willpower, effort, reflection, knowledge' is well-known, and it had a great influence on nineteenth-century criticism. But even in those days the discerning could see that it did not fit the facts. Maria Wagner, who as a girl of eighteen had been overwhelmed by the discovery of Schubert's songs, saw that the theory was quite inconsistent not only with his performance at the piano, but with 'his deep understanding of the finest and noblest poetry'.[1] And modern scholarship, by revealing the serious and deliberate nature of Schubert's ambitions as a composer, and the long process of preparation and drafting that preceded his important work, has ruled the whole idea out of court.

It has not, however, provided any convincing alternative, being content for the most part to treat all contemporary accounts of Schubert with impartial scepticism, to rely on the (essentially romantic) doctrine that, as Einstein puts it, 'great composers must also be great men', and to blame the obscurity of his life and the neglect of his work on the shortcomings of friends and relatives, and the wickedness of publishers. We have been so eager to discard the excesses of nineteenth-century Schubert mythology that we are in danger of destroying the man with the myth. Yet the very wealth of biographical material which survives, the proliferation of

[1] *Memoirs* (p. 298), *op. cit.*

anecdote, the strength of the Schubert myth itself, is evidence of the enduring fascination of his personality. However improbably, the work of the artist arose out of the experience of the man; the biographer's task is to throw what light he can on the relationship between the two.

This contrast between what Schubert could do and what he seemed to be lies at the root not only of the legend that surrounds his name, but of his social attitude also. Cut off by the intensity of his inner life, and by a shy introverted nature, from the conventional usages of polite society in which his art had established him, he was sustained by the certainty of his own genius and the loyalty of his own circle. His social unreliability becomes a sad joke. He seems to live on the Bohemian fringes of *Biedermeier* society, in it but not of it, but wearing his craft of composer as a kind of badge, a kind of status symbol in a society increasingly concerned with wealth and protocol, though still respectful of the title of tone poet. Had he not earned for himself the nickname *Kannevas*, from his habit of asking about any newcomer: What's he good at? This consciousness of his own genius set him apart—at no time more markedly than in 1827—but left him with no defence against his own moods, so that his friends remarked on a kind of dual personality, 'the Viennese gaiety being interwoven and ennobled by a trait of deep melancholy'. The phrase is Bauernfeld's, who is enough of an artist to recognise that the black-winged demon of sorrow and melancholy 'often brought out songs of the most agonising beauty'.[1]

We have to look for the sources of Schubert's depression in this dark year both in the pressure of external circumstance and in the contradictions of his own nature. As for the

[1] *Memoirs* (p. 234), *op. cit.*

former, he had two objectives, to establish his reputation, not simply as a song-writer, but as a great composer in the field of orchestral and instrumental forms, and to reach a position of reasonable economic security. Both aims now seemed further from fulfilment than ever. His hope of a performance for his symphony had come to nothing; the Music Society gave it a try-out, found it too long and too difficult, and set it aside indefinitely. In October 1826 the censor turned down the libretto of *The Count of Gleichen*. This ruled out a Vienna production, and though, in the hope of a production in Berlin, Schubert agreed to compose it, the heart had gone out of the project. It meant the end, for the time being anyway, of his hopes as an operatic and as a symphonic composer. Denied a hearing for what he regarded as his best work, Schubert turned to a more fashionable field, and in December 1826 wrote a virtuoso piece – the Rondo in B minor – for the young Bohemian violinist Josef Slavik, then rapidly building up a reputation as a new Paganini. It is not an ineffective piece, but long and rhetorical, lacking in Schubertian magic, as though the composer did not trouble to conceal the mood of cynicism in which the work was undertaken. It evidently impressed Artaria, however, for it did not have to wait long for publication, but appeared in April as opus 70.

In January the long-drawn-out affair of the vacant Vice-Kapellmeister post came to its inevitable conclusion. The appointment went to Josef Weigl, the conductor at the Court Theatres,[1] who had not applied for it; and on 27 January

[1] The appointment seems to have been, in part at least, an economy measure. For Weigl already received a salary of 1600 florins as Court Theatre conductor. He was given an additional 200 florins lodging allowance, and invited to take over the Vice-Kapellmeister's duties without the salary which normally amounted to 1000 florins (1800 florins was then worth £180).

Schubert's application was returned to him with a brief note indicating that the post had been filled. Schindler was doubtless right in maintaining that Schubert was quite unsuited for an official post of this kind, and would have been desperately unhappy if given it. Schubert himself, according to brother Ferdinand, acknowledged Weigl's superior claims to the post. None the less, the appointment meant the closing of one more door on hopes of material advancement. Bauernfeld's rather over-dramatised account of a meeting with Schubert in the summer of 1827, at which the composer contrasted his own poor financial prospects with his friend's rising hopes, does not have to be taken literally (it was written in 1869); but in substance there is no reason to doubt that the disappointment over the Vice-Kapellmeister post contributed to Schubert's general mood of hopelessness and disillusion at this time.[1]

This same month the negotiations with Probst of Leipzig, which had started promisingly in August, came to an abrupt end. On 15 January the publisher briefly acknowledged receipt of Schubert's three compositions, regretted that the fee asked was too high, added that he was in any case too busy at the moment with the collected edition of Kalkbrenner to take the matter further; and asked for Schubert's instructions as to the disposal of the Mss. One more door slammed!

The uncertainty of the financial prospect is reflected in Schubert's domestic arrangements. In prosperous times—as in 1821 and again in 1825—he preferred to live alone; when things got difficult he shared with friends, or lived at home. In the summer of 1826 he gave up his rooms in Fruhwirth's house in the Wieden suburb, where he had lived for more

---

[1] *Memoirs* (pp. 236–7), *op. cit.*

than a year, and spent most of the rest of the year with Schober either at Währing or in rooms on the Bäckerstrasse. At the end of 1826 he once again took rooms of his own, this time near the Caroline gate. But this arrangement did not last long, probably because of the need to cut expenses. Some time in February Schubert once again moved into Schober's house (next door to the Music Society's headquarters), where he lived on the second floor in two rooms and a study set aside for him, and this remained his permanent base for the rest of his life. Schober's hedonistic and dilettante way of life has not been treated very sympathetically by biographers, and in later years the surviving members of the Schubert circle turned against him. His attitude to the composer was curiously ambivalent and his influence dubious; yet the kindness of Schober and his mother to Schubert was in this respect unfailing. As at the beginning, so at the end of his life, Schober provided him with the means to compose unharassed by physical and financial embarrassments.

It is thus not difficult to give chapter and verse for Mayrhofer's much criticised judgment. 'He had been long and seriously ill, had gone through disheartening experiences, and life for him had shed its rosy colour.' It is tempting, however, to go further, and to see reflected in the events of this time an intensification of Schubert's occasional melancholia which may well have had its roots in the conflict between his sexuality and his idealism. For obvious reasons we know little of this side of his nature. It seems clear that once his adolescent love for Thérèse Grob faded, his relations with women suffered a kind of polarisation. No woman, after Thérèse, could engage his whole nature. His feeling for Karoline Esterházy may well have played a more important part in his life than is usually admitted, but it was an idealised devotion which must have stopped short of any overt physical expression. At the other end of the scale, Pepi Pöckelhofer, the 'complaisant chambermaid' of Zseliz, and the casual encounters Vienna offered in plenty, can have done no more than satisfy a physical appetite which, so the hints of his friends suggest, was naturally strong. Whether Schubert was capable of a more stable and integrated sexual relationship, and, if he was, what the effect on his creative imagination would have been had he achieved it—these questions are purely speculative. There are indications, however, that they have their relevance to the problem of Schubert's depression. If Schober is to be believed, there was a plan early in 1827 to get Schubert married to an attractive young woman called Auguste Grünwedel. The story comes to us at second hand, for Schober could never bring himself to write down in any orderly fashion his recollections of those years, but its very oddity carries conviction. 'Schober persuaded him that he ought to marry Gusti Grünwedel, a very charming girl of good family . . . who seemed very well disposed towards him. Schubert was in love with her, but he was "painfully modest"; he was firmly convinced that no woman could love him. At Schober's words he jumped up, rushed out without his hat, flushed with anger. The friends looked at one another in dismay. After half an hour he came quietly back and later related how, beside himself, he had run round St. Peter's Church, telling himself again and again that no happiness was granted to him on earth.

'Schubert then let himself go to pieces; he frequented the city outskirts and roamed around in taverns, at the same time admittedly composing his most beautiful songs in them, just as he did in the hospital too (the *Müllerlieder* according to

Hölzel), where he found himself as the result of excessively indulgent sensual living and its consequences.'[1]

This story was told by Schober to a journalist called Ludwig Frankl at a dinner-party some time in the 1860s. In such circumstances a man is not on oath; full allowance has to be made for journalistic exaggeration as well as for normal human frailty and inaccuracy. Yet curiously, Gusti Grünwedel appears twice in Franz Hartmann's diary for February 1827; she evidently attracted a good deal of attention in the Schubert circle, for Franz reports her as 'the loveliest dancer', and says she captivated Spaun!

As for the alleged sequel to the story, it calls to mind inevitably the brief encounter with Hoffmann at Grinzing in the following August, already described. In Hoffmann's diary his contemporary note of the occasion is even more vivid: '15 August 1827. . . . The old fiddler played Mozart. . . . Schubert with his girl we espied from our seat; he came to join us and did not show himself again. Franz Lachner, the fourth Musical Director at the Kärntnertor Theatre, also came to see us.' Not all the truth, as the French proverb says, is fit to be told. Evidently the situation bristled with embarrassment; evidently Franz Lachner, Schubert's old friend, was not 'with' him on that occasion, though they were drinking at the same inn. It certainly looks as though Schubert, at this time, still retained a taste for casual sexual adventures. And if the intensity of feeling in *Winterreise*, the sense of involvement and of alienation, contrasts strangely with the lightweight character of much else that belongs to these months, it is not unreasonable to see in this a reflection of his own sense of exclusion, his own separateness.

---

[1] *Memoirs* (pp. 265–6), *op. cit.*

Wunderlicher Alter, soll ich mit dir geh'n,
Willst zu meinen Liedern deine Leier dreh'n.[1]

The twenty-four songs of *Winterreise* were written, and published, in two instalments, each of twelve songs. The manuscript of Part I, dated February 1827, is a much revised document except for *Gute Nacht*, the first song, and *Rückblick*, the eighth, which appear to be fair copies; the inference is that these two songs had been so extensively worked over that a fair copy was necessary. The manuscript of Part II, on the other hand, is a clean copy throughout, dated October 1827. Both parts were published by Haslinger of Vienna, Part I in January 1828, Part II in December after Schubert's death.[2]

The explanation of this curious procedure is that Schubert did not come across the twelve poems of Part II until Part I was already finished and in Haslinger's hands. For Müller's verses were themselves published in instalments; the first twelve, which correspond exactly both in content and order with Schubert's Part I, appeared in a Leipzig annual in 1823, and it must have been an old copy of this annual, coming to Schubert's notice at the end of 1826, which first set his imagination afire. The complete cycle, in a revised order, was published in 1824 and dedicated to Carl Maria von Weber. What seems to have happened is that some time after composing the twelve songs of Part I Schubert came across the complete version of the cycle and decided to set the additional poems. But the publication of Part I was already in train; to postpone publication of the whole cycle until the

---

[1] Strange old man, shall I go with you?
Will you strum your music to my songs?
[2] A detailed discussion of the Mss. by Erwin Schaeffer is to be found in the *Musical Quarterly* for January 1938.

additional songs were finished and the complete set re-arranged in Müller's final order would have meant a lengthy delay, and possibly a long wait for the fee. So he set the additional poems as he found them with one minor change of order, the interchange of *Muth* with *Die Nebensonnen*, presumably made because Schubert felt the contrast between *Muth* and *Der Leiermann* was too violent to be artistically effective. This becomes clear if Müller's final order is set alongside Schubert's, with the additional poems of Part II italicised.

	Müller		*Schubert*
1	Gute Nacht	1	Gute Nacht
2	Die Wetterfahne	2	Die Wetterfahne
3	Gefrorne Thränen	3	Gefrorne Thränen
4	Erstarrung	4	Erstarrung
5	Der Lindenbaum	5	Der Lindenbaum
6	*Die Post*	6	Wasserfluth
7	Wasserfluth	7	Auf dem Flusse
8	Auf dem Flusse	8	Rückblick
9	Rückblick	9	Irrlicht
10	*Der greise Kopf*	10	Rast
11	*Die Krähe*	11	Frühlingstraum
12	*Letzte Hoffnung*	12	Einsamkeit
13	*Im Dorfe*	13	*Die Post*
14	*Der stürmische Morgen*	14	*Der greise Kopf*
15	*Täuschung*	15	*Die Krähe*
16	*Der Wegweiser*	16	*Letzte Hoffnung*
17	*Das Wirtshaus*	17	*Im Dorfe*
18	Irrlicht	18	*Der stürmische Morgen*
19	Rast	19	*Täuschung*
20	*Die Nebensonnen*	20	*Der Wegweiser*

	Muller		Schubert
21	Frühlingstraum	21	*Das Wirtshaus*
22	Einsamkeit	22	*Muth*
23	*Muth*	23	*Die Nebensonnen*
24	*Der Leiermann*	24	*Der Leiermann*

It appears therefore that the order of Schubert's greatest song cycle is, in part at least, due to chance. No doubt if he had discovered Müller's poems in the first place in their complete and final form, he would have kept to Müller's order. Indeed, a case can be made for reverting to that order, for there is no denying that it presents more effectively the wanderer's steady decline into hallucination, madness, and death. In particular, *Die Post* seems to take its place more naturally among the early songs, and *Frühlingstraum* and *Einsamkeit* among the later. But Schubert, who revised the proofs carefully himself, had no doubts on the matter, or if he had, left no hint of them.

The first song of Book I, as we have seen, carries on the Ms. the date February 1827, but this is not to be taken as marking the inception of the work, for *Gute Nacht* is itself a fair copy. More probably it represents the final stage of correction, collation, and copying where necessary. Most of these songs, if not all, must have existed in draft form,[1] and certainly the dated fair copy of Part II must represent the end of months of intermittent work. As Georg Kinsky says: 'Outward smoothness and lack of corrections in the Mss. of larger compositions are by no means to be regarded as proof of a seemingly effortless creation in Schubert's case, but are often to be explained by the fact that the first sketch or the

[1] I am indebted to Maurice Brown for the information that a most interesting sketch for *Muth* has recently come to light. A draft of *Nebensonnen* also exists.

revised first draft was destroyed and replaced by a clean copy.' The most reasonable assumption, therefore, is that the twelve songs of Part I were written in the first two months, and the remainder during the summer months, of 1827. It may well be that much of Part II was written at Dornbach, where Schubert stayed for several weeks in May and June.

Five of the songs, *Wasserfluth*, *Rast*, *Einsamkeit*, *Muth*, and *Der Leiermann*, were transposed to lower keys in the published version, at the insistence, so it is usually thought, of the publisher. The idea seems to have been to keep the voice within the normal baritone range. Vogl was, we remember, the first great exponent of *Winterreise*, and may have had some influence in the matter. On the other hand, Schubert may have had purely artistic reasons for the changes, for none offends, and one, the lowering of *Der Leiermann* from B minor to A minor, is a positive improvement. Just as the key of F major, the only flat key on the scale of C major, seems to express the essence of flatness more convincingly than any other, so A minor, the relative minor of C major, is the essential minor key, which surely matches the bleakness of that final song more effectively than B minor.

What distinguishes the work from the earlier cycle, and makes it uniquely representative of its composer, is not so much the preponderance of minor keys, which has often been noted, as the capacity to invest the tonic major with the colour, the very glow, of desolation and disillusion. No other composer has quite the same power to make the major mode sound even sadder and more poignant than the minor, though Mahler used the same device to good effect at the end of *Kindertotenlieder* and elsewhere. Certainly the most memorable moments in *Winterreise*—the pianissimo modulation to D major for the last verse of *Gute Nacht*, the infinite sadness of the final cadence of *Das Wirtshaus*, with its return to F major after the defiant bitterness of 'Nun weiter denn nur weiter', the *lento* sections of *Frühlingstraum*—are all associated with the major. The device is in a sense beyond analysis, for it takes effect not from the immediate context but from our apprehension of the whole Schubertian mode of expression, but *Frühlingstraum* deserves a special word, because of the classical economy of means by which the most imaginative stroke is achieved. The jejune little six-eight tune with which the song begins stands for the dream world of lost innocence, and the *vivace* interruptions for the harsh assault of reality. Then the raven's croak is silenced, and bare octaves in a slow halting rhythm signal a distancing of the imagination. Who drew those leaves on the window-pane, to mock the dreamer who dared to dream of flowers in mid-winter? (Example 13.)

On 4 March Schubert invited his friends along to his new rooms at Schober's to hear his new songs. Fritz von Hart-

Example 13

da? doch an... den Fen-ster-schei-ben, wer mal-te die Blät-ter da?

mann noted in his diary: 'We went to Schober's, where we met Spaun, Schwind, Bauernfeld and Kriehuber[1] with his wife and sister-in-law (the "Flower of the Land"), because Schubert, who is Schober's lodger, had invited us to hear some new compositions of his. Everybody was assembled, but friend Schubert did not come. At last Schwind undertook to sing several of Schubert's earlier songs, which enchanted us. At half past nine we all went to the "Castle of Eisenstadt", where Schubert too arrived soon after us and won all hearts by his amiable simplicity, although he had deceived our hopes by his artist's negligence.'[2] It is a reasonable guess that Schubert's intention had been to introduce his friends to the first twelve songs of *Winterreise*, and that for some reason he felt unable to go through with it. Perhaps the exposure of these intensely imagined songs to so large a gathering seemed, when the moment came, a kind of indecency, and he jibbed at it. It must have been at this time, on some similar occasion, that Spaun and Schober first heard them and their effect must have seemed to justify Schubert's hesitation, for as we have seen,[3] this first hearing left his friends puzzled and depressed. For them, at any rate, there was something in *Winterreise* that needed to be accounted for, and which the detachment of the artist could not altogether explain.

[1] Water-colourist and lithographer. Bauernfeld, and probably Schubert also, had attended his wedding on 31 January.

[2] *Documentary Biography* (No. 820), *op. cit.*   [3] See p. 103.

March was, for various reasons, an eventful month. It is further evidence of Schubert's need to improve his financial position that he suddenly appears as accompanist at a number of public concerts. For many years he had left the public performance of his work entirely to the professionals: then in less than two months, he made five appearances as accompanist to the tenor Ludwig Tietze, one at a private party and four at public concerts.[1] The Schubertians transferred their regular nightly custom from 'The Green Anchor' to 'The Castle of Eisenstadt'; the round of parties and concerts continued. But Vienna was pre-occupied with Beethoven's illness and death. On 29 March all the Schubertians went out to Währing to see the great man's funeral. The procession was flanked by thirty-six torchbearers, Schubert among them, clad in black and bearing white roses, and it paused at the entrance to the cemetery for Anschütz to deliver Grillparzer's funeral oration. The Hartmanns, who had gone out to Währing with Schober and Schwind, had a tedious wait of an hour and a half before the procession arrived. When it was all over Franz, who had been more emotionally moved by the whole event than his brother, went home; but Fritz went on to the 'Castle', and stayed talking with Schober, Schubert, and Schwind until one o'clock in the morning. 'Needless to say,' he wrote in his diary, 'we talked of nothing but Beethoven, his works and the well-merited honours paid to him today.'[2]

Schubert's veneration for the work of his great contemporary stopped only just short of idolatry. The evidence of his friends is unanimous. He never missed a Beethoven con-

---

[1] The list given by O. E. Deutsch [*Documentary Biography* (p. 938), *op. cit.*] is thus incomplete. It omits the charity concert in the University Hall on 6 May 1827.

[2] *Documentary Biography* (Nos. 839 and 840), *op. cit.*

cert. It is clear, also, that once he escaped from the bonds of Salieri's influence, it was the example of Beethoven that moulded his ambition as a composer, and often influenced the shape and lay-out of his work. The strength of his love for Beethoven's music was so strong that it is arguable whether it did not inhibit his own development. Certainly Schubert himself was sometimes aware of the daunting challenge of Beethoven's achievement. Spaun records an early occasion, probably in 1815, when he expressed pleasure in some new settings of Klopstock. 'He looked me frankly in the eyes and said, "Do you really think something will come of me?" I embraced him and said, "You have done much already, and time will enable you to do much more and great things too." Then he said, quite humbly: "Secretly, in my heart of hearts, I still hope to be able to make something out of myself, but who can do anything after Beethoven?" '[1] The wonder is, not that Beethoven's work so often provided the stimulus for his own, but that in spite of the powerful influence of that elemental figure in the background, he made his own way to his own goal.

What the personal relations were between the two men is the subject of wide disagreement. Such was Beethoven's physical disability and manner of life that any personal approach to him after about 1820 was a hazardous enterprise. Even for the self-confident and the thick-skinned—and Schubert was neither—establishing effective communication with the master was difficult, to say the least. We can be sure, therefore, that the two men were never intimate. Spaun, writing in 1864, declared that Schubert regretted at this time that he had never spoken to Beethoven. But Spaun was writing, in his old age, a somewhat polemical article on Kreissle's

[1] *Memoirs* (p. 128), *op. cit.*

biography, and it has to be remembered that he was away from Vienna, and out of touch with his friend, for five years, from 1821 to 1826. In any case, it seems injudicious to interpret Spaun's statement to mean that the two men never met. Vienna was a city about the size of modern Bradford. In terms of probability alone, it is almost inconceivable that two such eminent members of the Viennese musical world could live at such close quarters for so long without meeting. Besides, there is a good deal of evidence to contradict Spaun. Ferdinand Schubert, writing soon after his brother's death, said that he met Beethoven frequently, though he was never Beethoven's pupil; and both Johann Rochlitz and Sir Julius Benedict suggest that the two men were in contact in 1822 and 1823. The most probable explanation seems to be that Schubert held back because of his own reserve and *amour propre*; and because of the embarrassment of coping with Beethoven's deafness, never sought to advance from mere acquaintance with the great man to more intimate terms. As for Beethoven's attitude towards the younger composer, he seems to have known little or nothing of his work until the month before his death, when Schindler took a large batch of Schubert songs to show him. How Beethoven pored over them delightedly for days, recognising the 'divine spark' in Schubert's talent, is a story told with some self-congratulation by Schindler.[1] Though it rests on Schindler's word alone most commentators accept it, while remaining sceptical about the complementary story of the visit paid to Beethoven on his death-bed by Schubert, Schindler, Teltscher, and the Hüttenbrenner brothers. This seems a little inconsistent. True, Spaun denied the truth of the latter story. But the Hüttenbrenners confirmed it in the 1840s; further,

[1] Schindler, *op. cit.*, p. 321.

Beethoven's declared interest in Schubert's songs may have encouraged Schindler to arrange a meeting between the two composers while there was still time. Whatever the truth, Beethoven's death must have seemed to Schubert like the end of an age.

Among the visitors to Vienna in that eventful March was J. N. Hummel, come to make his peace with Beethoven, for the two men had been estranged for many years. Here we are on safer ground, for Spaun's account of the meeting between Hummel and Schubert at a party given by the singer Frau von Läszny is confirmed in some detail by Ferdinand Hiller, Hummel's companion. When they left for Vienna, Hiller tells us, they had never heard of Schubert. They were deeply impressed, however, when he and Vogl went on performing one beautiful song after another: 'The latter, already elderly, but full of fire and life, had very little voice left—and Schubert's piano playing, in spite of not inconsiderable fluency, was very far from being that of a master. And yet I have never again heard the Schubert songs sung as they were then! Vogl was able to make one forget his lack of voice by means of the utmost fervour and aptness of expression, and Schubert accompanied—as he could not help accompanying.' Hummel, celebrated *Kapellmeister*, composer and virtuoso, was deeply moved, and later improvised at the piano on the tune of *Der blinde Knabe*, which Vogl had just sung. Schubert was not to forget that evening either; it was his intention to dedicate the three great piano sonatas written in the following year to Hummel, had not death intervened.

Hiller's judgment on the performers cannot fail to raise our curiosity. Vogl went on singing Schubert to within a few years of his death at the age of seventy-two. If he had little voice left in 1827, what can he have been like, one wonders, ten years later? And what, even at their best, would the legendary combination of Schubert and Vogl, which brought tears to the eyes of Hummel and many another listener, sound like to a modern audience? So far as Vogl is concerned, the answer is, almost certainly mannered, quirky, and over-dramatic. He was a good man and a serious artist, but he had learnt his craft in the opera house. He regarded a song as a vehicle for the interpretation of the singer, and it is clear from many hints dropped by friends that Schubert often found the relationship irksome. One of them, Johann Ebner, goes so far as to suggest that Schubert at one time withdrew as accompanist in favour of Albert Schellmann—this was at Steyr—'who found no difficulty in adapting his accompaniments exactly to Vogl's style'.[1]

It is worth pausing to consider Sonnleithner's considered judgment on the interpretation of Schubert's songs, not only because it is by far the best and most illuminating account of Schubert's own style of performance, but also because it hints at the fundamental differences of approach which these legendary recitals somehow managed to transcend. Writing to Luib in 1858, he inveighs against the excessively declamatory fashion of singing Schubert songs then current, and goes on:

'I heard him accompany and rehearse his songs more than a hundred times. Above all, he always kept the most strict and even time, except in a few cases where he had expressly indicated in writing a ritardando, morendo, accelerando, etc. Furthermore he never allowed violent expression in performance. The lieder singer, as a rule, only relates experiences and feelings of others; he does not himself impersonate the characters whose feelings he describes. Poet, composer,

[1] *Memoirs* (p. 48), *op. cit.*

and singer must conceive the song *lyrically*, not *dramatically*. With Schubert especially the true expression, the deepest feeling, is already inherent in the melody as such, and is admirably enhanced by the accompaniment. Everything that hinders the flow of the melody and disturbs the evenly flowing accompaniment is, therefore, exactly contrary to the composer's intention and destroys the musical effect.'[1] And he goes on: 'Michael Vogl, it is true, overstepped the permissible limits more and more as he lost his voice, but nevertheless he always sang *strictly in time*; and he merely helped himself out as well as he could, in the manner of the experienced opera singer, where his voice and strength did not suffice. And Schubert would certainly not have approved his manner of performance as it developed in his last years.'

As for Schubert's skill at the keyboard, Hiller's estimate of him as a fluent but by no means brilliant pianist agrees with Anselm Hüttenbrenner's. But they bring us back once again to the Schubert mystery, to the transformation scene that seemed to take place when he played his own music. 'His young face lit up, he seemed to grow in stature, and when, having finished the song, he sank back into himself, turned round, with one arm on the back of his chair, asked me, as I stood there breathless and often in tears "Well, did you like it?" the earlier impression was certainly weakened but it did not disappear.'[2] The words are Marie Wagner's, who heard *Erlkönig* performed at the Music Society concert in December 1820 and was so moved that she escaped before the song was encored. She never cared for Vogl's performance, and thought no one sang Schubert songs as Schubert did, 'and that without a voice'.

There is little in the remaining compositions of these

---

[1] *Memoirs* (p. 116), *op. cit.*   [2] *Idem* (p. 298), *op. cit.*

months that calls for comment. Of the part-songs, *Grab und Mond* (September 1826) strikes a new and more sombre note. If, as O. E. Deutsch suggests, it can be identified as the song sung at Josef Merk's concert in the following April, it made little impression on the audience, according to the *Wiener Zeitschrift*. *Nachtgesang im Walde*, specially written in April for Josef Lewy's concert, makes effective use of its accompaniment of four horns. Perhaps the best of these part-songs, however, is the *Serenade*, composed at Anna Fröhlich's request to Grillparzer's words, so that Leopold Sonnleithner could give his fiancée Louise Gosmar a pleasant surprise on her birthday. Anna was fond of telling the story: how Schubert, after studying the verses for a few minutes, hit upon the idea for his setting, and presented her with the finished score three days later; how he absentmindedly set it for men's voices instead of women's, and made no trouble of transposing it; and how she failed repeatedly to get him to come and hear her pupils perform the work. The first performance took place outside Louise Gosmar's window at Döbling on 11 August 1827. Anna wrote:

'I had taken my pupils in three carriages to Döbling, where Fräulein Gosmar was living at the Langs' house; I had had the piano carried secretly under the garden window and had invited Schubert to the performance. But he did not come. The next day, when I asked him why he had stayed away, he apologized: "Oh dear! I forgot all about it." Then I gave a performance of the *Serenade* and invited him to it, repeating the invitation with emphasis. It was already time to begin and still I did not see our Schubert. . . . Heaven knows where he had got to this time. . . . Walcher had the excellent notion, "Perhaps he is at Wanner's *Zur Eiche*", for in those days musicians liked to go there because of the good beer. "I will run over there." Sure enough Schubert was sitting there, and came with him. But after the performance he appeared quite transfigured and said to me, "Do you know, I had no idea it was so beautiful".'[1] It should perhaps be added that the expedition to Döbling was not just an elaborate prank. Serenading was a long-established tradition in Vienna; any young woman with musical tastes and a fiancé might reason‑ ably expect an occasional tribute of this sort.

A curious piece of juvenilia issued from Diabelli's office in May as Schubert's opus 74. Called *Die Advokaten*, it seems to have been a very early version of a comic trio for male voices written in 1805 by one Anton Fischer.[2] It is significant that a work of similar scale and appeal, *Der Hochzeitsbraten*, to a libretto of sorts by Schober, was published shortly after Schubert's death by Diabelli. This latter is a kind of comic version of the *Schöne Müllerin* story, and is usually attributed to November 1827. Its appearance in this year, and the decision to publish *Die Advokaten* can only be seen as one more attempt to cash in on popular demand, in this case on the public's seemingly inexhaustible enthusiasm for comic opera of a conventional Italian type. *Der Hochzeitsbraten* is Schubert attempting to steal Rossini's clothes.

The twelve months from October 1826 to September 1827 are unique in Schubert's working life in being overshadowed by one work of supreme importance. As we have emphasised the gulf that separates *Winterreise*, however, from the other compositions of the period, it would be unfair to omit the one song that seems to herald a lifting of the clouds. In *Das Lied im Grünen* the sun shines again like a blessing. Schubert

---

[1] *Memoirs* (pp. 251–3), *op. cit.*

[2] On this highly problematical work, see a full discussion in *Essays on Schubert* (pp. 244–7) by Maurice J. E. Brown.

came across the verses while staying at Dornbach in June, presumably because he met the author there, an actor and amateur poet named Friedrich Reil. They are about spring the enchantress, and its perennial power of regeneration. The rondo form, and the cadential echo phrase–'in springtime, in springtime'–exactly match the easing of the spirit, the sense of time held at bay, that belong to a perfect spring day; and though the quaver figure in the pianist's right hand moves unceasingly yet unhurriedly from beginning to end–like a rippling stream–Schubert's uncanny instinct for melodic variation delights us to the end. Indeed, he reserves his best surprises for the last verse, which reminds us that we are only young once. In spring, it says, everything seems possible, so why not make the most of our luck and our dreams while we can?

> *Ins Grüne, ins Grüne,*
> *Lasst heiter uns folgen dem freundlichen Knaben!*
> *Grünt einst uns das Leben nicht fürder, so haben*
> *Wir klüglich die grünende Zeit nicht versäumt,*
> *Und wann es gegolten, doch glücklich geträumt*
> *Im Grünen.*[1]

First the running quavers, with no trouble but a repeated bar, became the running feet of the boys at play; then, at the words 'Grünt einst uns das Leben nicht fürder', D minor comes like a touch of mortality, almost but not quite break-

[1] 'Let's gaily follow Spring, the friendly boy, into the open. Then, when one day life is no longer green, we shall be able to say that we have wisely not missed the springtime of life, and while it lasted we were happy, dreaming in springtime.' Under these verses the author wrote: 'Was often sung in the meadows here and there this summer by a merry party to an agreeable cheerful melody by Schubert.' The note was published, with the verses, in the *Theaterzeitung* of 13 October 1827.

ing the even flow of the song. Then, shrugging off such thoughts, the singer reaches to a top A natural before return-ing for the last time to the carefree cadence – 'in springtime.'

Schubert had been in and about Vienna for two years. He had not much longer to wait, however, for the holiday he needed. There was a long-standing invitation for him to visit Graz, the Styrian capital, with his friend Johann Baptist Jenger, and stay with Dr. Pachler, an enthusiastic and well-to-do amateur, and his family. Jenger had been secretary of the Music Society at Graz in 1823, when the Society pre-sented Schubert with a diploma of honour. He was now an official of the War Ministry in Vienna. The plan for joining forces in a visit to Graz had been mooted long ago, but in 1826 it fell through for lack of money. Now, at last, it was to come off. The two friends set off on Sunday evening, September 2nd, by coach, and reached Graz the following night. For Schubert, it was to be his first glimpse of the mountains for two years, and the last holiday of his life. And with it, the depression of his year seems to lift, heralding a new phase in his life and art.

A Note on Schubert's Dots

True to his conservative bent, Schubert never found any occasion to modify the conventions of musical notation he learnt from Salieri. There was nothing in him, as Sonnleith-ner said, of a musician of the future; the saying applies as much to his notation as to his attitude to the trend of public taste. So it is that in playing his music the performer is often called upon to make the same use of his interpretative skill as he would in playing Mozart and Haydn. Most modern editions give reasonable guidance in these matters, except in one respect, the treatment of the dotted quaver, in association with triplet rhythms. In Schubert's music, with its addiction to dance rhythms, this problem cannot be ignored; and since *Winterreise* offers a number of leading cases, a note on it may not be out of place here.

The basic fact is that Schubert, following the usual eighteenth-century practice,' never in his later work uses ♩♪ as a triplet group. He writes ♪♫ instead. It cannot be said that ♩♪ never occurs in his work. There are clear examples in *Geisternähe* (D. 100 written in April 1814), in *Auf einen Kirchhof* (D. 151 February 1815), and in the male-voice quartet *Im Gegenwärtigen Vergangenes* (D.710). But it never seems to occur in his mature years; and the proof that ♪♫ is used ambiguously, sometimes to represent ♩♪ and sometimes with its modern connotation is that when the parts lie close together Schubert will often link the semi-quaver following the dotted note with the third note of the triplet group. Thus in *Erstarrung* (bar 24) we have:

Example 14

There are similar examples at bar 20 of *Heimliches Lieben*, written at Graz in September 1827, and in the piano sonatas. These do no more than confirm our intuitive feeling that, given Schubert's liking for triplet rhythms, and his conservative aversion to the notation ♩♪ as a group, ♪♫ must often be played in triplet rhythm. There seems little doubt, for instance, that the following passage from the D major piano sonata:

Example 15

should be played throughout in triplets. And so, to come nearer home, should the accompaniment to *Der Lindenbaum* in the middle section:

Example 16

where the dotted rhythm sounds intolerably jerky. The same principle should surely apply in songs like *Ungeduld* and *Lob der Thränen*, as it does in countless passages in the keyboard duet works. Yet when Benjamin Britten played the accompaniment of *Wasserfluth* in triplets rather than dotted rhythms in 1965 a long correspondence erupted in the columns of the *Musical Times* which showed how little the conventions of the age had been thought to apply to Schubert's music. It would seem to be time for editors to give some guidance in this, as they do in other notational questions; and the more one considers the matter, the more the purely musical arguments suggest that the triplet rhythm should normally be sustained in these ambiguous passages. Remembering Sonnleithner's warning–'Everything that hinders the flow of the melody and disturbs the evenly flowing accompaniment is . . . exactly contrary to the composer's intention and destroys the musical effect'–one suspects that Schubert would have been on Britten's side. There are certainly cases, however, where the dotted rhythm is obviously intended to make its own accent against the triplet. A good example can be found in the Adagio of the C minor sonata of 1828, where the dotted rhythms throughout the middle section give tautness and strength to the piece.

Even where there are no adjacent triplets to alert the performer, we frequently come upon extended passages in Schubert which seem to fall naturally into a triplet rhythm, though written with dotted notes. His 'run up to the wicket', a formula which occurs frequently in the sonatas and symphonies, is a case in point. Take, for example, the very characteristic sonata in A minor (D.784), written in 1823, at bar 23.

Example 17

It is difficult to play such passages as these, and the many similar ones scattered throughout the keyboard works, and retain the strict dotted rhythm. It seems more than likely that a triplet rhythm is the composer's intention here, in such movements as the scherzo of the piano sonata in D major, and even in the dotted quavers which accompany the scurrying triplets in the last movement of the Great C Major symphony. His practice, evidently, was to leave these things to the discretion of the performer. As for his own example, we would give a great deal for a faithful recording of Schubert playing his own music. All we know is that his emphasis was always upon a smooth legato touch, unhurried steady tempi, and a singing melodic line. He belonged to the 'old school of good pianoforte players', according to Schober, 'whose fingers had not yet begun to attack the poor keys like birds of prey'. And he told his father that he hated the 'accursed chopping' in which the new generation of pianoforte virtuosi indulged. Conservative in all musical matters, Schubert, it seems, never imagined that his dotted notes might mislead performers as they most certainly do today.

It is a curious fact, however, that while it is generally agreed in the case of baroque music that faithfulness to the composer's intentions can only be achieved by an act of conscious and considered interpretation, based on a knowledge of the contemporary conventions, in playing Beethoven and Schubert the assumption is that we can safely take the notes to mean exactly what they say. The evidence proves otherwise; that eighteenth-century conventions lingered on long into the nineteenth century, and that a well-intentioned insistence on playing 'what the composer wrote' can be as misguided in playing Beethoven as in playing Bach. Certainly Schubert calls for skilled and sophisticated interpretation at every point. Anyone who sings the recitative of *Der Sänger* (D. 149) as Schubert wrote it will not be proving faithful to the composer's intentions, for it should be sung with appoggiaturas, just as if it came from a Handel opera. The mordents in *Pause*, and the grace notes in the pianist's left hand throughout the accompaniment of *Im Dorfe*, should fall on the beat and not, as written, before. As for Schubert's indiscriminate use of ♪, sometimes as an acciaccatura and sometimes as an appoggiatura, this calls for constant care and imaginative interpretation on the part of the performer.

We are also, at long last, beginning to realise to what extent the modern grand piano can falsify the musical sense of what Schubert wrote. Play the opening chord of *Am Meer* on a modern piano, and the result too often is an ugly 'clumph'. These close-set harmonies in the lower half of the keyboard were written for the lighter resonance of the contemporary instrument. Come to that, do we know how Schubert's rippling accompaniment figures should sound until we have heard them on the instrument for which they were written? It may be that we are due for a revaluation of early nineteenth-century music in terms of the conditions of the age, and that in twenty years' time it will seem as normal and natural to play Schubert on a contemporary instrument as it does now to play Bach on a harpsichord.

V

STYRIAN INTERLUDE:
SEPTEMBER 1827

Those were the happiest days I have passed
for a long time.
                    Schubert to Carl Pachler,
                    27 September 1827

Schubert felt as though he had a new lease
of life.
                                Faust Pachler

In August the Schubertians began to disperse for the
holidays. Schwind left for Munich early in the month to
pursue his art studies, and went on to Upper Austria to join
up with the Linz circle in September. The Hartmann brothers,
after a brush with the university authorities over the necessary travel permit, left, severally, a few weeks later, and we
hear no more of events in Vienna until November, when
Franz returned to continue his studies, this time with a
younger brother, Louis. Meanwhile Bauernfeld, engrossed in
his writing and in his official duties, which seem to have
proved less onerous and dull than he anticipated, retires
somewhat to the background. Indeed, until early in 1828,
when the revival of the reading parties brought back a sense
of purpose to the regular meetings of the friends, the circle
wears a faded *fin de siècle* air. Bauernfeld, always the most
intellectually self-conscious of the group, catches the note in
his diary:

'Moritz to Munich, on 7th August. Gap in the friendly

circle. By the way, see Kotzebue's "Philibert, or Circumstances". What is to become of us all?'

The invitation to Graz was of long standing, as we have seen, and what special circumstances made it possible to accept now it is difficult to say. O. E. Deutsch suggests that the two recent publications of that summer—op. 75 in July (four polonaises for piano duet) and the song-book op. 84/87[1] in August—may have provided the funds. But these were no more than routine publications, and the fifty florins or so they brought in would hardly have done more than pay day-to-day living expenses. It seems more likely that Schubert set aside a more substantial sum, possibly the fee for Part I of *Winterreise*, which must by then have been with Haslinger, or the money he got from the exceptional series of engagements as accompanist a few months earlier. One can sense, too, a new determination in the preliminary correspondence that this time the plan must be brought off; as though Schubert's friends recognised his need to escape from Vienna, and the unhappy effects of his failure to do so in 1826. We find Jenger writing to Marie Pachler as early as December 1826: 'Friend Schubert is firmly resolved to go to Graz next year; but if he does not get there with me, it will again come to nothing, like this year.' So it is likely that Jenger not only made the trip possible by conducting the negotiations with the Pachlers, but also looked after the financial arrangements.

Dr. Carl Pachler, in whose house the friends stayed, was an advocate who also took a prominent part in local artistic affairs. He and his wife Marie, a talented pianist who had won the warm approval of Beethoven when they met in

[1] The book was first published as op. 84. But Weigl had already (misleadingly) used this opus number for the second and third movements of his duet sonata. So the song-book became op. 87.

1817, kept open house for visiting artists appearing at the
Opera House, or at concerts; and the impression one gets of
the musical life of this large provincial capital is that, like
Linz, it was more conservative in taste than Vienna, less distracted by what Schubert called 'wretched fashionable stuff',
and therefore much more willing to lionise conservatively-
minded composers like Schubert and Beethoven. In Graz
Schubert had both professional and personal links, dating
back to his election as an honorary member of the Styrian
Musical Society in April 1823, and indeed earlier, to his
friendship with the Hüttenbrenners, whose home it was; and
with the opera house there the links were especially close.
Carl Pachler was a close friend of the manager, Johann
Stöger, whose assistant and secretary was Schubert's old
friend Josef Kupelwieser, the librettist of *Fierrabras*. Johann
Nestroy, a regular performer of Schubert songs at Music
Society concerts in Vienna, and who later became well-
known as a dramatist, was also employed at the Graz opera.
With no lack of friends at court, circumstances encouraged
Schubert to make one more attempt to get a hearing for his
operas. During his stay a Graz production of *Alfonso and
Estrella* was seriously discussed, and Schubert later sent the
Ms. score to Carl Pachler. In the end the plan came to
nothing, possibly because resources were lacking to mount
so large and problematic a production; but the score remained for many years with the Pachlers, until Ferdinand
Schubert reclaimed it.[1]

No sooner had Schubert and Jenger arrived than they were
plunged into a busy round of visits and parties. On the 5th
the friends joined up with the Hüttenbrenners to visit Meyer-
beer's *The Crusader in Egypt* at the Opera House. Three days

[1] See *Memoirs* (pp. 402, 412), *op. cit.*

later a grand charity concert was held, advertised as 'with the kind collaboration of an artistic and greatly celebrated composer from the metropolis'. Schubert accompanied three of his own songs, *Normans Gesang* from the *Lady of the Lake* group (curious how all-pervasive the Walter Scott craze seems to have been), and two part-songs, *Gott in der Natur*, written in 1822 but not yet published, and *Geist der Liebe*, which struck the right nature-worshipping note: 'Where the pulse of Creation beats, there the spirit of Love works and strives'—both songs set in Schubert's favourite key of C major. There were also excursions to nearby Wildbach, where the party was royally entertained by Dr. Pachler's aunt, Frau Massegg, a Schubertiad was held, and a good deal of the local wine drunk. Frau Massegg had six daughters, one of whom—'my darling Netti' to Jenger—wrote to Marie Pachler:

'We shall never forget the day you spent with us with the other dear company . . . and I have often thought quietly to myself how gladly I would recall it. . . .'

One can indeed imagine that the arrival of two distinguished musical visitors would be an event to remember in the lives of six attractive young women, even if one turned out to be a shy genius and the other a confirmed bachelor. Schubert blossomed, admired the singing of the eldest daughter, and played duets with Jenger. Back within sight of the mountains, and made much of by friends who admired, even if they did not fully comprehend, his genius, he seemed to take on a new lease of life.

The social round, however, left little time for composition. A visit had also to be paid to Haller's Castle, where the Pachlers usually spent the summer months, south-east of Graz. On that occasion there were two Franz Schuberts in the party, for a namesake of the composer's, an instrument-maker living in Graz and a member of the musical society, wrote an account of it for Luib many years later:

'We thought we were paying Schubert a special honour that evening by performing several of his compositions; but after a time he said to me: "Stop playing my compositions now, I hear them enough in Vienna; I would rather hear something Styrian." When following this a Fräulein Kathi von Graveneck sang a number of Styrian songs, Schubert was quite enchanted with them.'[1]

The evenings at the Pachlers' house were also filled with music, in which Marie Pachler took her share as a performer. A talented pianist, she seem to have anticipated an Elgarian notion by playing musical portraits of her friends, and she was also a lover of poetry. She introduced Schubert to the verses of Karl Leitner, several of which he later set, and the two songs he did write at Graz, the setting of the ballad *Edward* in Herder's translation and *Heimliches Lieben* were, according to Kreissle, composed at her suggestion. Schubert had a great liking and respect for her, as we shall see, and paid his debt not only by dedicating the songs of opus 106 to her,[2] but by writing a special duet, with easy part for *primo*, for her to play with her eight-year old son Faust on his father's nameday. Warned perhaps about Schubert's forgetfulness in matters of social obligation, Marie took care to send Jenger a written reminder on the day the two friends left to return to Vienna by easy stages. After a final Schubertiad on the 19th (for which Schubert found himself obliged to cancel another engagement) they left the following morning on a four-day

[1] See *Memoirs* (p. 105), *op. cit.*
[2] The book included the two Leitner songs written on Schubert's return from Graz—*Das Weinen* and *Vor meiner Wiege*—and *An Sylvia*. Also *Heimliches Lieben*.

journey home. On the 27th Jenger wrote a long account of the journey to Frau Pachler, and enclosed with his own letter a note of thanks from Schubert:

'Madam, Already it becomes clear to me that I was only too happy at Graz, and I cannot as yet get accustomed to Vienna. True, it is rather large, but then it is empty of cordiality, candour, genuine thought, reasonable words, and especially of intelligent deeds. . . . Above all, I shall never forget the kindly home where, with its dear hostess, and the sturdy "Pachleros" [Dr. Carl], as well as little Faust, I spent the happiest days I have had for a long time. . . . P.S. The opera libretto I hope to be able to send in a few days.'[1]

Marie arranged for her son, Faust, to write himself to Jenger asking him to remind Schubert of his promise. The letter arrived on 10 October, and two days later the Ms. of the Children's March (D.928) was dispatched with warm and appropriate messages from both Schubert and Jenger. Here is one composition, therefore, that can be confidently and precisely dated—11 October 1827. It is an unpretentiously cheerful and attractive little piece, and admirable for its purpose. There seems to be almost a touch of false modesty in Schubert's apologetic accompanying note. 'I fear I shall not earn his [Faust's] applause, since I do not feel that I am exactly made for this kind of composition.'

One commission Schubert was still not able to perform. The libretto of *Alfonso and Estrella*, which he had promised to send, was still at the Kärntnertor Theatre, and Schubert had so far failed to get it back. It seems that the new management, in its search for original German works, had decided to take another look at it, and had briefed a certain Herr Gottdank, an old associate of Schubert's, to read it. What happened

---

[1] *Documentary Biography* (No. 948), *op. cit.*

was that Schubert sent the full score to Graz instead, where it remained until 1842, when brother Ferdinand asked for it back.[1] It was Liszt who, with typical generosity, eventually brought to the stage the work of his one-time secretary Schober together with Schubert's score of *Alfonso*. The production, in a much edited version prepared by Liszt, took place at Weimar in 1854, and stimulated—so Schwind wrote to Bauernfeld—kind words about the music and much satirical comment about the text.[2] It has become a critical cliché to poke fun at Schubert's libretti, and certainly it is difficult enough to take them seriously. But to infer from this that Schubert was the victim of incompetent collaborators, or that he was an operatic composer dogged by ill-luck and insensitive managements, is to ignore the salient facts of the situation; first, that many operas with libretti quite as outrageous as *Alfonso* successfully reached the stage (indeed the trouble with Schubert's texts is that they keep much too close to the narrow and faded conventions of fashionable historical romance; what they offer is a kind of poor man's Walter Scott, minus his genius); that with Vogl's backing he had a good start in the operatic field, achieved more than a *succès d'estime* with his early work, and was for a time taken on to the staff of the Kärntnertor; and finally that he never shows the operatic composer's instinctive aversion to a bad libretto, and the kind of ruthless discrimination that might have given him a good one. True, Schubert was unfortunate in that his creative years coincided with a period when German opera was fighting a losing battle

[1] See note on page 75.

[2] Schober himself, in later years, characterised his own libretto as 'such a miserable, stillborn, bungling piece of work that even so great a genius as Schubert was not able to bring it to life.' *Memoirs* (p. 208), *op. cit.*

against the new wave of Rossini. Even a slight acquaintance with *Alfonso*, however, leads one to doubt whether Schubert had the opera composer's flair for a stage situation, the knack of allowing that situation to develop plausibly and at the appropriate dramatic (rather than lyrical) pace which alone can ensure the temporary suspension of disbelief. That inexorable rule of the gods which seems to decree that the lyric muse and the dramatic muse are on bad terms, so that no age, and few men, can claim equal friendship with both, makes no exception for composers. By and large, the great song-writers leave opera alone, and the giants of opera are too much taken up with the theatre to be concerned with the salon, the home of the *Lied*. *Alfonso* is full of good music in Schubert's *Schöne Müllerin* manner, and we would like to hear it on the stage; but it seems doubtful whether any stage production, however good, would invalidate the judgment that his best operas are the two song-cycles.

'Schubert returned from Graz recently, full of enthusiasm, but richer by only two songs,' wrote Feuchtersleben in October. It would be pleasant to be able to point to those songs as evidence of Schubert's return to his best creative form, but unfortunately this is not possible. *Heimliches Lieben* is, for the text, a gushing sentimental piece, though better than most of the nineteenth-century drawing-room love-songs of which it is the ancestor. Schubert's music is damned with faint praise by Capell, and treated with reproachful silence by Alec Robertson;[1] surely a little unfairly. The tune flows above the accompanist's triplets with a serenity and grace that is unmistakably Schubertian, even if it does suggest that the singer's secret passion is well under control. And the short linking passages between the verses have a very

[1] *Schubert: A Symposium* (p. 174), *op. cit.*

characteristic turn of phrase. The setting of *Edward*, however, fails entirely to match the quality of that splendid dramatic poem. In seeking to keep the piece within the conventions of drawing-room performance—a strophic form, a simple tune in (of all things) six-eight rhythm—Schubert completely misses the cumulative force of the unfolding tragedy. It is a strange miscalculation for the composer of *Erlkönig* to make; to be sure, it might have led to embarrassment to bring alive the raw emotions of lust and murder in those comfortable provincial salons, but in that case why set the poem at all?

Feuchtersleben's *mot*—'richer by only two songs'—is not strictly true, for we must assume that the twelve Grazer waltzes of opus 91, published by Haslinger in January 1828, were begun, if not completed, at Graz, and in some ways they are the most interesting product of that holiday month. For one thing, they represent a return to a genre to which Schubert had paid little attention for years. It has to be accepted that the chronology of the waltz compositions is beyond detailed unravelling,[1] but clearly the well-known collections (with the possible exception of the Valses Nobles of opus 77) were all written before the end of 1824. Apart from occasional contributions to periodicals, Schubert had since then left the waltz to Lanner (who established his orchestra in 1824) and to Strauss. The Grazer waltzes thus offer an interesting comparison with earlier collections. Before we look at them, however, a comment on the importance of the dance compositions and their place in Schubert's creative output may not be amiss.

Modern criticism has in general played down the waltzes as artistically unimportant. But there are at least two good

[1] See, however, Maurice Brown's chapter on the dance music manuscripts in *Essays*; much the most informative account.

reasons why they are worth serious study, quite apart from the continuing delight they give to succeeding generations of pianists. Schubert of all composers is the poet of tonality, and it is in the waltzes above all that he reveals his infinitely subtle command of the resources of the tonal system he inherited. He used his melodic gift not merely to explore the inexhaustible riches of the musical world that lay concealed within the tonal horizons of tonic, dominant, and sub-dominant, but also to probe the boundaries, so to speak, of that world; so that if one wants to illustrate the curiously modal quality of some of Schubert's writing, or his habit of opening ambiguously, by way of the relative minor (or even its dominant) on his way to the tonic, or his command of remote keys, it is to the waltzes one can turn as readily as to the chamber music. Maurice Brown has suggested that these dances played the part of sketch-books in the composer's life, and it does indeed seem possible to illustrate from them his growingly expressive use of the dance forms which play an important part also in his larger compositions. They thus sum up many of the unique attributes of his work, its spontaneity—for most of them must originally have been improvised at the keyboard—its facility, and its universality. Of all the great composers, Schubert has the broadest appeal. Even more than Beethoven's, his music speaks with equal directness and force to the connoisseur and to the musically unsophisticated, and this is an aspect of his genius that is not to be explained away by pretending that the waltzes were unconsidered trifles tossed off in the intervals of more serious composition. One might call the dances light music at its best, were it not for the unfortunate associations the term has acquired. Enthusiasm for class distinction is often carried to the length of regarding light music as something necessarily second-rate, thus adding the spice of snobbishness to the pleasure of connoisseurship; and the principle is even extended so as to imply that 'serious' and 'popular' music are mutually exclusive terms, a notion most eighteenth-century composers would have found incomprehensible. We should therefore approach this element in Schubert's work not apologetically, but as a central and unifying part of it, witnessing to the homogeneity of his creative imagination and to its universality. Apart only from the difference of scale, his genius is as richly involved in the best dance music as it is in the string quintet or the Great C Major symphony.

Superficially considered, the Gräzer waltzes show more freedom of form than their predecessors in that they escape more frequently from the two-sentence structure—each of eight bars—which provides the pattern for almost all of the earlier dances. The eight-bar unit of course remains the basis, but instead of AA BB (32 bars) or A B A (24 bars), five of the twelve extend the second half to 16 bars, giving more scope for modulatory excursions, and the last has a first section of 16 bars, and a final section of 32 bars, both repeated so that its shape is AA (ending at the dominant) BA BA. This final number has a brilliance and a corresponding thinness of harmonic texture which suggests Johann Strauss rather than Schubert:

Example 18

The set begins and ends in E major, and never ventures (except for No. 11 in G major) beyond the adjacent territory of A major, A minor, and C major. In variety of mood and freshness of appeal it does not rival, for instance, the opus 33 set of 1823/4; but if there is nothing quite to match the best of the earlier sets, many of the dances splendidly illustrate Schubert's ability to achieve his expressive purpose with the simplest melodic and harmonic means; as he does in number 9:

Example 19

At least waltzes were still a saleable commodity, and Haslinger lost no time in getting out the new set. It appeared, without opus number, on the same day as Part I of *Winterreise*, 14 January 1828. Schubert was to have much more trouble selling his new piano trio, the work with which he signalled his return to chamber music after more than a year, in November, and on which he now pinned his hopes of establishing his reputation as an instrumental composer.

VI

OCTOBER 1827–FEBRUARY 1828

*Relationship is everything. And if you
want to give it a more precise name, it is
ambiguity.*

*Do you know what I find? That music turns
the equivocal into a system.*

Thomas Mann: *Dr. Faustus*

In the autumn of 1827 Schubert turned to the composition
of short keyboard pieces—the so-called *Moments Musicaux*
and *Impromptus*—which, in their free and original treatment of
simple dance-like tunes, provide a link between the dance
music proper and works of a more ambitious scale. They
belong to the diversified literature of short pieces which
grew up as the potentialities of the new pianos, and the
expressive impulses of romantic composers, came to be
realised, a literature variously represented by Field's
nocturnes, Beethoven's bagatelles, and Chopin's waltzes,
experimental in technique and romantic in feeling, which
was to be brilliantly exploited in their different ways by
Chopin, Liszt, Mendelssohn, Brahms, and many others. The
importance of Schubert's opus 94, however, is far from purely
historical. These six pieces—let us call them simply *Moments*,
since Leidesdorf's schoolboy French has hopelessly confused
the issue[1]—uniquely illustrate his creative genius as a key-

[1] They were published originally as *Momens musicales*, and on the cover
as *Momens musicals*, with reckless indifference to the susceptibilities of
the French language.

board composer and his contribution to the development of tonality. It is as though, looking back to the achievements of his most productive years, from which the third and the last of these pieces date, he takes up again the exploration of the remoter regions of the tonal universe, and, using the simplest material, indeed, confining himself for the most part to the eight-bar sentence and its answer, decides to sum up definitively the characteristics of his own musical thought and style as a keyboard composer. This is not of course meant to suggest that there was a conscious change of direction. Much else was written during these months, including the E flat major piano trio and—in a different vein altogether—*Der Hochzeitsbraten*. Of this varied and uneven output, however, nothing is more important than the *Moments* and the *Impromptus*, because nothing is as perfectly realised, as unmistakably Schubertian, as they are. The popularity of these pieces is not, therefore, to be taken as evidence of their slightness. As so often, it is in his most popular work that Schubert reveals himself best. In their purity of style, absence of rhetoric, and variety of mood, always however preserving the note of transcendental nostalgia which seemed 'mystical' to Schubert's contemporaries,[1] these pieces are quintessential. And since they provide a *locus classicus* for the discussion of Schubert's contribution to the development of tonality, it may be worth while to preface that discussion with a brief account of the theoretical basis on which it is to be conducted.

Though notes, in themselves, lack the conceptual content of words, the language of music shares with verbal language that dependence on recognition of the whole, of the *Gestalt*,

[1] See *Documentary Biography* (No. 669), *op. cit.* 'He always talked very mystically.'

which characterises all forms of perception. It is by virtue of this fundamental psychological principle that a combination of musical sounds, either vertically as in a chord, or horizontally in a tune, sets up an expectation in the mind of the listener which 'turns the equivocal into a system' and makes possible the art and craft of composition; for the business of the composer is so to play upon the listener's expectations, first satisfying them, then suspending them, that his interest and delight are constantly held and intensified. So, at the simplest level, an interrupted cadence cheats and delights the listener by leading him to expect a full close; and so, at a more complex architectural level, the whole shape of a symphonic movement is designed to heighten and intensify our perception of the main tunes when, refined and illumined by the composer's exploration of their nature, they return with enhanced effect at the end.

Even more than words therefore, musical sounds take their sense from their context. In itself a meaningless noise, the chord E♯, G♯, A, B can take on associations of infinite tenderness in the opening bars of Strauss's song *Die Nacht*,

Example 20

and quite different associations in other contexts. Schubert's power of tonal association is so strong that he can disguise the tonic key as a remote region far from home—as he does in the B flat major piano sonata just before the recapitulation of the first movement. This inherent ambiguity in the nature of musical sounds is sometimes contrasted with verbal language, and used as an argument to support the doctrine that music is 'just notes', an autonomous art set apart in a kind of intellectual ghetto from the world of ideas, emotions, and from any 'real' meaning. But this argument misconceives both the nature of verbal language, which is as inherently ambiguous and as dependent upon context as music, and the nature of music, which has its own vocabulary and semantics, more precise and more expressive to the composer than those that belong to words. As Mendelssohn put it, music expresses thoughts too definite to put into words.[1] As for the supposedly unequivocal nature of verbal language, every writer knows that the process of using words with point and precision is like hewing a statue out of a block of marble. String several words together, and what you have in normal everyday usage is something which can be interpreted in several different ways; in their different ways poets, lawyers, administrators, and stand-up comics all earn their daily bread by exploiting the fact.

The development of sonata form, and of more complex rondo and aria forms, which marks the work of the great classical composers, depended of course upon the exploitation of the ambiguity inherent in the character of musical

[1] To a gentleman who wrote to him about the 'meaning' of the *Songs without Words*, Mendelssohn replied: 'There is so much talk about music and so little really said. My belief is, in fact, that words are insufficient for the purpose, and if ever I found that they were sufficient I should ultimately never write any more music. People generally complain that music is capable of so many interpretations; they are so uncertain what they ought to understand by it whereas everybody would understand words. To me it is just the other way . . .only the song can say the same thing to one person as to another, can awaken the same feelings in him—feelings, however, which cannot be expressed on every occasion by the same words.'

language; so that the listener's enjoyment comes in large measure from what Hanslick describes as 'the intellectual satisfaction which he derives from continually following and anticipating the composer's intentions—now to see his expectations fulfilled, and now to find himself agreeably mistaken'.[1] (This process Hanslick, in a striking phrase, calls a 'pondering of the imagination'.) To those of us who were brought up to take the supremacy of the classical Viennese composers for granted, pleasure of this kind may be said to reach its peak in listening to a performance of, say, a Beethoven quartet.

One way of attempting to define Schubert's musical personality is to point to the instinctive feeling he showed for the expressive possibilities latent in tonal ambiguity. The G major quartet, we have seen, is in one aspect an extended essay on the tonality of the mediant. At a much simpler level, however, it can be shown that certain sequences and harmonic positions had an inherent fascination for Schubert, because of their power to evoke a wide range of tonal associations. The chord that we hear at the beginning of *Schöne Welt, wo bist du?* (a seminal song) lies poised between the tonic, the relative minor, and the major of the mediant.

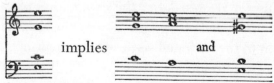

It is significant that this sequence is further explored in the A minor quartet and many other works of the middle years; indeed, the opening bars of the Great C Major symphony are no more than a translation into melodic terms of the same idea.

Alongside Schubert's predilection for ambiguous harmonic

[1] Hanslick: *The Beautiful in Music*, English edition, p. 135.

positions we have to put his love of the that other ambiguous device, the appoggiatura.

For Schubert 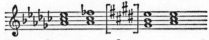 implies

and the reader will recognise the germ not only of the Andante of the A major sonata of 1819 (D.664) but also of the Scherzo of the G major quartet. If one starts from the minor chord in its root position the possibilities opened up by the appoggiatura are even more fascinating, because they invite enharmonic development; and much of Schubert's most characteristic writing, as we shall see, stems from sequences such as these:

Like his eighteenth-century forerunners, Schubert rarely ventures into these remote regions in his early instrumental works; it is to the songs we have to go for evidence of his precocious tonal sense. About the year 1822, however— and it may be taken as the mark of his full maturity as a composer—a new note sounds. It is heard above all in the *Unfinished Symphony*, that incomparable diptych of a work which, in its display of enharmonic relations, seemed to widen the expressive frontiers of music; but also in a more frequent use of remote keys, the exploration of the enharmonic no-man's-land of Ab/G♯, Gb/F♯, the increased use of modulation to the flattened sixth and the mediant, the subtle interplay of major and minor, indeed of all those harmonic devices which we have come to regard as Schubertian fingerprints.[1] These characteristics are so generally apparent and so well recognised that they do not need illustration. Two

[1] Schubert did not invent the enharmonic modulation. It is not certain who did, though Mozart certainly used it. But Schubert made it, with his fondness for the keys of the mediant and the flattened sixth, part of the composer's normal equipment.

further observations should be made, however, before we return to the *Moments musicaux*. The concept of the *Gestalt*, of the composer's creative manipulation of the *double entendre*, applies to all the elements of musical expression, to pulse and melody as much as to harmony. Schubert's rhythmical sense is strong, but he does not in the sonatas, as Haydn and Beethoven for instance often do, take a sophisticated delight in cross-rhythms, though the ambivalent pulse of the second subject of the first movement of the *Unfinished Symphony* has played a part in its popularity. His power of melodic variation and extension—that is, his skill in exploiting melodic ambiguity—is however superb. At its best, as in the slow movement of the G major piano sonata, or the Impromptu in C minor of opus 90, it becomes the main structural component of the music. Finally, it is worth remarking that this instinctive feeling for the ambivalent nature of musical language, and its exploitation as a form of poetic expression, show to their fullest effect in compositions of the years 1824 and 1825. The Theme and Variations in A flat for piano duet, written at Zseliz, a major work and surely a more characteristically Schubertian one than the contemporary Grand Duo sonata, is a *locus classicus* (see especially variations V, VII, and VIII); and so are the piano sonatas of 1825, where one comes across passages which hover indeterminately in a state of suspended motion, before taking off in a new direction. The first movement of the 'Relique' Sonata in C major has a good example at bar 75:

Example 21

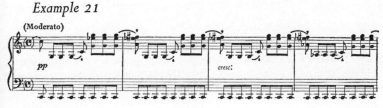

This game of musical blind man's buff occurs, it is interesting
to note, in the exposition. The waywardness of the passage,
and the structural link with the second subject, charm the
ear of the Schubertian,[1] though one has to admit that the
arrival at the dominant in the end seems fortuitous.

Of the six pieces which make up opus 94, published in
July 1828, two date from Schubert's middle years. No. 3 in
F minor had first appeared in December 1823 as a contribution to Leidesdorf's Christmas annual, entitled *Air Russe*;
and No. 6, fancifully titled *Plainte d'un Troubadour*, appeared
in the same publication in December 1824. The others were
all written in autumn 1827, possibly in October after the
return from Graz, and the homogeneity of style, in view of
the time lapse, is noteworthy. So too is the fact that, with the
exception of number one in C major, they all inhabit the
same tonal territory, centred on A flat major and its near
relations F minor/major and D flat minor/major (D flat minor
written enharmonically as C sharp minor). Even the first
piece seems designed to illustrate the 'pull' of C minor and
E flat major against the tonic key.

[1] Not, however, that of the anti-Schubertian. Was it this passage
which provoked Professor Norman Suckling into a protest against
Schubert's 'unadventurous pottering, like a penned sheep, within the
bounds of an outworn musical language'?

Example 22

In the subtlety of their internal thematic relations, and the sense of inevitability and economy in the writing, these pieces well illustrate Schubert's skill in development when relieved of the formal responsibilities of sonata form. In the first the second section in G major, and the third section in D major have a clear relationship with A and B in example 22:

Example 23

At the risk of drawing invidious distinctions, it may be said that the most beautiful of these six pieces, and those that most effectively display Schubert's command of tonal exploration, are number two in A flat minor and number 4 in C sharp minor. The key signatures conceal an identity of tonal interest, for both are concerned with the enharmonic potentialities of C sharp/D flat, with a sequence that might be expressed in skeleton form thus:

Example 24

Number 2 is a kind of lyrical sarabande which takes as its starting point the first chord of this sequence and 'takes off' into a gentle rocking motion hinged on the dominant. It gives an effect of rapt and wistful contemplation tinged with melancholy, which looks forward to the adagio of the C major string quintet. The fourth piece counterpoints a running legato figure in the right hand and staccato quavers in the left with Bach-like security and charm. Its tonal scheme is summed up in the last four chords of the sequence quoted in Example 24, and the middle section, written in D flat major, adds a touch of rhythmical ambiguity by leaving us uncertain whether it begins on an up-beat or a down-beat:

Example 25

This elliptical waltz tune written in square time, with its curiously Bohemian flavour, leads us into F flat major before we return to C sharp minor. But at the last Schubert breaks off enigmatically and inserts two bars of the waltz tune pianissimo before closing in C sharp minor, as though to assert that the only way to end an argument about tonality is to accept its ambiguity gracefully.

The four *Impromptus* of opus 90, the first two of which were published by Haslinger in December, must also belong to the second half of 1827. Like the *Moments*, they reveal Schubert's power of thematic development within a basic ABA structure at its best. Rudolph Retí has shown in some detail[1] how, in number 4 in A flat, the piece grows from a single idea, and how this seminal idea is adapted to provide the contrasts of mood and dynamic inherent in the ABA plan. He could equally well have made his point with any of the other three, for their organic unity is just as striking. The *Impromptus* show the same characteristics as the *Moments Musicaux*, the same delight in remote modulation, often in the same keys (for the *Impromptus* also live on the flat side), and the same reliance on internal thematic development to shape the music within the requirements of a comparatively simple external form; for all these pieces,[2] despite their subtly varied effects, are built up on a single eight-bar sentence. But the scale is extended to the length of a sonata movement, and the lyrical line is stronger. Their variety is strongly marked. Number three in G flat major is a nocturne; number two is a *moto perpetuo* of gossamer-like delicacy and lightness; number four once again explores the tonal region where extremes meet, where A flat minor merges with E major and C sharp minor, and the rhythmical ambiguity of a pulse which seems now triple, now duple; while in number one Schubert provides an object-lesson in the art of building up a full-length tightly constructed movement from a single idea by variation and extension.

[1] Retí, *The Thematic Process in Music* (pp. 151–6), London 1961.
[2] Except number four, which has a subtly changing pattern of six-beat or twelve-beat phrases.

Example 26

This statement, and its answer, is reiterated for forty bars in such a way as to establish and hold the key of C minor stubbornly against the pull of C major, G major, and E flat major. Then Schubert allows us to hear it in a kind of second-subject dress:

Example 27

This tune immediately turns to the minor, and then to a variant which forms the basis of a lovely passage with moving inner parts in the left hand. The relationship is shown in the following example:

Example 28

and so on for nine pages of development which never loses sight of that opening seminal four-bar phrase but which surprises and delights the listener to the end.

These pieces deserve close examination, both because they reveal Schubert's creative imagination working in its most confident and characteristic way, and because he evidently took trouble over them. A full sketch of opus 90 number 1 exists, and it is a reasonable assumption that the other numbers were also sketched. Their certainty of purpose and clarity of form, which contrast so markedly with the comparatively wayward and diffuse quality of many of Schubert's later sonata movements, raise an inevitable question. His genius seems to favour a process of what might be called continuous development. His tendency to introduce ideas more suited to development in the exposition of sonata movements is one aspect—but only the negative aspect—of this; the other side is the expressive mastery of organic structure he displayed when set free of the formal requirements of first movement form. Does this entitle us to say that Schubert was not by nature a sonata composer? Hardly, for to assent to this proposition would be to write off not only the great sonatas of his middle years—the two in A minor, opus 143 and opus 42, in particular—which successfully effect a marriage between Schubert's idiom and sonata form; but also the last three posthumous works of 1828 which, if not great sonatas, are certainly great music. It would be more reasonable to suggest that his intuitive grasp of the possibilities for thematic development inherent in the ambiguous nature of the musical language itself—his grasp, that is, of the indigenous aspects of development—was exceptionally strong, and that it did not always display itself to best advantage within the external constraints of sonata form.

In an illuminating passage on Shakespeare's creative manner, Coleridge contrasts it with that of Ben Jonson, Beaumont and Fletcher. 'The latter,' he says, 'see the totality of the sentence or passage, and then project it entire. Shakespeare goes on creating and evolving B out of A, C out of B, and so on, just as a serpent moves, which makes a fulcrum out of its own body, and seems for ever twisting and untwisting its own strength.' This last sentence seems to characterise Schubert's compositional method as it is revealed in the *Moments* and the *Impromptus* of opus 90 vividly and precisely. This is exactly how his best movements, and his best songs, grow from the initial impulse (often little more than a pianistic figure or a short phrase), steadily and cumulatively gathering strength and interest as they unwind. Indeed, it is tempting to take the analogy further, and to see in Coleridge's comment a distinction between two sorts of composers. The contrast between Schubert's creative method and Beethoven's comes immediately to mind. For the latter did see the totality of a work, often it seems in conceptual verbal terms, before the process of composition began. Beethoven is unique in this capacity to sustain the idea of a work through years of gestation, slowly and laboriously working away at the raw material of notes and tunes, as a sculptor releases the image from a block of stone, until it begins to correspond to the pre-conceived conceptual idea of the work. So it is often difficult to believe that the finished theme grew from the ordinary little tune which first appeared in the sketch-books. Schubert works quite differently. His sketches are first drafts, but finished drafts. His second thoughts are often masterly improvements, but they are improvements to an already completely realised work. There is nothing analogous to Beethoven's painful struggle to release a conceptual idea; the work is done in the process of composition, not before it. And for that reason, perhaps, his best music never loses its freshness and spontaneity.

It is possible to see in the compositions of Schubert's later years a conflict between his natural genius for internal thematic development, which works best from a single musical idea, and the external requirements of sonata form, based as a rule upon two contrasted themes. An examination of his second-subjects, especially in his most characteristic sonatas, shows how closely they derive from the first. It is noteworthy also that as Schubert's powers matured the contrast between the strength of his monothematic structures and the comparative diffuseness of his sonata movements forces itself more and more upon our attention. In the early years all is satisfactorily contained within the eighteenth-century conventions of *Spielmusik*. But in the autumn of 1827 nobody can fail to appreciate the contrast between the assurance of the *Moments* and the *Impromptus* (opus 90) on the one hand, and the structural weakness of the Piano Trio in E flat, written possibly a month or two later, on the other. To say this is not to suggest that Schubert was a miniaturist. It was his nature (and his ambition) to write at 'heavenly length'; and in the perspective of the long history of the romantic symphony, we can safely say that mastery of sonata form is not the minimum qualification for entry to the great symphonic composers' club. It is a question not of scale, but of two quite different methods of composition.

In the piano trio in E flat, opus 100, written in November, we can see Schubert's intention to write a full-length chamber work based on the best models, with strongly contrasted themes and an integrated structure; but something goes wrong. The work is much longer than the earlier B flat trio, and it has many delightful passages of unmistakably Schubertian quality; but it has never won the affection of listeners as has the earlier work, and for good reasons. It lacks the internal thematic unity of the B flat trio, and becomes prolix and repetitive. In the last movement Schubert first charms us by inserting quotations from earlier movements in a new and attractive dress, a graceful gesture, so to speak, in the direction of structural unity, and then allows the device to outstay its welcome. The sound is often enchanting, but we miss the support of a strong design.

This point is well illustrated by a comparison of the two first movements. That of the B flat trio (surely one of the best Schubert wrote) is built on two beautifully related themes, the first vigorous and positive, the other sensuous and passive, both strongly lyrical:

Example 29

In the development section Schubert combines these tunes in a new and exciting way, so that our delight in both is heightened.

Example 30

The recapitulation is beautifully prepared, and an eloquent coda rounds off a movement of splendid coherence and charm.

The first movement of opus 100 is built up on two groups of themes strongly contrasted in tone and shape. At the outset we have a unison theme, all vigorous assertion, subsiding dramatically into the relative minor:

Example 31

Almost immediately there is a counter-subject:

Example 32

and this carries us strongly along for fifty bars, after which Schubert introduces his second subject. First we hear a strongly contrasted theme, a diffident little tune in Schubert's favourite rhythm:

Example 33

Fifty bars further ahead we are involved in a development of the tune we heard at the beginning, which now becomes:

Example 34

But there is still a surprise in store; forty bars later we come upon a new version of this which tugs at the heart strings with wonderful effect:

Example 35

Here's richness indeed; one wonders what Schubert will make of this wealth of material when he gets to the development proper. Alas, the answer is very little. He combines Example 35 above with a catchy little arpeggio figure for the pianist, and finding that it works well, uses the formula three times over, up a fifth each time. Several pages of right hand piano triplets later we are back at the recapitulation. It is, to say the least, a disappointment.

It is worth looking at these two movements in detail, for it seems impossible to resist the conclusion, first, that the raw material of the E flat trio is splendidly rich and amenable to development, more varied indeed than the main themes of the earlier trio, and richer in emotional overtones; and second, that the formal strength of the first movement of opus 99 is conspicuously lacking in its successor. This cannot be because Schubert's creative powers had waned. As we have seen, he had in these same months produced piano works which display his structural powers at their best; and he was in the next few months to give new evidence, in the F minor duet fantasia, of his ability to give formal unity and cumulative effect to a four movement work in a quite original and unconventional way. Why then did he choose, in the trio, to follow the conventional model but allow the thing to sprawl? The answer seems to lie in his estimate of the audience. He had professional players to hand, and a public concert in the offing. He needed to make an effect which was something more than a *succès d'estime*. Sonata form was beginning to look old-fashioned, and its architectural aspects failed to attract much interest. The public mood was for virtuosity, sentiment, and an easy sociability; and it seemed no more than prudent to try to live up to its expectations.

The two middle movements of the trio are the best. The Andante, supposedly based on a Swedish folk song (and certainly it seems to bear little thematic relation to the other movements) is a very attractive piece so long as it is played 'con moto', as Schubert instructs. The pulse is similar to that of the second movement of the Great C Major—also marked *andante con moto*—or to *Gute Nacht* at the beginning of *Winterreise*, a brisk steady pacing movement; if the movement is played *lento* its character is completely altered. Moreover, it should be played at a pace which prepares us for its magical reappearance in the last movement, when it emerges *piano* and *appassionato* from the cello against the pianist's syncopated right hand quavers. This is a stroke of extraordinary originality, and perhaps the most effective single moment in the whole work. It can hardly be denied, however, that the last movement as a whole still seems over-long, though Schubert cut it before publication.

Drawing comparisons between the two piano trios has been a favourite pastime of critics ever since Schumann, welcoming opus 99 on its first appearance, characterised it as 'passive, feminine, lyrical' in contrast with the 'active, masculine, dramatic' opus 100. Choosing between them is, in the last resort, a matter of taste and temperament. To the listener prepared to accept Schubert on his own terms the E flat trio is a richly rewarding work, in spite of its structural weaknesses, and it has a kind of emotional maturity not to be found in the earlier work. But when Schumann goes on to suggest that in the style of opus 99 'there is absolutely no evidence of any earlier period' he is surely wide of the mark. It may have seemed so in the 1830s, but today the two works seem far apart in manner as well as matter.

We learn from the official list of musical events in Vienna that a 'new trio' by Schubert was performed at a Musical Society concert on 26 December by Bocklet, Schuppanzigh, and Linke, and the obvious inference has been drawn by O. E. Deutsch and most other commentators that this was the first performance of the E flat trio. In fact this seems doubtful. Maurice Brown gives some reasons[1] for believing that the trio played at this concert was the earlier B flat work, and the suggestion gains credence from a statement of Schubert's. Writing to Anselm Hüttenbrenner on 18 January, he says: 'Recently a new Trio of mine for pianoforte, violin, and violoncello was performed at Schuppanzigh's, and pleased very much.' There must therefore have been two performances, one at the Musical Society and one at Schuppanzigh's; if the E flat trio was played at both, why did Schubert only mention the private performance in his letter? It seems more probable that the new work was written for the public concert planned for March, and that its first public performance took place there. In that case the performance at Schuppanzigh's was a kind of private pre-view for a select few; while the appearance of the B flat trio in the Music Society programme in December could be explained as

[1] See *Essays on Schubert* (pp. 255–7), *op. cit.*

advance publicity for the concert in March. In itself, of course, the description 'new trio' means nothing. The conventions of the time demanded the adjective even when, as often with Schubert, the work was several years old.

Through these autumn months, richly productive as they were, the routine of Schubert's personal and social life went on uneventfully. After his return from Graz he was unwell, complaining to Frau Pachler in the letter which accompanied the *Kindermarsch* for Faust that 'my usual headaches are assailing me again'.[1] And a few days later he excuses himself from Anna Hönig's party because 'I am ill, and in a way which totally unfits me for such a gathering.'[2] But it seems to have been no more than a passing gastric infection, a mild attack possibly of that endemic typhoid from which he eventually died. For within a few weeks the old routine had re-established itself. Franz von Hartmann, who returned to Vienna in November, notes:

'Every Wednesday and Saturday we go to the alehouse, where Enk, Schober, Schubert and Spaun are to be met. Nearly every day to Bogner's coffee house. . . .'

The pub currently in favour was 'The Wolf Preached at by the Geese', but the life seems to have gone out of the party. We hear nothing of Schwind and Bauernfeld, who were busy with their own professional and artistic concerns. Spaun was shortly to announce his engagement. Schober was, as usual, at odds with the Linz set. It was not until the New Year, when the resumption of the reading parties was to give point and purpose once again to the meetings of the friends, that the group took on a new lease of life. Meanwhile Schubert had

---

[1] *Documentary Biography* (No. 957), *op. cit.*
[2] Brown, *Critical Biography* (p. 280).

his own more serious concern, the projected public concert, to consider. If Bauernfeld is to be believed, this idea took definite root in Schubert's mind some time in the summer of 1827, but it had been talked about for years. It was mooted first in 1823, and Beethoven's public concert of May 1824, at which the D Minor Symphony was first performed, certainly aroused Schubert's interest in the possibility of organising a similar concert of his own works, for he mentions his intention to do so in a letter to Kupelwieser. He seems to have been unwilling however, or perhaps unable, to accept the financial risks involved, in spite of the encouragement of his friends.[1] According to Bauernfeld, his diffidence was only shaken off when he (Bauernfeld) assured him that all his friends would rally round to make the concert a success.[2] Jenger, then secretary of the Music Society, agreed to help with the arrangements, and made the Society's hall available free of charge. It has already been suggested that Schubert wrote the E flat piano trio in November with the forthcoming concert in mind, and that its easy-going manner owes something to his hope of making his mark with the general audience. It is characteristic of the compositions of the period that Schubert seems to have reconciled himself to the limitations imposed by the trend of public taste, and to the need to employ his talents (prostitute seems too strong a word perhaps) where they would find reward. So, alongside the *Impromptus* and the *Moments Musicaux*, we find him busy in these months with exercises in the Rossini manner (the three Italian songs of opus 83, published this September), with dramatic pot-boilers like *Der Hochzeitsbraten* (written in November), and with show pieces like the Fantasia in C for

---

[1] *Documentary Biography* (Nos. 415, 456), *op. cit.*
[2] *Memoirs* (p. 237), *op. cit.*

piano and violin, written in December for Josef Slavik's concert on 20 January 1828.

A point of interest in this last piece is that its opening idea anticipates that of the string quintet written in the following summer:

Example 36

a) Fantasia (simplified)

b) Quintet (simplified)

This opening theme is brought back at the slow movement, an elaborate set of variations on the tune of *Sei mir gegrüsst*, and is then adapted to provide the subject of a final movement of great brilliance but little heart. Into this last movement Schubert inserts, before the peroration, a pianissimo reminiscence of the tune of the variations. The plan appears to be to achieve an effect of unity by overt cross-references, whilst the soloist dazzles us with fireworks. The piece can be brought off by two players of great sensibility and skill, but what impresses the student of Schubert's development is the striking contrast between the superficiality of this Fantasia, written for Slavik, and the profundity of the F minor Fantasia composed immediately afterwards, dedicated to Karoline Esterházy, and written, it seems probable, as a result of a renewal of his old friendship with her.

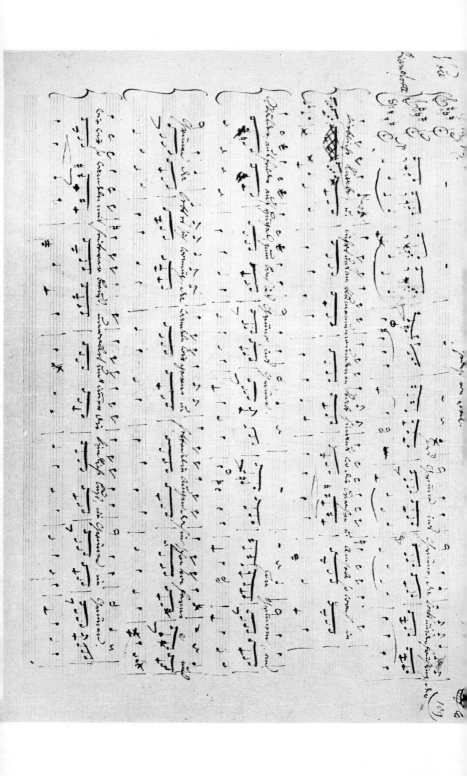

Above, a view of the City Hall and the Church from the Square in Graz.
Below, 'Promenade at the City Gate', 1827, by Moritz von Schwind.
This picture foreshadows Schwind's decision to leave Vienna for
Munich. Studying the map, is Schwind himself. Anna Hőnig, his
betrothed, peeps anxiously over the garden wall, but the promenaders
in the middle of the picture, among whom Schubert, Vogl and Bauernfeld can be discerned, seem to be taking little interest

Our knowledge of the attachment between Schubert and the young Countess Karoline rests mainly on the testimony of Bauernfeld, but it seems to have been accepted as a fact by his friends. When in the 1860s Schwind came to conceive the idea of painting a picture which would be both a documentary record and a reincarnation of the spirit of the Schubertiad, he incorporated Karoline's portrait, which hangs on the back wall of Spaun's room in his famous *Schubert Abend bei Josef von Spaun*; and he would hardly have done that if he had not felt that Karoline had a right to be there, that she in some way represented the idealistic side of Schubert's nature.[1] One does not need to sentimentalise the situation to believe that Schubert's feeling for his young pupil played an important part in his life. The phenomenon is common enough, and an attachment of this kind, hopeless in a practical sense but capable of engaging strong feelings of affection and respect, would appeal to a nature like Schubert's.[2] At all events, Karoline's association with the piano duet Fantasia in F minor is proved, not simply by the dedication, but by the music itself, the Hungarian flavour of which looks back to the *Divertissement à la Hongroïse*. Spaun actually links these two works as both resulting from the visit to Zseliz in 1824,[3] and in the sense that they stem from common sources he may be right. What is quite certain, however, is that the F minor Fantasia took shape in January 1828, and not before. If one wants to believe that Schubert's association with the young Countess was renewed about this time, it is not difficult to

---

[1] For a full and fascinating account of the origins of this picture, see 'Schwind's *Schubert Abend bei Josef von Spaun*' in Maurice Brown's *Essays on Schubert*.

[2] One of Schubert's favourite heroes, Wilhelm Meister, also fell in love with a countess.

[3] *Memoirs* (p. 134), *op. cit.*

think of plausible explanations. On 1st December 1827 Karoline's sister Marie (Schubert's other, but not so favourite pupil) married Count Breunner Enkevoerth, an occasion which may well have brought their music teacher back into the family circle again. Whether this, or some similar social occasion, brought them together we do not know; but that they were still in touch is clearly shown, not merely by the dedication of the Fantasia, but by the fact that Schubert gave Karoline the manuscript of the E flat trio, just completed. It remained with her through what seems to have been a not very happy lifetime.

The Fantasia is Schubert's finest work for piano duet, and arguably his finest keyboard composition. A single movement from a sonata—the *andante sostenuto* from the very last for instance—may move us as deeply; the *Impromptus* and the *Moments Musicaux* may seem more beautifully idiosyncratic; but the Fantasia's unity of form and content is unique. It sustains its initial impetus over what is in effect a four movement work with cumulative effect. The familiar Schubertian devices, minor/major shifts, canonic imitation, work here with fresh and unsurpassed effect. The scherzo in F sharp minor, in a sense the centre of gravity of the work (though what distinguishes the piece is that each section plays its part in the whole) is a miracle of grace and lightness. The fugal finale is unique, Apollonian in its concern simply with 'the notes in their relations', yet providing a logical and satisfying conclusion to the musical argument, achieving an effect analogous (was that what Schubert intended?) with the fugal episodes in the finale of Beethoven's opus 110. What a step forward this is from the bravura gestures which serve the *Wanderer* Fantasy for finale. It is not, perhaps, quite true to say that reservations about the work do not exist. It is possible to feel that the Rossini-inspired tune in the second (Largo) section is out of place (equally possible to believe that Schubert here brought off an effective stylistic marriage); it is possible to think that Schubert's fugal finale is a little short-winded, which, if true, would not be surprising. It is not possible, however, to deny that in the Fantasia he broke new ground, and produced a work which in its structural organisation, economy of form, and emotional depth represents his art at its peak.

Rudolph Réti has shown, in an illuminating analysis of the *Wanderer* Fantasy, how the themes of that expansive work are related in such a way as to give it formal unity.[1] By comparison with the rhetorical richness of the *Wanderer*, the F minor *Fantasia* seems almost epigrammatic. Yet its thematic unity is all the more striking. In its insistent reiteration of dominant and tonic, the opening tune establishes its kinship with the first subject of the Great C Major symphony,[2] the minor mode and the dotted rhythm combining to give an effect of restrained strength and passion. Thereafter the unity of the work turns upon two elements, a tonal scheme which contrasts two outer movements in F minor/major with two inner movements in the Neapolitan key of F sharp minor/major, and a series of contrasted but related themes which all explore the relationship between tonic and dominant. As for the tonal scheme, it is perhaps worth pointing out that, like the second and fourth of the *Moments Musicaux*, it exploits the enharmonic relationship of C sharp and D flat. Schubert himself makes the point explicit in the link-passage leading into the restatement of the opening tune after the scherzo, where a repeated forte

---

[1] *The Thematic Process in Music* (pp. 101–4), *op. cit.*

[2] Still more, of course, with that first subject in its original form, a fourfold repetition of tonic and dominant in dotted rhythm.

C sharp, dominant to F sharp major, leads to a double forte tonic chord of D flat, and thence back to F minor. For the tunes, it is sufficient to set them side by side to show their close family resemblance.

The complete autograph bears the date, April 1828, and the opus number, 103, in Schubert's hand, but this is one further proof of the danger of taking his dates at their face value. Outline sketches exist dated January 1828, showing that the first two movements were complete in all essentials, and the third well on its way to a final form at that date. A sketch of the finale also exists, on different paper and possibly later, which, apart from some filling out of the climax, is identical with the final version. What seems to have happened is that Schubert drafted the work in January, but found the right shape for the scherzo elusive and put it aside, possibly to concentrate on preparing for his concert. When this was out of the way he returned to the Fantasia, polished up the first two movements, drastically cut the third, completed the finale, and wrote out the fair copy. He and Lachner played the new work for the first time in Bauernfeld's lodgings on 9 May and on the same day he treated Bauernfeld to Paganini's concert.

A study of these sketches throws a fascinating light on the way Schubert composed. The first two movements are all there, in outline; only the accompaniment remains to be filled in, with an occasional improvement to the tune and an added bar here and there to give impetus. Examples of felicitous second thoughts are not difficult to find. The opening tune itself is strengthened in bars four and five, and an extra bar a little later is inserted to give more attack to the repeat of the tune. So bars 10–14 originally stood thus:

Example 37

instead of as in the final version:

Example 38

Perhaps the most surprising thing is to find that the most breathtakingly Schubertian moment in the whole work, at the switch to F major at bar 38, is an improved version of a passage that first stood thus:

Example 39

Only some elaboration of the tune and other minor amendments distinguish the sketch of the Largo from the final version, but with the scherzo Schubert seems to have run into difficulty, particularly over the middle section. The *con delicatezza* theme is there, but in the sketch it is preceded by a longish march section, based on this not very exciting tune:

Example 40

Fortunately Schubert realised that this would lower the temperature of the whole piece, and discarded it. In the finale he heightened the climax by expanding the double forte passages with triplet runs. A more dubious alteration this perhaps; but the extension of the coda, which originally ran like this

Example 41

is a splendid improvement. Schubert added five bars to bring a touch of poetic rhetoric to the ending of the piece.

Example 42

It is unfortunate in one sense that one of Schubert's greatest works is written for the now unfashionable medium of piano duet, for the Fantasia is possibly the best example of its composer's mature keyboard style, comparable in this regard with Mozart's great F major duet sonata K.497. Its only chance of public performance comes with a duo recital, now happily not quite so rare a phenomenon as a few years ago. In another sense it seems appropriate, however, that Schubert, the most sociable of composers, should have reserved one of his most inspired compositions for two musicians playing for themselves and their friends at one keyboard. If its poetry and grace owe something to the attractions of that 'certain star' the Countess Karoline, to whom it was dedicated, generations of Schubertians have reason to remember her with gratitude. Before we leave this enchanting work, however, it may be worth pointing out once again how Schubert's most movingly poetic moments turn out on analysis to be due to his feeling for tonal ambiguity. At the very outset of the work, after thirty-seven bars of F minor tonality, we find ourselves, all the more firmly because of that uncompromising opening, in F major. No sooner there, however, than the B natural grace note, and the

G sharp (A flat) in the bass, dart like a flicker of shadow across the listener's mind, as though to remind him that

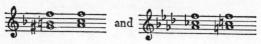

identical notes on the keyboard, are very different in their associations and tonal relations.

Example 43

(simplified)

(Allegro molto moderato)

On New Year's Eve the usual party was held at Schober's. Franz von Hartman recorded it in his diary.

'1st January 1828: At Schober's. On the stroke of 12 we (Spaun, Enk, Schober, Schubert, Gahy, Edward Rössler—a young medical student from Pest—Bauernfeld, Schwind, and we two) drank mutually to a happy new year. . . . Bauernfeld then read a poem on the time of year. At 2 o'clock we went home.'

Bauernfeld's poem is a more serious (and duller) affair than his *jeu d'esprit* of two years earlier, a little sermon in the conventional manner on time's inexorable way with young men and young women, including poets and musicians.

'The spells of the poet, the pleasures of singing,
They too will be gone, be they true as they may;
No longer will songs in our party be ringing,
For the singer too will be called away.
The waters from source to the sea must throng,
The singer at last will be lost in his song.'

The verses seem oddly prophetic, but they are no more than an illustration of the well-worn theme that time and tide wait for no man. And, so far as Schubert is concerned, the dawn of 1828 must have seemed a much brighter affair than that of 1827. His public concert lay ahead, and his creative powers were fully engaged. The first part of *Winterreise* was due from the publishers any day. He had not yet, it is true, established a place for himself commensurate with his genius, nor was he within sight of financial security. Slowly his work was attracting more attention, however. The G major piano sonata, which had appeared in April 1827, attracted notices in the autumn from Frankfort—condescending and uncomprehending—and from Leipzig—a considered and sympathetic piece from G. W. Fink, the editor of the *Allgemeine Musikalische Zeitung*, who of all German observers seems to be the only one, with the possible exception of Rochlitz, who paid any serious attention to Schubert's published work. Fink had already written sympathetically on the A minor sonata (opus 42);[1] he now published articles on two recent books of songs, and on the four-handed variations on a theme from Hérold's *Marie*, in addition to that on the G major sonata. His essays are interesting both in tone and content; he strikes a nice balance between respectful encouragement on the one hand and paternal admonition on the other, praising Schubert's obvious intention to find his own way, while pointing out the dangers of doing so too hastily and wilfully— the tone, indicative perhaps of the hierarchical social structure which applied even in artistic matters, resembles that of a headmaster addressing a gifted sixth-form pupil. As for content, there are the predictable sounds of alarm at abrupt transitions, 'surprise attacks with strange chords',

[1] *Documentary Biography* (No. 632), *op. cit.*

and incessant modulation, but awareness too of Schubert's originality. In an interesting passage on Schubert's merits as a song-writer for instance, Fink singles out (1) his ability to choose poems which are good in themselves and suitable for musical treatment, (2) his skill in finding a musical equivalent for the basic poetic idea, and (3) his use of the accompaniment for descriptive heightening of the sense. This is just, and the conventional complaints about extravagant use of modulation and dramatic contrast are after all no more than were usually levelled at Beethoven, whose reputation, however, gave him a special status. One of Fink's more interesting passages elaborates on the dangers for a young composer like Schubert of being unduly influenced by the great example of Beethoven. (He regards it as evident that in his piano sonatas 'he has chosen Beethoven as a model'). The later Beethoven is unique, and 'his most original ways suit him alone'; those who follow in the steps of the master usually end in mediocrity; better to follow them as far as we can, but then to take our own way.[1]

Where this contemporary point of view finds contact with modern criticism is in recognising the problem posed for Schubert by the very existence and pre-eminence of a composer of Beethoven's stature. To us, what seems remarkable is the way the individuality of the younger composer took root and grew under the shadow of that towering figure; to contemporary observers like Fink the obvious point was that Schubert risked his own originality in following Beethoven so closely. And Fink was after all a representative of the more old-fashioned school. Popular taste regarded both Beethoven and Schubert as equally outmoded.

Josef Slavik's concert took place on 20 January, and the

[1] *Documentary Biography* (Nos. 984, 1014, 1023, 1032), *op. cit.*

C major Fantasia was accompanied by Bocklet. If this work was intended to catch the public mood for brilliant virtuosity, it seems to have miscarried. The Leipzig correspondent reported that it 'failed to please in any way', and the *Sammler* noted unkindly that the hall gradually emptied. Doubtless the piece was under-rehearsed, for the *Theaterzeitung* declared that it showed up Slavik's shortcomings, and thought it could only be appreciated by an audience of 'true connoisseurs'. Whatever the reason, it missed the mark.

By this time, however, Schubert was busy with the F minor Fantasia, and the records of these months show no signs of depression or disappointment. The first part of *Winterreise* appeared on 14 January, and by way of advance publicity Tietze sang the first song in the cycle, *Gute Nacht*, at a Little Society concert on the 10th. The news of Spaun's engagement to Fanny Roner leaked out, and was the occasion for some innocent fun at the pub, for a grand Schubertiad which took place at the end of the month in Spaun's lodgings, and for a party at Witteczek's two days later. At Spaun's party, Bocklet, Schuppanzigh and Linke played Schubert's piano trio (presumably, though not certainly, the recent one in E flat), and Schubert and Bocklet played duets. Franz von Hartmann was entranced by the music, everybody became happily tipsy, and the inner circle of the Schubertians went on to the coffee house, where they stayed gossiping till 2.30 in the morning. Spaun was 39, and his Fanny was 32, a fairly advanced age to be saying farewell to youth and bachelordom. Schubert spared no pains to make the music worthy of the occasion, as a way of paying tribute to his oldest friend. Years later Spaun recalled this party with affection as the last of its kind. The wedding was in April.

Meanwhile the reading parties, resumed at the beginning

of the month, were held every Saturday at Schober's. On the menu, so to speak, in these first weeks were two novels of Heinrich von Kleist, poems by Josef Zedlitz, and the first part of Heine's *Reisebilder*, which Franz von Hartmann enjoyed, but with reservations about Heine's political views.

'12 January 1828. To Schober, when the splendid *Story of the Marquise von O.* by Kleist was read to the end, a book *Travel Notions* by Heine begun. Some pleasant things. Much wit. False tendencies. . . . To the pub, where we stayed until after midnight.'

Schubert took his six Heine songs from the opening sequence of the *Reisebilder*, so it is a reasonable presumption that he made their acquaintance through these readings, and went on to compose them in the first two months of the year. They represent his art as a song-writer at its peak. *Die Stadt* shows his power of pictorial suggestion straining at the limits of the musical language he inherited; it looks forward to Debussy rather than to his immediate successors. *Der Doppelgänger* looks forward rather to Wolf, in its complete sharing of the musical and dramatic interest between voice and piano, in the reduction of the vocal line to a form of declamation, and in its splendidly controlled climax. (Significantly, *Doppelgänger* is built on a kind of ground bass, which recalls both the key and the seminal idea of the Unfinished Symphony, that most revealing and personal of all its composer's utterances.)[1] And *Am Meer* is in a sense Schubert's last word in the art of the strophic song. In these six wonderful songs, each a masterpiece in its own way, Schubert brought the art of the *Lied* to a peak of expressiveness it has never surpassed, before or since.

[1] The point is well made by Mosco Carner in his essay on Schubert's orchestral music in *Schubert: A Symposium* (p. 65), *op. cit.*

The provenance of the Heine songs has been confused by their accidental inclusion with the Rellstab group in the entirely factitious *Schwanengesang* collection, which has influenced biographers into believing that they do indeed belong to the last months of Schubert's life. The composer intended them to be published separately, however. There is also Schönstein's clear recollection, first written down in 1857 in a letter to Luib, that on a visit to Schubert 'some years' before his death he found Heine's *Buch der Lieder* lying on the composer's desk and borrowed it, Schubert having clearly indicated that he had finished with it. Schönstein later modified his account, when it was pointed out that the *Buch der Lieder* was not published until October 1827, but continued to insist that the inclusion of the Heine songs in *Schwanengesang* was entirely misleading, and that the incident happened long before Schubert's death. Schönstein is an honest level-headed witness, and the possibility that he invented or dreamed up the story can be dismissed. Moreover, the facts in regard to the publication of the *Heimkehr* cycle, from which Schubert chose his six Heine settings, are not quite so simple as this summary of them suggests, for though the complete *Buch der Lieder* was not published till October 1827 the *Heimkehr* cycle appeared first, in the first part of *Reisebilder*, in May 1826.[1] One point seems not to have been noticed, however. Schönstein clearly recalls that his visit took place 'when Schubert was still living at Schober's, *unter den Tuchlauben*'; and it was not till the beginning of March 1827 that Schubert moved in with Schober. It looks as though the Heine songs may have been composed towards the end of 1827, rather than as a result of the readings in January. Almost certainly they belong not to the last months of

[1] See *Documentary Biography* (note following No. 1000), *op. cit.*

Schubert's life, but to the preceding winter. These supreme examples of his genius as a song-writer take their place, in their clarity of form and economy of style, beside the great keyboard compositions we have been discussing, as evidence of the final flowering of his genius which took place in this last winter of his life.

In February the possibility of a further visit to Graz was mooted, in circumstances which require a little explanation. Jenger's superior at the War Office was Rafael von Kiesewetter, an enthusiastic amateur at whose *salon* Schubert's work was always in request, and one of the pioneers in the study of ancient and medieval music. His daughter Irene, now seventeen, was a very capable and attractive young woman who frequently performed at her father's *soirées*; Jenger's admiration for her was so unstinted that Frau Pachler evidently concluded the feelings involved were not entirely aesthetic, for the correspondence between Vienna and Graz contains a good deal of indignant protestation and sly allusion on the matter. Schubert, too, was an admirer of Irene's talent; when she recovered from a serious illness in December 1827, he set some occasional verses for male voices accompanied by two pianos, doubtless for performance in her honour and to celebrate her reappearance at the party. As a way of completing her convalescence, Jenger now writes to suggest that he and Schubert should escort her to Graz for a short holiday and a taste of mountain air. The plan perhaps assumed that Irene's father would make a generous contribution towards the expenses; but it also suggests that Schubert's affairs were not so disordered as to rule such a holiday out. Jenger takes the opportunity to mention two other commissions for Schubert. Would she allow Irene Kiesewetter to accept on her behalf the dedication of opus

106 (including the two songs written at Graz in the previous September) and to sign the proof accordingly? And would she ask her husband to put in a word for Schubert's brother Carl, who had applied for the post of art master at the Graz training school? Schubert had already written to Anselm Hüttenbrenner on the last matter, a letter which shows that then, as now, the influence of local celebrities in such things was not thought to be without effect.

'Vienna, 18 January 1828: My dear old Hüttenbrenner, You must be surprised at my writing for once. I too. But if I do write, it is because I have a purpose. Listen, then: there is a drawing-master's post vacant at your Graz, and the competition for it is announced. My brother Carl, whom perhaps you know too, wishes to obtain this post. He is greatly skilled, both as landscape painter and as draughtsman. Now if you could do something for him in this matter, I should be infinitely obliged to you. You are a powerful man in Graz and may know somebody on the county council or someone else who has influence. . . . Recently a new Trio of mine for pianoforte, violin, and violoncello was performed at Schuppanzigh's, and pleased very much. . . . Have you done nothing new?'[1]

It is sad to note that so much well-intended pulling of strings proved fruitless, but so it was. Carl did not get the job; nor did the projected trip to Graz materialise.

Early in February, however, affairs took an altogether more hopeful turn, which prompts the speculation that someone else may have been pulling strings on Schubert's behalf. He received letters from Probst of Leipzig, and Schott of Mainz, both written on 9 February, offering to consider any

---

[1] *Documentary Biography* (No. 1007). The original of this letter is in the British Museum.

works he had available for publication, indeed asking for his manuscripts to be sent, and inviting him, in the case of Schott's letter, to 'kindly fix the fee'. That these friendly overtures should have been made at all seems remarkable; that they should have been made on the same day is too much to be accepted as a coincidence. Possibly Fink's recent articles had excited the publishers' interest; we do not know. But Schubert's reply to these letters throws an interesting light on the two major problems of chronology posed by the work of his later years, the date of the B flat major trio, and that of the Great C Major Symphony, already discussed in an earlier chapter. The significance of this new evidence has now to be considered, and it brings us to a critical month in Schubert's life.

Badgastein as it was in Schubert's day, an engraving by J. Axmann after the painting by Jakob Alt; *below*, Schubert's sketch for the first movement of the Fantasia in F minor for piano duet, January 1828

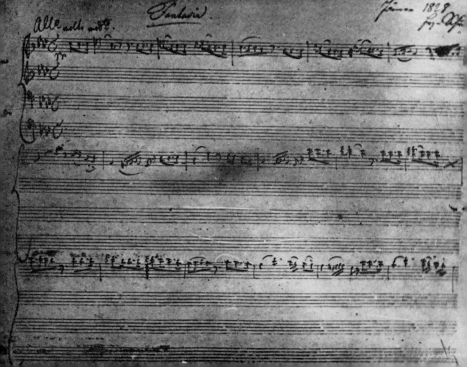

Schubert's manuscript of the Great C Major Symphony showing bars 154 to 179 of the last movement. Between these two pages the composer had written a fugato-like theme, which he then cancelled

VII

MARCH 1828

'*On the 26th was Schubert's concert. Enor-*
mous applause, good receipts.'
Bauernfeld's Diary

'*26 March 1828.*

With Louis and Enk to Schubert's con-
cert. I shall never forget how glorious that
was . . . To the "Snail", where we jubi-
lated till midnight.'
Franz von Hartmann's Diary

If the sketches for the F minor Fantasia had not survived,
we should no doubt have assumed that Schubert began
work on it in April 1828, since that date appears at the head
of the autograph. No sketches for the Great C Major Symphony have survived, and in their absence we assume that the
work was begun in March 1828, because that date appears on
the manuscript. It is a simple, indeed a fundamentalist view,
which involves the faithful believer, as we shall see, in greater
violations of common-sense than it is designed to obviate.
In Chapter III the case for a missing symphony presented by
Grove in 1881 was examined and found to be groundless. But
disposing of Grove's theory only raises a further problem. If
the symphony presented to the Music Society in 1826 and the
Great C Major are one and the same, what is the status of
the existing dated manuscript? Were there two manuscripts?
If so, where is the earlier one? Or does the existing autograph
date from 1826? Let us consider the alternatives before we

return to Schubert's correspondence with the publishers.

Theoretically, three possibilities exist: (1) that the two symphonies were quite distinct, and that the earlier one has disappeared, (2) that there was one symphony, but two manuscripts, one written in 1826 and the other in 1828, the earlier Ms. having disappeared, and (3) that there was one symphony and one manuscript, written in 1826 and revised and dated in March 1828. The first of these possibilities has already been considered and rejected. Apart from the fact that there is no contemporary evidence whatever to suggest that the 1825/26 symphony disappeared, we have explicit statements from Spaun and from Sonnleithner linking the Great C Major with the Gastein holiday of 1825 and with the presentation of October 1826. The stylistic evidence is of a different order, but equally conclusive; there are frequent cross-references between the Great C Major and the works of 1825, and the spirit of the work clearly belongs not to 1828 but to the optimistic phase of Schubert's middle years. The second view, which would regard the existing autograph as a new version of an earlier work, is more plausible, but there are serious objections to it. It has already been pointed out that the autograph had been revised some time after its original completion, that two quite distinct creative strata are, so to speak, compressed within it. If it is itself a revision, we are faced with a degree of complexity unique in Schubert, though not impossible. There is a further point, however. If the date on the autograph, March 1828, refers to the earlier of the two stages represented in it, when did Schubert find time to make the final revision? The output of the final few months of his life is already impressive, and if the autograph is a major reconstruction of an earlier work, it must have kept him busy over a period of months. If, on the other hand, the date is assumed to be that of the final recension, there is no compelling reason for regarding the manuscript as distinct from the earlier one, for it may well have incorporated large parts, indeed whole movements of it. On this view, our second and third possibilities cease to be distinguishable.

To the third possibility, that the original Ms. presented to the Music Society in October 1826 was revised and dated in March 1828, the objection is that it seems to involve the composer in an act of dissimulation, even of deception. But is this really so? Let us look at the situation in February 1828, when Schubert received promising enquiries from two of the foremost publishers in Germany, in the light both of his own practice and the conventions of the time, and ask ourselves whether this course of action is in any way improbable or improper.

We must first rid ourselves of the notion that Schubert's dates are an infallible guide to the chronology of a major work. It was his habit to date work in progress, *and* fair copies. What is true of the first piano sonata (D.157) of 1815, at the outset of his working life, and of the F minor duet Fantasia of 1828 at the end, must also be true of many other works in between; the dated fair copies of these works represent the last stage of composition, not the first, not even the most important, stage. Often, indeed, the dated final autograph is no more than a clean copy of earlier work. Sometimes it represents the final stage of filling in the detail of a work already complete in all essentials, or preparing a work for the publisher long after the hard work has been done, much as the author of a book may write and date an introduction as a final task long after the book itself is finished. It is therefore uncritical to allow our estimate of the chronology of a work to depend upon the accident of chance, whether

or not the sketches have survived. We know the F minor
Fantasia was not started in April, because the sketches exist
to prove that it reached an advanced stage in January. If the
sketches for the Great C Major Symphony ever come to light,
they could hardly convict Schubert of acting uncharacteristi-
cally, if they were to prove that in dating the Great C Major,
March 1828, he was registering the date of the final and
definitive version.[1]

It is not difficult, either, to see that there were some
advantages for Schubert, in hopes of getting 'this, my
symphony' published, of offering it as a new work. Publishers then, as now, liked to know that they were being
offered the latest flowering of genius; it was a convention of
the time, when new music was fashionable, when concerts of
'ancient music' were put on for sophisticated minority
tastes, to attach the label 'new' to works often years old. (So
Schubert's Octet, written early in 1824, was billed at
Schuppanzigh's concert of 16 April 1827 as a 'new great
octet'; and at his own concert in March the first movement
of the G major quartet, written in the spring of 1826, was
presented as a 'new string quartet'.) It is perhaps significant
that in his letter to Schubert of 9 February 1828 Probst
stresses his willingness to consider 'some of the later products
of your mind', as though to suggest that the failure of the
earlier negotiations owed something to the fact that the
works offered were early ones. At all events, an old symphony, and one in the possession of the Music Society, was
obviously a less saleable property than a 'new' one.

We have to take into account also the Society's failure

---

[1] That dated autographs can mislead with other composers too is
generally accepted. Beethoven's op. 119 no. 1 is a case in point. But
Schubert's dates seem to be regarded with special sacrosanctity, and
certainly he was meticulous in such matters.

to perform the symphony, and Schubert's keen disappointment that his greatest orchestral work should have been set
aside; but to say this is not to imply that there was anything
irregular in offering to a publisher a work which had been
presented to the Music Society. At a time when rights of
authorship were still uncodified and largely unrecognised, a
composer was obliged to strike the best bargain he could,
and it was recognised that a private presentation or dedication
in no way inhibted him from disposing of a work on the
most favourable terms available. Schubert did not display
Beethoven's ruthless skill in conducting simultaneous negotiations with several publishers (and patrons) over the
same work, but he did offer the Octet, commissioned by
Troyer, to Probst in 1826, and would obviously not need to
feel any compunction in selling the Symphony if an opportunity occurred.

In February 1828 it looked as though an opportunity might
occur. Probst's letter begins by regretting that the earlier
correspondence came to nothing, and goes on to express
admiration for recently published songs and piano duets. He
is still a little wary, however, of the more esoteric aspect of
Schubert's work ('Kindly, therefore, send me . . . songs,
vocal pieces or romances which, without sacrificing any of
your individuality, are yet not difficult to grasp'), and
introduces a tactfully worded warning not to expect much
higher fees than the Viennese publishers offered. Schott is
more concerned to emphasise the importance of his international connections, and his association with Beethoven; he
too singles out vocal pieces and piano works for special
mention, with an eye on the rapidly growing amateur market,
but he ends by inviting Schubert to send a list of what he has
in stock.

Both letters were addressed simply to Franz Schubert Esq., Famous Composer (or 'Musician and Composer' in Probst's case), Vienna, and one was delayed in consequence. On 21 February Schubert replied to Schott from his lodgings at Schober's.

'Gentlemen, I feel much honoured by your letter of 8th February (*recte* 9th) and enter with pleasure into closer relations with so reputable an art establishment, which is so fit to give my works great currency abroad.

'I have the following compositions in stock:

(a) Trio for pianoforte, violin, and violoncello, which has has been produced here with much success.

(b) Two string Quartets (G major and D minor).

(c) Four Impromptus for pianoforte solo, which might be published separately or all four together.

(d) Fantasy for pianoforte duet, dedicated to Countess Karoline Esterhazy.

(e) Fantasy for pianoforte and violin.

(f) Songs for one voice with pianoforte accompaniment, poems by Schiller, Goethe, Klopstock, etc., etc., and Seidl, Schober, Leitner, Schulze, etc., etc.

(g) Four part choruses for male voices as well as for female voices with pianoforte accompaniment, two of them with a solo voice, poems by Grillparzer and Seidl.

(h) A five-part song for male voices, poem by Schober.

(i) 'Battle Song' by Klopstock, double chorus for eight male voices.

(k) Comic Trio, 'The Wedding Roast', by Schober, for soprano, tenor, and bass, which has been performed with success.

'This is the list of my finished compositions, excepting three operas, a Mass, and a symphony. These last compositions I mention only in order to make you acquainted with my strivings after the highest in art.'

The list has a comprehensive air about it, and it enables us to draw some important conclusions. The first point is that, though Schubert includes both the unpublished string quartets of his later years, no mention is made of the B flat piano trio, though the E flat trio is given pride of place. This fact is impossible to reconcile with the conventional attribution of the B flat trio to the year 1827. It must have been finished and disposed of long before. The remaining items are fairly easy to identify. It is interesting that Schubert regards the F Minor Fantasia as finished and available, though the work was still only in draft. The Impromptus are presumably the second set (D.935) of opus 142, since Haslinger had already embarked on the publication of opus 90. Schubert's parade of etceteras in item (f) is fully justified when one remembers that only about 160 of his songs had so far appeared. As for the touchingly modest last paragraph, the Mass is the one in A flat major, finished in 1822, the operas are presumably *Alfonso*, *Fierabras*, and *Die Verschworenen*, and the symphony is the Great C Major, since October 1826 in the possession of the Music Society.[1]

The faintly apologetic tone of Sonnleithner's comment on the circumstances surrounding the composition of the Great C Major, already referred to in Chapter III, suggests that Schubert's disappointment over the Society's failure to

[1] O. E. Deutsch's note on this reads as follows: 'the one among his seven finished symphonies he singles out is doubtless that of Gmunden and Gastein of 1825 (for the Great C Major was not begun until March).' He does not attempt to explain why, with one symphony already in the Society's library, still unperformed, in February, Schubert should have started another for the Society in March. Nor is there any evidence at all to suggest that Schubert dedicated two symphonies to the Music Society.

perform the work was keen, and that the honorarium of 100 florins was felt to be a rather ungenerous solution to an admittedly awkward situation. There is no evidence, however, of any estrangement between Schubert and the Society. His work continues to appear in the programmes of the Society's regular concerts, and Schubert was in close touch both with Sonnleithner and with the Fröhlich sisters—stalwarts of the Society—over the composition of the four-part *Ständchen* in July 1827 and of *Miriams Siegesgesang* in this March. There could on the other hand be no objection on the part of the Society if Schubert withdrew the autograph to revise it for publication, and that in all probability is what happened.

What remains is a textual problem. If the Ms. of March 1828 is, essentially, the one presented to the Music Society in October 1826, how much revision had it undergone? It is possible that a thorough examination of the autograph with the aid of scientific techniques might throw further light on this, for as Grove long ago pointed out, the autograph of the Great C Major is unique among Schubert's symphonies in the number and importance of its alterations and revisions; and these revisions include changes in the main themes throughout the work. There is, however, an important qualification, which Grove also noted:

'In the Finale there are but few alterations, and those of no importance. It has evidently been written straight off, and towards the end the pen seems to have rushed on at an impetuous speed, almost equalling that of the glorious music itself. The first four movements [*sic*], on the other hand, are literally crowded with alterations; so much so that the work looks as if it were made up of afterthoughts.'[1]

[1] See Grove's appendix, Kreissle von Hellborn (vol. II, p. 323), *op. cit.*

There is, in fact, a quite clear indication in the Ms. itself that the revision of March 1828 may have involved a much more radical re-writing of the last movement than of the earlier movements. At bar 163 of that movement, which brings us to the bottom of the page, and before the entry of the second subject, there is a break in the writing. The next page shows the following theme, first written out for horns and flutes, then comprehensively cancelled.

Example 44

At the top of the next page we have the two silent bars which precede the entry of the second subject, then the familiar tune itself, but in a script significantly different from the first 163 bars, resembling Schubert's copying hand much more than his composing hand.

The usual explanation of this curious procedure is that Schubert, in the full flood of composition, first thought of the theme quoted above either as a second subject or as a link with the true second subject, but changed his mind, and reverted to the tune we know so well. But if the theme was simply a wrong turning, recognised as such as soon as written down and immediately corrected, why the change in the look of the page? Moreover, the second subject, with its impetuous pounding rhythm, seems worlds away from this rather unpromising fugue-like subject. Is it possible that they belong to the same period of the composer's life, to the same creative impulse? The former has a long ancestry in Schubert's work, and close associations with the A minor and C major sonatas of 1825. It is of the essence of the symphony, so closely and organically related to the work as a whole that one cannot believe it to have been the result of the revision of March 1828. We know, however, that Schubert's interest in fugue was re-aroused some time early in 1828, partly as the result of his study of Handel's scores; and we can see the results of that renewed interest not only in the finale of the F Minor Fantasia, but in the choral work *Miriams Siegesgesang* written in this very month of March 1828, a work which concludes with the first fully worked fugue he had composed since the completion of the A flat mass in 1822.

No obvious solution to this puzzle presents itself, but at least two possibilities exist. One is that the association of the cancelled theme with the symphony is entirely accidental; that in the course of revision Schubert unwittingly took up a piece of paper which happened to have been used. But the placing of the notes on the page, with the orchestral scoring indicated, makes this theory improbable, to say the least. A more plausible explanation is that he was influenced by the views of his friends (Schindler among them) that the symphony was too long and too difficult, and decided to attempt a shorter more contrapuntal finale, similar perhaps to that of the F Minor Fantasia; but realising that such a finale would be out of character with the symphony as a whole, gave up the idea, and reverted to the original material, possibly in a shortened form. Either way, it seems likely that the revision of March 1828 involved a substantial reshaping of the last movement, the final version of which was copied out in that month and incorporated with the original score.

One final conjecture ought, perhaps, to be mentioned, though it belongs to the category of possible-improbable solutions usually rejected by writers of detective stories. It is not beyond the bounds of possibility that the date on the manuscript, March 1828, is simply a mistake for March 1826. Such mistakes were sometimes made; manuscripts had not then acquired the status of historical documents which protects them today, and wrong dates are not unknown in the Schubert documents and outside them. In this controversy with Grove, Pohl quoted the case of the Mozart *Requiem*, which bears a posthumous date in its composer's own hand! But this is a case more of eager anticipation perhaps than of error. He could have found a more interesting parallel nearer home. On a revised copy of the chorus *Wo sich die Pulse*, written in September 1822 for the opening of the Josefstadt Theatre, Beethoven wrote: 'Written towards the end of September 1823, performed on October 3, at the Josefstadt Theatre', and the same misleading information appears on the copies of the other music written for this occasion.[1] Was this just a slip, or was Beethoven 'updating' the revised copies? If one feels disinclined to take the idea of an accidental mistake seriously in the case of the Great C Major, it is not because it is inherently unlikely, but because of the special importance Schubert himself attached to the work.

Schubert's other main concern in this month of March 1828 was with the cantata *Miriams Siegesgesang*, for contralto solo,[2] chorus, and orchestra. The piece was intended for performance at a Music Society concert, probably in the forthcoming winter season, but death intervened before Schubert could orchestrate it. At the first performance at the Memorial Concert of 30 January 1829, Tietze sang the solo part to piano accompaniment, but a full performance was given two months later to an orchestral accompaniment

[1] See Thayer's *Beethoven* (vol. ii, p. 807), London 1968.

[2] In the reference books this work is said to be for soprano solo and chorus. But the solo part was intended for Josefine Fröhlich, a contralto, and the tessitura is well within the contralto range.

made by Franz Lachner. In completing the work in March, Schubert may have intended to include it in his own concert later that month; but if so he changed his mind, presumably because there was insufficient time to rehearse it.

The cantata is the sole expression (if we except the naïve allusion to 'Comfort ye' in the first of the three *Klavierstücke* written in May) of Schubert's well-attested enthusiasm for Handel, which he seems to have inherited, along with some Handel scores, from Beethoven. Indeed, the fact that a large-scale work was projected, to words specially written by Grillparzer, and that the whole plan was conceived in close association with the Music Society, suggests that Schubert may have to some extent cast himself in the role of Beethoven's heir. It was well known that the Music Society had commissioned an oratorio from Beethoven and had advanced 400 florins as early as 1819 as a consideration for the work. It was well known also that Beethoven intended in this work to give expression to his lifelong devotion to Handel's music, to create something in the very spirit and manner of his long-revered master; and to this end he spent long hours, in those last years of his life, in the study of Handel scores, particularly 'Alexander's Feast', 'Messiah', and 'Saul'. The oratorio was never written, however; it was one of several projects left uncompleted at his death, along with the tenth symphony, the operas, and the string quintet. Meanwhile the Music Society, accepting the inevitable, wrote off the 400 florins in 1825 and made Beethoven an honorary member. The same compliment was paid to Schubert in June 1827.

After Beethoven's death, the forty-volume edition of Handel's works in the Samuel Arnold edition, which J. A. Stumpff had sent him a few months earlier, was put up for

auction and bought by Haslinger for 102 florins. It is usually
assumed that it was this edition which came into Schubert's
possession, as a loan from the publisher, but this seems doubtful. For one thing Haslinger had bought the volumes as an
investment, and promptly put them on sale again for 450
florins. Those were substantial sums, equal to at least as many
pounds at present-day values, and one may question whether
Haslinger's generosity would run to the loan of so valuable a
property. In addition to the complete edition, however,
Beethoven owned six volumes of Handel's works, including
'Alexander's Feast' in orchestral score, 'Messiah', and a
volume of miscellaneous choruses.[1] These may well have
passed to Schindler, along with other music and papers, on
Beethoven's death, and have found their way into Schubert's
possession towards the end of 1827, about the time when, as
we know from other evidence, his interest in Handel's work
began to be aroused.

According to Sonnleithner, Schubert visited the Fröhlich
family 'a few months before his death' and told them about
the Handel scores. 'Now for the first time I see what I lack,'
he said.[2] Josef Hauer, who played second fiddle at the first
performance of the D minor quartet, and lived long enough
to become a respected musicologist, described in later years
how Schubert discovered Handel. 'How often did he say,
"My dear Hauer, do come to my place and let's study Handel
together".'[3] About this time too, there was a rapprochement
between Schubert and the Fröhlich family, which Kathi
Fröhlich described in moving terms to Gerhard von Breun-
ing.[4] Out of these circumstances the plan for the cantata

[1] See 'Beethoven and Handel' by Donald MacArdle in *Music and
Letters*, January 1960. [2] *Memoirs* (p. 114), *op. cit.*
[3] *Memoirs* (p. 177), *op. cit.* [4] *Memoirs* (pp. 244–5).

seems to have been born. Kathi's beloved Grillparzer would write the words, 'Pepi' Fröhlich would sing the solo, Anna would train the choir, and the Music Society should after all have a choral work which would do honour to the memory of Handel.

Schubert's intuitive sympathy with the music of the classical masters, his negative capability, to use Keats' phrase, enabled him to wear his borrowed robes with an air. The idiom is unmistakably Handelian, not simply in the allusive phrase, or the metaphorical writing descriptive of the Red Sea crossing, but in the style and texture of the piece; yet even in the following passage the echo phrase in the accompaniment is Schubert rather than Handel.

Example 45

In retrospect, however, the whole episode seems curiously misguided. Is it not extraordinary that the composer of *Winterreise*, of the *Impromptus* and the *F Minor Fantasia*, should move on to the writing of a work which so narrowly

escapes the charge of *pastiche*? *Miriam Siegesgesang* seems
to throw into relief–like the decision this same year to
take lessons of Simon Sechter–the whole sad story of
Schubert's relations with the age he lived in. It seems
inexplicable unless we take into account the immeasurable
influence which Beethoven still wielded. For Beethoven too,
it must be remembered, had considered withdrawing into the
life of a Kapellmeister at one time. Beethoven also professed
nothing but contempt for contemporary taste, and found in
the study of fugue a kind of answer to the aesthetic problems
posed by his most profound creative conceptions; and it was
Beethoven who had said, in answer to Stumpff's question
' Whom do you consider the greatest composer who ever
lived?'–'Handel, to him I bow the knee.' Where Beethoven
led the way, it could not be wrong to follow.

A more fashionable idol monopolised the attention of
musical Vienna during March. Paganini arrived on 16 March,
and held his first concert on the 29th, three days after
Schubert's. As the correspondent of the Dresden *Evening
News* put it, 'There is but one voice within our walls, and
that cries "Hear Paganini!"' He expresses a certain sympathy
with lesser mortals whose musical activities are overshadowed by the great man's arrival, including 'the favourite
composer Schubert', whose concert he reports; for 'un-
questionably there was much that was good about it all'. It
had to be accepted, however, as one of the sad but ineluctable
facts of life, that 'the minor stars paled before the radiance
of this comet in the musical heavens'. Brief notices of the
concert appeared also in Leipzig and Berlin, but the Vienna
papers were too full of Paganini to find space for it.

Originally planned for Friday, 21 March, the concert was
postponed for a week, possibly because Linke was too busy

with the arrangements for his Beethoven memorial concert on the 23rd to attend. The programme was lithographed with the new date 28 March on it. There must have been a second change of plan, however, for the date is corrected by hand to 26 March. Possibly it was felt to be overbold to hold a concert the night before Paganini's first appearance; or Schubert may have had reasons of sentiment for preferring the anniversary of Beethoven's death. In the event, any doubts or misgivings were swept aside. The concert, held in the Music Society hall, was well attended, there was great enthusiasm, and several items—vocal ones, no doubt—were repeated. The Schubertians went off to the 'Snail' afterwards to celebrate their triumph.

The programme offered an interesting mixture of the immortal composer and the man of his age. It opened with a performance of the first movement of a 'new string quartet', doubtless the G major quartet written two years earlier, by Böhm, Holz, Weiss, and Linke. This cannot have been a very good performance even by the modest technical standards of the time, for there had been little time for rehearsal; one cannot help wondering what the players and the audience made of this difficult movement. The next item had been advertised in the preliminary announcement as 'four new songs', to be performed by Herr Vogl, but in the programme the epithet was dropped, reasonably enough. For the group consisted of two Leitner songs (*Der Kreuzzug* and *Die Sterne*) written a few months earlier, *Fischerweise*, written in March 1826, and the setting of a chorus from Aeschylus written as long ago as June 1816. It seems to have been designed to illustrate the catholicity of Schubert's literary tastes, and the variety of mood in his work, rather than his greatness as a composer; we can at least share the enthusiasm of the audience for *Fischerweise*. Next followed a performance of *Ständchen*, the choral work written for Louise Gosmer's name-day celebration in July 1827, and of the E flat piano trio, by Bocklet, Böhm, and Linke. Item number five was a *bonne bouche*, a setting of Rellstab's *Auf dem Strome* for tenor (Tietze) and horn obbligato (Lewy), specially written for the concert. And after a performance of Pyrker's *Die Allmacht* by Vogl, the male chorus of the Music Society provided a rousing climax with a version of Klopstock's *Schlachtgesang* for double chorus.

The repercussions of this great event echoed round musical Vienna. A group of Schubert admirers wrote enthusiastically to the *Wiener Zeitschrift* demanding a repeat performance. The editor, Johann Schickh, sent the article on to Schubert, pointing out that he was not really in a position to comply with the request, though he fully shared the sentiments expressed! Marie von Pratobevera, whose letters to her lover Josef Bergmann provide an interesting inside view of events at this period, describes a visit to Währing on the anniversary of Beethoven's death, and goes on: 'Enough of graves and death; I must tell you about fresh and blossoming life, which prevailed at a concert given by Schubert on 26 March. Only compositions by *himself* were given, and *gloriously*. Everybody was lost in a frenzy of admiration and rapture.'[1] It seemed like a new beginning. Vienna had at last paid its tribute to Schubert's genius, and on the anniversary of Beethoven's death. A public audience had at long last listened eagerly—yes, to his songs—but also to his chamber music. And the foremost publishers in Germany had asked him for his manuscripts.

By an odd coincidence, there appeared on the 29 March in the *Theaterzeitung*, the first critical notice of Schubert's work which seems to take the measure of his genius. The

[1] *Documentary Biography* (No. 1071A), *op. cit.*

anonymous reviewer of the first part of *Winterreise* speaks of
Schubert's intuitive sympathy with Müller, who 'sets against
outward nature a parallel of some passionate soul-state,
which takes its colour and significance from the former';
and goes on to examine the union in these songs of the
'gentle pain of the constricting present' and 'premonitions of
the infinite'. 'It is this spirit that is breathed by the present
songs; it expresses itself through them even when the subject
seems to point to entirely different paths; and in this logical
establishing of harmony between outward and inward things
lies the chief merit of both poets, the speaking and the singing
one.' Ominously, the reviewer concludes by expressing the
hope that Part II would not fail to appear.

For the moment, the future looked bright. The reading
parties met regularly, absorbed in the novels of Tieck. The
affairs of the Schubertians, even their financial affairs, seemed
to be settling down; for Schubert had made a useful profit
out of his concert, and his friends were increasingly taken up
with matrimony, or with their professions, or both. Schwind,
bracing himself against the philistine pretensions of his
beloved's family, made his formal request for the hand of
Netti Hönig at the end of the month, much to the amusement
of Schubert and Bauernfeld, who waited for him in the pub
after his gruesome experience. Spaun's marriage took place
a few days later. Schubert, his self-confidence renewed by
success, planned a whole series of new works, sonatas, a new
mass, the long-projected opera with Bauernfeld, perhaps a
string quintet (which Beethoven had talked about but never
begun), and many more. To Schubert himself, as to Marie
von Pratobevera, it all seemed to offer, in this spring of 1828,
the hope of fresh and blossoming life. But the hope was to be
short-lived.

VIII

APRIL—NOVEMBER 1828

'Sometimes it seems to me as though I no
longer belong to this world.'
Schubert to Anschutz, summer 1828

Cases of typhoid take the following course:

When the fever is at its height, life calls to the patient; calls
out to him as he wanders in his distant dream, and summons
him in no uncertain voice. The harsh imperious call reaches
the spirit on that remote path that leads into the shadows, the
coolness and peace. He hears the call of life, the clear, fresh,
mocking summons to return to that distant scene which he had
already left so far behind him, and already forgotten. And
there may well up in him something like a feeling of shame for
a neglected duty; a sense of renewed energy, courage, and
hope; he may recognise a bond existing still between him and
that stirring, colourful, callous existence which he thought he
had left so far behind him. Then, however far he may have
wandered on his distant path, he will turn back—and live.
But if he shudders when he hears life's voice, if the memory of
that vanished scene and the sound of that lusty summons make
him shake his head, make him put out his hand to ward off as
he flies forward in the way of escape that has opened to him—
then it is clear that the patient will die.

Thomas Mann: *Buddenbrooks*

On the eve of his death he called his brother to his bedside
with these words: 'Ferdinand! put your ear to my mouth',
and then said quite mysteriously: 'You: what is the matter

with me?—Ferdinand replied: 'Dear Franz! we are all very anxious to make you well again, and the doctor assures us, too, that you will soon be restored to health; only you must be good and keep in bed!'—All day long he wanted to get up, and he continued to imagine he was in a strange room.

A few hours later the doctor appeared, who persuaded him in similar words. But Schubert looked fixedly into the doctor's eyes, grasped at the wall with a feeble hand, and said slowly and seriously: 'Here, here is my end!'

Ferdinand Schubert
on his brother's death

Fortified by the success of his public concert, Schubert felt able to assume a more self-confident tone in his negotiations with the publishers. Schott had written on 29 February, in reply to Schubert's list of available works, requesting that they should all be sent to him except the string quartets (evidently too much of a gamble) and the solo songs, a line which was in danger of being played out; and promising that all these works would be published 'by degrees'. Schubert left the letter unanswered until after his concert. Then, on 10 April, he wrote to offer the E flat Trio for 100 florins, and two other works, the four Impromptus of opus 142 and the vocal quintet *Mondenschein*, for 60. His main concern is clearly to get the Trio published; he takes the opportunity to tell Schott of its enthusiastic reception at the concert, and throws in the two more marketable pieces at a modest fee, presumably to make an attractive package deal. In the meantime, however, Probst's delayed letter had reached him, and he replies to it at the same time.

'It may perhaps not be without interest to you if I inform you that not only was the concert in question, at which all the pieces were of my composition, crammed full, but also that

I received extraordinary approbation. A Trio for pianoforte, violin, and violoncello, in particular found general approval, so much so, indeed, that I have been invited to give a second concert (*quasi* as a repeat performance). For the rest, I can assign to you some works with pleasure, if you are inclined to agree to the reasonable fee of 60 florins A.C. per sizeable book.' This was perhaps a little disingenuous. The intention seems to have been to invite a counter-bid for the Trio from Probst; and failing that, to let Schott have the Trio, and Probst the other works at 60 florins each. However that may be, Probst appears to see through this ploy; for he replies by return of post, accepting the Trio for 60 florins, and enclosing the money! Having thus secured the major work at a cheap rate, he goes on to ask for 'some selected trifles for the voice or for four hands, a trio being as a rule but an honorary article and rarely capable of bringing in anything'.[1] Schubert felt cheated. He was in no position to return good money, and at least he would soon see the Trio in print. But it was a bad omen for the future.

His immediate financial anxieties relieved by a profit of 320 florins on his concert, Schubert set to work on the final version of the F minor duet *Fantasia*. The misconception over the date of the Great C Major has thrown the chronology of the works written in last months of his life into confusion, and given the impression of an uninterrupted stream of masterpieces issuing from his pen at incredibly short intervals. The output of this last spring and summer is, on any showing, impressive, but once the attempt to fit in the Great C Major is abandoned there is no need to postulate miracles. Compared with the achievements of 1815, or even of 1824, those of 1828 can be seen to be well within Schubert's

[1] *Documentary Biography* (Nos. 1076, 1077, 1081), *op. cit.*

phenomenal powers. Nor is the output of this final year of consistently high quality. On the contrary, at no time is the contrast between his best work and his weakest so striking as it is in 1828: on the one hand supreme expressions of the Schubertian spirit like the string quintet, the A major Rondo for piano duet, and the B flat piano sonata, on the other commissioned liturgical pieces which lapse into soggy 'harmonium music'—like the Hymn to the Holy Spirit (D.964)—or academic chromaticism. Within single works the same unevenness is often observable. Not even the most enthusiastic admirers of the E flat Mass would claim that the fugal sections of that work reach the same level as the best of it, and the *Drei Klavierstücke* exhibit, alongside a splendid piece of *echt* Schubert in the first half of number 2, long passages of comparatively uninspired material.

Another point to bear in mind in any reassessment of the work of this year is that it was by now Schubert's normal practice to sketch out a new work, and then to go back to it after an interval. Sketches exist even of minor works like the *Hymn to the Holy Spirit*, and the sketches for the three final piano sonatas reveal such a wide gap between the composer's first thoughts and the final version that it is difficult to believe the whole process of composition was concentrated within the month of September. No sketches for the string quintet are extant, but they must certainly have existed; a work of this scale and importance could hardly have emerged complete and finished on to the page, particularly from a composer who found it worth while to sketch *Die Taubenpost*. With these considerations in mind, it may be helpful to set out the possible course of creative events, month by month, during this period.

April	Completion of F Minor Fantasia.
	Rellstab songs.
May	*Hymnus* an den heiligen Geist (second version).
	Drei Klavierstücke (D.946).
	Allegro in A minor (*Lebensstürme*) for piano duet (D.947).
	Sketches for piano sonatas.
June	Mass in E flat.
	Rondo in A major for piano duet (D.951).
July	Completion of E flat Mass.
	Setting of 92nd Psalm in Hebrew (D.953).
August	Final version of Rellstab songs.
	String quintet sketched.
September	Piano sonatas in C minor, A major, B flat major.
	String quintet (possibly completed in October).
October	*Die Taubenpost.*
	Der Hirt auf dem Felsen.
	Tantum ergo in E flat, Vocal Quartet, Chorus, Orchestra (D.962).
	Offertorium *Intende Voci*, Tenor solo, Chorus and Orchestra (D.963).
	Orchestration of *Hymnus* an den Heiligen Geist.
	Alternative *Benedictus* for Mass in C of 1816.[1]

This schedule, which is to some extent conjectural, at least presents a programme of work which, though heavy, is quite credible on Schubert's standards of industry. It also makes clear the extent to which Schubert's energies, in these last months of his life, were diverted to the composition of liturgical pieces alien to his genius. He had little sympathy

[1] Omitted from the list are *Widerschein*, nothing more than a transposition of an earlier song, and the Fugue in E Minor, little more than a *jeu d'esprit*.

with orthodox expressions of Christian belief, and reacted strongly against his father's honest unsophisticated conformism. His religion, if it can be called such, was a Wordsworthian natural piety, vaguely pantheistic, but deeply felt. His God was the creator of the visible universe, whom he celebrated in countless songs, in the great chamber works written at Zseliz, and in the Great C Major. Not insignificantly perhaps, when he came to set the first phrase of the *Credo* in his first full-scale mass, he used the simple rising third—C, D, E—which was to be the opening statement and the germinal idea of that symphony.

Example 46

Yet he devoted most of June and July, it seems, and almost the whole of October to liturgical works, evidently in an attempt to establish himself in a field which at least offered opportunities for lucrative employment. Several of these pieces we know were commissioned, two of them by the Franciscan church at Alsergrund, where Beethoven's body was blessed before burial; the probability is that all of them were. For it is difficult to believe that Schubert would have embarked on a work like the offertory hymn *Intende Voci*, for tenor solo, chorus, and orchestra, which occupies thirty-six pages of the supplement to the Collected Edition in full score, without a clear and substantial inducement. If much of this work suggests that Schubert was trying to write in a foreign language, the probable explanation is that he was. Writing music for the church was a highly specialised and technical business, in which it was important to heed the customer's requirements. Josef Hauer recalled Schubert's telling him about the rejection of his A flat Mass. 'He said to me: "Not long ago I took a Mass to Court *Kapellmeister* Eybler for performance in the Court Chapel. . . . When, some weeks later, I went to find out my child's fate, Eybler said the Mass was good, but was not composed in the style the Emperor liked. So I took my leave and said to myself: So I am not fortunate enough to be able to write in the Imperial style."'[1] To us, it may seem tragic that Schubert should have felt obliged to devote his time and creative energy to a series of works that too often seem to bring out the worst in him; it is possible, however, that success as a liturgical composer would have been more damaging than failure.

The much-deprecated decision, later in the year, to go to Simon Sechter for lessons in fugue must be looked at in the same context. This was no sudden whim, no irrational loss of confidence in his own genius. In an age when the profession of composer had no independent status, the patronage of the church, or that of the impresario, offered the only choice open to a composer who, like Schubert, was unable or unwilling to make a career as a virtuoso. Even Beethoven, exasperated at the steady erosion of his pension by inflation, toyed with the idea of becoming a *Kapellmeister*, while Hummel, not without stresses and strains, held official posts at Eisenstadt, Stuttgart, and Weimar throughout most of his working life. In looking to the church, therefore, Schubert was following a course for which there were good precedents, and which had been in his mind for many years. According to

[1] *Memoirs* (p. 177), *op. cit.*

Schindler, lessons with Sechter had been suggested years
earlier, and only Carl Pinterics among Schubert's friends
doubted the wisdom of the proposal. Certainly a post at
court had been very much in his mind in 1826, as we have
seen. While the idea is not in itself so outrageous as might
first appear, however, it suggests an almost cynical surrender
to current standards of taste when taken in combination with
the sort of liturgical music Schubert was writing in 1828.
What is alarming is not the quantity of that music, but its
quality. It looks forward, not to the expressive aspects of
chromaticism, but to the sentimental. *Lazarus*, the unfinished
Easter cantata written early in 1820, is not without a tinge
of religiosity in the music, but it is an extraordinarily forward-
looking work, through-composed on Wagnerian lines, and
consistently interesting in its purely musical inventiveness.
As an attempt to illustrate the character of this work, here is
a short extract from the beginning of Act II, where Simon
the Sadducee, wandering apprehensively in the graveyard,
comes upon the open grave prepared for Lazarus.

Example 47

Now it is true that *Lazarus* was never finished; perhaps on this occasion also Schubert's music was too unconventional to please its sponsor. But when we compare this music with, say, the *Hymn to the Holy Spirit*, over which Schubert appears to take so much trouble in 1828, we can only exclaim at the pity of it.

Example 48

Lazarus is perhaps a special case, and it could be argued that the 1828 *Hymn* is an unimportant work designed to please the customer. Many good critics would agree, however, that the same weaknesses obtrude in parts of the E flat mass. Schubert is never at his greatest in his liturgical pieces; the gulf that separates them from his best work is widest in the last year of his life.

Throughout April the talk in Vienna was all of Paganini. His first appearance on 29 March was followed by two more concerts in April. Jenger, writing to Frau Pachler on 26 April, is so taken up with the new wonder that he forgets to mention the success of Schubert's own concert.

'Well, one star has risen for me on the musical horizon, one that stands alone and solitary in this world, and that is the greatest violin virtuoso who has ever existed and will ever be born—to wit, Paganini, whom I have heard twice already. What you, dear lady, will read about him in all the papers—and he receives much praise—is all too little. One can only hear, admire, and wonder at him. More I cannot say.' But he does report that the four songs of opus 106, including the two written at Graz, are in the engraver's hands, and promises to bring some copies with him 'when Schubert and I come to you, which will doubtless be at the end of August'.[1] For the Styrian holiday in company with Irene Kiesewetter and her mother was still on the cards, though it had had to be postponed because of the death of Irene's aunt. Schubert, too, fell under the spell of the wonder violinist. Enraptured by that splendid *cantabile*, he wrote to Hüttenbrenner that he 'heard an angel sing in the *adagio*' (presumably of Paganini's second violin concerto, played at his first concert); and on 4 May he insisted on paying Bauernfeld's admission fee so that he too should hear the great man. Bauernfeld, increasingly taken up with his official duties and with his literary ambitions–his first comedy was to be produced in September–seems less involved with the Schubert circle than formerly, and took no part in the weekly reading parties which continued throughout the spring. Perhaps he found Schober's dilettantism a little difficult to stomach. But in truth he was not the only one of the circle to forsake the old ways. On 14 April Spaun and Fanny Roner were married in Vienna. Schubert's old friend was forty. Witteczek, with whom Spaun had shared lodgings in Schubert's schoolmastering days, and whose collection of Schubert songs is a major source, was a witness, and there was a great gathering of the Linz friends. Schwind, too, had reached an understanding with Netti Hönig, though it was not to last. Three weeks later there was another wedding. Leopold von Sonnleithner and Louise Gosmar, for

[1] *Documentary Biography* (No. 1088). Jenger includes *Edward* as the last song of the four intended for op. 106. In fact *An Sylvia* was later substituted for it.

whom Schubert had written the four-part vocal *Serenade* a year earlier, were married on 6 May. Schubert must have been present at both these weddings, but we do not hear of any special Schubertiads. The grand parties held to mark Spaun's engagement in January seem also to have marked the end of an age.

The reply from Schott to Schubert's offer of the E flat Trio, which reached him at the end of April, cannot have added much to his peace of mind. Accepting the Impromptus and the vocal quintet *Mondenschein* for 60 florins (i.e. 30 florins each) Schott added: 'The Trio is probably long, and as we have recently published several trios, and short of doing ourselves harm, we shall be obliged to defer that kind of composition until a little later, which might not after all be to your advantage.' This, in a way, was fortunate, in that the Trio had in the meantime been accepted and paid for by Probst; but it left Schubert feeling out-smarted. He had hoped for 100 florins for the Trio, and 60 each for the smaller works; instead, Probst had snapped up the Trio for 60, and Schott had closed with his own offer of the two other works 'together for 60 florins'. Not unnaturally perhaps, Schubert attempted to put matters right by changing his terms. 'I send you the two desired compositions,' he writes on 23 May, 'each at the rate of 60 florins currency,' and asks for six copies of each work. To this Schott replied with a long silence; and when in October Schubert wrote to ask whether the publication was in hand, with a further haggle over the fee. Meanwhile, on 10 May, Schubert sent off the Trio to Probst accompanied by a letter which seems to strike a new and poignant note of resignation. Protesting that he never intended to let the work go for 60 florins, he goes on: 'In order, however, to make a beginning at last, I would only ask for the speediest possible publication, and for the dispatch of 6 copies. The cuts indicated in the last movement are to be most scrupulously observed. Be sure to have it performed for the first time by capable people, and most particularly see to a continual uniformity of tempo at the changes of the time-signature in the last movement. The minuet at a moderate pace and *piano* throughout, the Trio, on the other hand, vigorous except where p and pp are marked.'[1] Even then, matters refused to go right. For some unexplained reason, the Ms. took ten weeks to reach Leipzig, and when Schubert at last heard from Probst, it was only with a request for details of the opus number and the dedication.

It is suggested above that in April Schubert took up again his settings of Rellstab songs which were later to appear as part of *Schwanengesang*. That these poems were in his mind at least is proved by the fact that on 28 April he copied into the album of Heinrich Panofka—the same whose unavailing efforts to introduce Schubert to Fallersleben in the previous August we have already described—the setting of *Herbst* written probably in the previous summer. For there is no good reason to doubt the truth of Schindler's statement that these poems came to Schubert from Beethoven's *Nachlass* and that his attention was first drawn to them in the months after Beethoven's death by Schindler himself. Unfortunately the whole question has been bedevilled, first by the accidental association of the Rellstab and the Heine group in the so-called *Schwanengesang* cycle; secondly by the fact that Schubert prepared fair copies of some of these songs in August 1828; and finally by the almost universal tendency among biographers to discount anything Schindler says as the product of his over-heated imagination. It is surely unscholarly, however,

[1] *Documentary Biography* (No. 1096), *op. cit.*

to allow one's distaste for Schindler's self-importance to colour one's judgment of his generally over-dramatised testimony. That Rellstab sent his verses to Beethoven is quite clear, and certainly Schindler had access to Beethoven's papers. It would be very much in character for him to draw Schubert's attention to them, and Schubert's veneration for Beethoven's memory would guarantee his interest in them. Moreover, the fact that the fair copy of *Liebesbotschaft* is dated August 1828 gives no ground for believing that *Liebesbotschaft* itself was composed in that month, still less for assuming, as is often done, that the whole cycle belongs to August and September. On the contrary, the sketch of *Liebesbotschaft* (and that of *Frühlingssehnsucht*) is associated with the unfinished *Lebensmut*, generally thought to have been composed much earlier, possibly as early as the summer of 1827. Haslinger's fatal instinct for a good title has done its work all too well; nothing short of an act of Parliament can now, it seems, restore to independent existence the disparate elements that were bundled together after Schubert's death to make a profitable package for the publisher. None the less, the attempt must be made. Let us begin by stressing that the six Heine songs, so different in tone and intensity from the Rellstab group, were intended for separate publication, and were to be dedicated, according to Spaun, to the composer's friends. In itself this strengthens the case for regarding them as a kind of by-product of the reading parties, which took up the Heine poems on their resumption in January 1828. The last song in Haslinger's collection, *Die Taubenpost*, has of course no connection either with Heine or Rellstab. Written in October, it is a comparatively lightweight piece thrown in by the publisher for good measure.

It seems reasonable to suppose that some of the Rellstab songs were composed in the summer of 1827, and that the others were written in the following spring. Schindler's own account dates from 1857. He declares that he met Schubert frequently after Beethoven's death. 'During these visits, certain portions of Beethoven's literary estate had engaged his very special attention, among them once more the lyric poems of all kinds which had been sent to the great master. A collection of perhaps twenty items absorbed his attention, because I was able to tell him that Beethoven had earmarked several of them to compose himself. . . . Only two days later he brought me *Liebesbotschaft Kriegers Ahnung*, and *Aufenthalt* set to music.'[1] Once again there is no real inconsistency between the dated fair copy – August 1828 – and Schindler's account, inaccurate as that may possibly be in detail. Schindler himself, in his chronological catalogue of Schubert's work, allocated to 1828 'many songs, among them several which are included in the *Schwanengesang*'. And not even his most severe critics suppose that the whole cycle was composed in August 1828.

In their fluency and charm, the Rellstab songs seem to represent a return to Schubert's best 'Maid of the Mill' manner. Once again, the lover's changing moods are mirrored in the changing face of nature. *Liebesbotschaft* is, as Richard Capell remarks, the last of the brook songs; but nearer in sentiment to *Des Müllers Blumen* than to *Des Baches Wiegenlied*. *In der Ferne*, in Schubert's 'tragic' key of B minor, is nearer in spirit to *Das Wandern* than to *Der Leiermann*. *Frühlingssehnsucht*

---

[1] *Memoirs* (p. 319,) *op. cit.* O. E. Deutsch notes that the dated fair copy 'disproves Schindler's anecdote', but even he accepts, in the Thematic Catalogue, that the cycle 'was sketched, possibly as early as the summer of 1827'.

has the lyrical attack, the sense of joy, of *Mein*. The dark intensity of the *Winterreise* cycle—and of the Heine songs—is missing; instead we are delighted to recognise the old Schubertian finger-prints—the echo-phrase in the accompaniment, the subtly effective movement of inner parts to transform what might be only a good tune into something gloriously different, the masterly alternation of major and minor—in a group of love-songs inspired by the sense of life and hope. For that reason we need not regret the popularity of *Ständchen*, for it is the most ardent and magical of Schubert's love-songs. But *Aufenthalt* is an equally fine song, and *Abschied* can be irresistible in the hands of two performers ready to surrender good-humouredly to its jog-trot rhythm. Altogether the Rellstab songs enable us to conclude that, though Schubert's musical personality has been deepened and intensified during the dark days of 1827, there is a remarkable continuity in the themes which he chose to celebrate in his lyrical art. *Aufenthalt* is, so to speak, the Wanderer twelve years later, free of youthful illusions; and the nightingale pleading for the lover in Rellstab's serenade has a sadder tale to tell than those earlier nightingales of Hölty and Claudius.

During May and June Schubert wrote two works for piano duet which are among the greatest of his mature years. What impresses us in the *Allegro in A Minor* is first the thorough-going nature of the formal treatment—it is a full-length first movement in sonata form with one of the best developments Schubert ever wrote; and secondly the orchestral texture. Even more than the Grand Duo sonata, which has so often been mistaken for a symphony in disguise, in spite of the composer's unambiguous title-page, the *Allegro* cries out for orchestration; with brass passages—

Example 49

pizzicato strings leading to a melting second-subject theme
for woodwind

Example 50

and passages for full orchestra all clearly adumbrated. It may
be said that much of Schubert's writing for four hands has this
orchestral quality, and so it has. But not all; the F Minor
Fantasia, for instance, sounds purely pianistic by comparison.
In style, too, the movement has a spaciousness which recalls
the symphonic works of 1824 and 1825, particularly the
Grand Duo sonata and the Great C Major symphony. Was this,
then, some kind of preparatory work for a second 'great'
symphony? It is not impossible. And curiously, there is
evidence in this very month of an intention on Schubert's
part to return to Gmunden, where 'this, my symphony' had
been born. Ferdinand Traweger, with whom Schubert and

Vogl had stayed in the happy days of June 1825, wrote on 19 May to say that he had heard from Franz Zierer, a flautist on tour with the opera orchestra, that he (Schubert) would like to visit Gmunden again, and would like to know Traweger's terms. 'You really embarrass me; if I did not know you and your open guileless way of thinking, and if I did not fear you might not come, I should ask nothing. But in order to get the idea out of your head that you might be a burden to anyone, and so that you may stay on as long as you like, listen: for your room, which you know, including breakfast, lunch, and supper, you will pay me 50 Kreuzer V.C.[1] per day, and pay extra for what you wish to drink.' To this tactful and affectionate letter there is no reply. All plans for a holiday, whether at Gmunden or Graz, faded as Schubert's circumstances worsened once again: and by September he was ill.

This A minor allegro was published in 1840 by Diabelli under the spurious title of 'Life's Storms', which at least suggests a composition of serious intent. The Grand Rondo in A major, on the other hand, was published at the end of the year by Artaria, at whose request it is said to have been written. Yet the two pieces surely belong together, as movements of a major work for piano duet which, for some reason, was never completed in the form originally envisaged. Since Artaria's manuscripts were acquired by Diabelli a few years after Schubert's death, it seems possible that both pieces went originally to Artaria, and that he decided to publish the rondo separately as the easier and more approachable of the two movements. The Grand Rondo is an altogether delightful

[1] Viennese currency. At contemporary rates, this was equal to about 4p a day: perhaps 50p a day by twentieth-century standards, very approximately.

work which illustrates Schubert's capacity to build up a full-length movement on extended lyrical themes, and strikes a note of relaxed romanticism which seems new. As a formal structure it sounds more convincing than the first movement of the B flat piano sonata, where the problem is the integration of lyrical themes in sonata form; a fact which should be taken into account by those critics who interpret any criticism of Schubert's command of form as a failure to understand the composer's intentions.

In comparison with these two masterly compositions, the three *Klavierstücke*, also dating from April/May 1828, are uneven and unconvincing. O. E. Deutsch calls these pieces Impromptus, and suggests that Schubert intended an opus of four numbers comparable with op. 90 and op. 142. If so, they represent a sad falling off in quality. Only the wistful barcarolle which opens the second piece, and its *misterioso* first episode, really live up to the memory of opus 90, and there seems every justification for playing this piece in simple A B A form separately, as Myra Hess used to do; for the second episode is inferior, and over-long. If there seems to be something almost anachronistic about this hauntingly beautiful *Allegretto*, coming as it does in the middle of some rather pedestrian writing, it is no wonder; for it is a kind of free transcription of the chorus music sung by Emma and her maidens at the beginning of Act III of *Fierrabras*. Indeed, the lovely little ritornello in that scene is taken over unchanged:

Example 51

The comparatively casual linking and grouping of these ideas suggests, rather than a considered opus, a stringing together of various pieces which for one reason or another had not been incorporated in any of the new piano sonatas. Unfortunately none of the sketches for these sonatas is dated; it seems unlikely, however, that no thought was given to them until after the completion of the String Quintet, and the probability is that they were sketched in April/May and given their final shape in September. Whatever their provenance, the *Drei Klavierstücke* appear to have been lost sight of after the composer's death. Schindler was evidently aware of their existence, for he lists among the 1828 compositions a 'Sonata in E flat minor'; but they did not appear until 1868, when Brahms took them up and edited them.

The three piano sonatas, however, passed to Diabelli on Schubert's death, and appeared in 1838 under the title of 'Franz Schubert's Last Compositions: Three Grand Sonatas'. Schubert had intended to dedicate them to Hummel, in gratitude perhaps for the warmth and admiration displayed by the old *Kapellmeister* towards the young composer in the dark days of March 1827. But Hummel having died in 1837, Diabelli transferred the dedication to the new champion of Schubert's genius, Robert Schumann. The composer annotated the fair copies Sonata I, Sonata II, and Sonata III, as though to emphasise that this was a new beginning, and regardless of the fact that the Sonata in A Minor (D.845) had already in 1825 been published as a 'Premier Grande Sonate' (not to mention its many distinguished predecessors). The critic, also, is bound to recognise the qualities in these sonatas which mark them off from earlier work, making them a kind of touchstone in Schubert criticism; their poetry, spaciousness, and a certain nobility of conception that gives to each sonata its own expressive character in keeping with its key, the first in C minor sombre and turbulent, the second in A major flowing and lyrical, the last in B flat serenely contemplative and tinged with romantic melancholy. They are now more highly prized, and more often played, than all the rest of Schubert's keyboard compositions, and the B flat sonata in particular has become a 'must' for recitalists, old and young. Thus the twentieth century has more than made up for the neglect accorded to these works in the nineteenth, and it may be time to ask whether the pendulum has not swung too far. Because of their scale and emotional range, not to mention the difficulties posed by their elaborate architecture, these sonatas must remain the supreme test of the Schubert pianist's powers of interpretation. This is not to say, however, that they are the most characteristically Schubertian of the sonatas, still less that they represent Schubert's intended 'last word' for the piano. On the contrary, a careful study of them in comparison with the great sonatas of 1819, 1823, and 1825 will show to what extent they represent turning back on Schubert's previous line of development.

One of the interesting features of these sonatas—and the same may be said of the *Drei Klavierstücke*[1] —is the large number of musical cross-references to be found in them. The

[1] Note for instance the close affinity between the opening bars of no. 1 and those of the Introduction and Variations on an Original Theme in B flat for Piano Duet (D.603): a point of some importance since the authenticity of the latter work was doubted by Nottebohm.

influence of Beethoven is frequently apparent, especially in the
C minor sonata; but much more remarkable is the number of
self-quotations and self-allusions, which must on some
occasions at least have been conscious and deliberate. It
seems impossible to suppose that Schubert, in writing the
Rondo finale of the A major sonata, was unaware of the virtual
identity of the theme with that of the *Allegretto quasi andantino*
of the A minor sonata of 1817 (D.537). Clearly Schubert
decided to 'realise' one of his own tunes, as he used the B flat
Rosamunde entr'acte for the *Andante* of the A minor quartet,
and for the third impromptu of opus 142. Was he also aware
of the close kinship between the *Andantino* theme in the same
sonata and the song *Pilgerweise* of April 1823? Or of the family
resemblance between the theme of the Menuetto of the C
minor sonata and the *Presto vivace* of the early string quartet in
mixed keys (D.18)? The most curious cases of all occur in
the B flat sonata. In December 1814 Schubert set to music the
cathedral scene from *Faust*, in which the Evil Spirit taunts
Gretchen in her wretchedness, while the strains of the *Dies
Irae* are heard from the choir. The piece opens with an
expressive six-note theme which might almost be called, in
Wagnerian terms, the motif of Gretchen's Doom.

Example 52

This theme will be recognised at once as one that plays an
important part in the development of the first movement of
the B flat sonata, not least in the magical passage that leads
back to the recapitulation. The resemblance might reasonably be explained as coincidence, or as a quirk of unconscious

memory, were it not that another passage from the *Faust* scene gives us in thinly disguised form the main tune itself of the sonata movement. At the words 'Quid sum miser tum dicturus' the choir sings:

Example 53

It may be said that this is a long way in texture and feeling from

Example 54

but many a recognisable variation strays much farther from its theme.

The following movement of this sonata, *Andante sostenuto*, takes us, like the parallel movement in the string quintet, 'to the still point of the turning world', and holds us breathless in a mood of hushed expectancy. It is one of Schubert's most splendid and sustained achievements. The middle section does not, perhaps, quite match up to the rest, making one wonder whether it would not have been even more effective as a monothematic movement; but such doubts seem unworthy in the face of those apocalyptic modulations. Once again, Schubert explores the tonality of C sharp minor, com-

bining a gently moving succession of thirds with a dotted
octave figure which accents the second beat of each bar.

Example 55

This very distinctive rhythm has one precedent in Schubert,
in the *Notturno* for piano trio, of uncertain date, supposedly
based on the rhythm of the pile-drivers' song, in which the
silent second beat of each bar marks the unison fall of the
sledge-hammers. Schubert was said to have heard this action-
song at Gastein during his holiday in 1825, and to have used
the rhythm in the middle section of his *Notturno*, which runs

Example 56

for many (rather too many) bars. The *Notturno* is not a very
effective piece, and Schubert did not include it in the B flat
piano trio for which it was probably intended. But three years
later, his thoughts turning once more to the mountains, he
finds the exact musical equivalent of the pile-drivers' 'strike'
on the second beat of each bar, and uses it to give shape and
rhythmical tension to a movement of mystical intensity. It is a
luminous example of the transmuting of experience, in this
case a fairly mundane experience, into the material of the
highest art.[1]

[1] I am indebted to Dr. Roger Fiske for first drawing my attention to
this link between the *Notturno* and the B flat piano sonata.

These examples of self-borrowing are quoted not with the intention of showing the last three sonatas to be derivative– Schubert would no doubt have been proud to admit to a practice so brilliantly exemplified in the works of Bach, Handel, Beethoven, and many others–and for that reason inferior; if the first subject of the B flat sonata is indeed derived from the *Faust* scene, it illustrates the genius of its composer no less. There is, however, a specially retrospective quality about these sonatas which contrasts with the sonatas of the middle years, in which the allusions are mainly contemporary. The sonatas of 1825 have many associations with the Great C Major symphony. The 1828 set look rather to the early work of 1816 and 1817, sometimes in direct quotation, more often in a general affinity of mood and material. So the Scherzo of the A major sonata reminds us forcibly of the A major Scherzo of the five-movement sonata of August 1816 (D.459); the middle section of the Adagio of the C minor sonata recalls with its triplet chords the Andante of the E flat sonata of 1817; while the characteristic cadence that hovers between A major and A flat major in the beautiful coda of this same movement finds its earliest precedent in the Allegro Vivace of the A minor sonata of 1817, where a somewhat similar passage hovers ambiguously between B flat major and A minor.

The spaciousness of these works enables Schubert to deploy his love of tonal ambiguity within the limitations of sonata form, and in his hands the form itself becomes attractively discursive. The result is not achieved without loss, however. We look in vain for a movement with the epigrammatic quality of the sonata in A minor of 1823. Nothing quite matches, in economy as well as poetry, the Andante of that sonata, or the parallel movement from the A major sonata of 1819. The second movement of the A major sonata of 1828 goes quite to the other extreme, sacrificing formal unity for the sake of a programmatic episode full of bravura passage-work, presumably in the search for dramatic contrast. This experiment must owe something to the growing vogue for fantasy pieces and the decline in the status of the sonata; but whatever the reason, the effect seems wayward and contrived. What is weakened, in these last sonatas, is the unity of form and content. Not that less attention is paid to the superficial requirements of sonata form. On the contrary, the elaborate finale to the C minor sonata–Schubert's longest keyboard movement–falls readily into the standard compartments, and if the exposition includes a section that sounds like development and the development begins with a new tune that sounds like a second subject, this is Schubert's way. But when we turn to the finale of the 1823 sonata in A minor, very similar in mood to the later work, we find a movement which defies precise analysis along conventional lines, and yet has a coherence which the later movement lacks. It seems to be a matter partly of impetus, of the inevitability with which bar follows bar, and partly of Schubert's intention in the later works to achieve his effect over the broadest timescale. It is significant that the sketches to the instrumental works of these last years show that his second thoughts were usually in the direction of expansion, not concentration. It is a process which makes large demands on the performer's powers of formal integration, and nowhere more so than in the first movement of the B flat sonata, where the last page of the exposition moves so deliberately that the impetus is difficult to sustain. The sonata idea is, in essentials, the architectural aspect of musical composition; its strength can be measured not by conformity to a conventional pattern, still less by length, but by the inevitability with which the musical argument unfolds; on this ground, at least, and leaving much else unsaid, it is possible to affirm, as many goods critics have, that the greatest Schubert sonatas are those of his middle years.

At the beginning of June Schubert made a short visit to Baden. The circumstances are thus described by Franz Lachner:

'In the year 1828, on 3 June, Schubert and I were invited by the editor of the *Modezeitung*, Herr Schickh, on an excursion to Baden near Vienna; in the evening Schickh said to us: we will go to Heiligenkreuz first thing tomorrow morning in order to hear the famous organ there; perhaps you could compose some little thing and perform it there?–Schubert proposed the composition of a fugue each and towards midnight we had both finished. The next day–at 6 o'clock in the morning–we drove to Heiligenkreuz, where both fugues were performed in the presence of several monks from the monastery.'[1] The little Fugue in E minor for four hands is Schubert's only composition for organ, little more than an exercise as one might expect from the circumstances, but significant as evidence of his growing interest in liturgical composition. Schickh, who had recently been in correspondence with Schubert over the proposal to repeat the public concert, was something of a Schubertian himself, to judge from the enthusiastic tone of the notices that appear about this time in his paper, the *Wiener Zeitschrift für Kunst*.[2]

There is also further evidence this month, though slight, of Schubert's growing reputation in Germany. On 4 June an

[1] *Memoirs* (p. 195), *op. cit.*

[2] See, for example, the write-up of the Rondo Brilliant op. 70 quoted in *Documentary Biography* (No. 1107), *op. cit.*, on 7 June 1828.

acquaintance of Schober's, Johann Mosewius, writes to Schubert from Breslau to enlist his interest in a young musician shortly arriving in the capital, and takes the opportunity to enclose a note to Schober declaring his newly-found enthusiasm for the song-cycles. And a few days later the publisher Karl Bruggemann, of Halberstadt, sends an invitation for Schubert to contribute to his monthly anthology of piano pieces, with an assurance that nothing will be included which 'might stand unworthily side by side with your contributions'. The answer was evidently favourable, for Bruggemann wrote again in August to confirm the arrangement, and express his interest in publishing other larger works, but the plan was prevented by Schubert's illness.

Meanwhile the financial position was once again deteriorating. There was no news from Probst of the receipt of the E flat Piano Trio till 18 July, when the publisher wrote to ask for the title, dedication, and opus number, and to explain that it could not be ready for about six weeks, because of the delay. Schubert's reply expresses, briefly and brusquely, his exasperation.

'Sir, The opus number of the Trio is 100. I request that the edition should be faultless and look forward to it longingly. This work is to be dedicated to nobody, save those who find pleasure in it. That is the most profitable dedication. With all respect, Frz. Schubert.' From Berlin and from Munich came insensitive and satirical notices of *Winterreise*, Part I, and in July the appearance of a group of Goethe settings (op. 92) and the two books of *Moments Musicaux* from Leidesdorf marks the first Schubert publication to appear since January. It comes as no surprise to find Jenger, at the beginning of July, writing to Frau Pachler to put off indefinitely the visit to Graz, because of the difficulty of getting away from the office and 'the not very brilliant financial circumstances of friend Schubert'. Jenger, who was an official in the War Office, refers ominously to the possibility that the Russians and the Turks might 'queer my pitch'. He still holds out hopes of a visit in September, but the tone of the letter belies his hopes:

'Schubert had in any case planned to spend part of the summer at Gmunden and its environs—whence he has already received several invitations—from accepting which he has however so far been prevented by the above-mentioned financial embarrassments. . . . He is still here at present, works diligently at a new Mass, and only awaits still—wherever it may come from—the necessary money to take his flight into Upper Austria.'[1]

This picture of the composer in the last summer of his life is supplemented by references in the documents to two other incidents which took place in June. Earlier in the year Schubert had dedicated a group of songs (op. 96) to Charlotte, Princess von Kinsky, the widow of Beethoven's benefactor, and about this time Schubert accompanied Schönstein to a reception at her Vienna residence. Her note of thanks, enclosing an honorarium, has survived,[2] but Spaun's gloss on the occasion is more revealing. Remarking on Schubert's modesty and dislike of the social limelight, he says: 'Once when he was invited, with Baron Schönstein, to a princely house in order to perform his songs before a very aristocratic audience, the enraptured audience surrounded Baron Schönstein with the most ardent appreciation (and with congratulations on his performance). But when no one showed any sign of vouchsafing so much as a look or a word

---

[1] *Documentary Biography* (No. 1117), *op. cit.*
[2] *Idem* (No. 1119), *op. cit.*

to the composer sitting at the piano, the noble hostess, Princess K., tried to make amends for this neglect and greeted Schubert with the highest encomiums, at the same time intimating that he might overlook the fact that the audience, having been absolutely carried away by the singer, paid homage only to him. Schubert replied that he thanked the Princess very much but she was not to bother herself in the least about him, he was quite used to not being noticed, indeed he was really very glad of it, as it caused him less embarrassment.'[1] An expedition to Grinzing at the end of the month turned into a gay party, according to Hartmann, with all four friends 'tipsy more or less, but Schubert especially'; not in itself an event of any importance, one might think, had not biographers, taking their cue from Spaun, shown them-selves extraordinarily touchy on the subject, as though great composers have all been noted for their sobriety. Sonnleithner and Bauernfeld both testify to the fact that Schubert occa-sionally took too much to drink in convivial company; what seems to have caused comment was that on rare occasions he did so in the presence of strangers or social 'superiors'. But an evening of high spirits in Grinzing can have been no more than a moment of relaxation in a summer of steady and concentrated work, intended it seems to establish himself in the field of church music and equip him-self for the *Kapellmeister* post which would offer him the security he needed. He set the words of the 92nd Psalm, in Hebrew, for the cantor of the synagogue in Vienna, and also wrote a charmingly Haydnesque setting of a hymn—Faith, Hope, and Charity—for four-part chorus for the dedication of the recast bell at the Minorite church at Alsergrund. Then, as though to demonstrate the versatility of the composer

---

[1] *Memoirs* (p. 135), *op. cit.*

of *Gebrauchsmusik*, he wrote a quite different and more Schubertian version of the same text as a solo song. But his main concern was the E flat Mass, begun early in June and finished in July, also intended, it seems, for the newly formed music society at the Alsergrund church. It shows, more revealingly perhaps than any other work, the schizophrenic nature of Schubert's musical personality in this last year of his life. Conceived on traditional lines, with a conventional key-scheme and fully-worked fugues in all the right places, the Mass seems to have been designed to catch the eye of *Kapellmeister* Eybler. Its lapses into sentimentality, and into academicism, make it an indigestible work to bring off in the concert hall; yet its best moments show how nearly Schubert got to producing a great setting of the sacred text. The opening of the *Sanctus*, with its bare sequence of E flat major, B minor, and G minor, is splendidly dramatic; the contrapuntal writing in the *Agnus Dei*, and still more in *Et Incarnatus*, is ravishing; and the change of colour and rhythm at *Domine Deus* movingly effective. For the most part, however, it seems as though Schubert is holding his natural genius in check. The melodic material of the *Benedictus* is flaccid, and that of the *Dona Nobis* dull; as for the fugues, for which Schubert seems to have accepted 'safe'–i.e. traditional–subjects, it takes a very good performance to reconcile the listener to their not very heavenly lengths. There is more of the real Schubert (and a more consistently high level of creative inspiration) in the earlier A flat major Mass than there is in this uneven work.

Yet the string quintet in C major, to which he turned his attention in August, is not only essential Schubert, not only his greatest piece of chamber music, but on any reckoning a supremely poetic expression of the romantic spirit in music.

The sense of cosmic nostalgia, the yearning for a lost paradise, the tradition of European romanticism which believes the dream to be more potent than the reality, the search more important than the discovery, the unconcerned regard for easeful death—it is only by recourse to such high-sounding phrases as these that one can convey something of the unique quality of this work, both as a musical document expressing a particular mode of thought and feeling in the first decades of the nineteenth century, and as a summing-up of Schubert's own musical idiom. For all these things have been found in it, and more besides. The easy-going finale, for instance, is not, to the sophisticated Schubertian, an anti-climax. It is a recognition that one cannot live on the philosophical heights all the time, and that the romantic vision—intimations of immortality in the world of everyday—is the handmaid not only of joy, but of a more sober and sociable optimism. 'We were the happiest people in all the world,' said Spaun in later years, with pardonable and misleading exaggeration. But even if the social life of the Schubertians were not so fully documented, this says as much:

Example 57

And it is right that it has its place in Schubert's musical last will and testament alongside this:

Example 58

technically a second subject, first heard in the unconventional key of the flattened mediant, and in the recapitulation in that of the flattened sub-mediant; but emotionally the centre of the first movement, and in its lyrical intensity, heightened by Schubert's contrapuntal genius, a marvellously apt expression of the inward and sensuous joy which his contemporaries described as *mystisch*.[1] Surprisingly, it plays little part in the development, the main emphasis of which is put upon quite a different tune, an enigmatic little theme which Schubert introduces at the end of the exposition almost as an afterthought: and yet perhaps not surprisingly, for the asperities of the development give the movement much more shape and discipline than the corresponding movement of the E flat major piano trio, where the nostalgic second subject theme runs away with the development.

This quizzical little four-bar theme

Example 59

hesitating characteristically between the dominant and its relative minor, illustrates Schubert's growing skill in giving structural significance to themes which are, in themselves, little more than everyday chord sequences. The opening theme of the quintet, itself adapted, as we have seen, from the violin and piano Fantasia written in November 1827, is a case in point, and so is that of the trio. What is new—though it is to an extent a reversion to earlier practice—is the

[1] *Documentary Biography* (No. 669), *op. cit.*

assurance with which Schubert integrates these harmonic motifs with the lyrical elements. The lovely second subject itself, quoted above, is beautifully introduced in E flat major as an approach to the dominant G major, and then melodically varied and extended until example 59 appears as a questioning voice to keep the discussion open. The dominant chord sounds only momentarily, as a kind of punctuation mark, before an unceremonious lurch into A major opens the development. For the work has its own tonal points of reference. Not until the finale do we hear much of G major. The tonal landscape is bounded by the 'circle of thirds', on the flat side E flat and A flat, on the sharp side E and A major, not by the normal landmarks of dominant and sub-dominant. The other clue to the tonal scheme is Schubert's fondness for the Neapolitan relationship. Not for nothing does the work end with an accented unison appoggiatura D flat/C.

These tendencies find their clearest illustration—and the whole work finds its emotional centre—in the trio. In all his earlier chamber music Schubert had reserved this movement, whatever the character of the work, for a moment of spiritual release. He never fails to respond to the lilt, and the spirit, of the *Ländler*, with a touch of innocent lyricism. But not now. Marking the piece andante sostenuto and choosing a steady 4/4 rhythm, he begins tentatively, as though feeling his way towards the simple sequence of subdominant, tonic, dominant, tonic, which represents, so to speak, the total harmonic content of the movement. It is as though, choosing the Neapolitan key of D flat major in opposition to the assured certainties of the Scherzo's C major, he is questioning, with a kind of wistful tenderness, the very essence of the tonal system on which his own work, and that of his great predecessors and contemporaries, had been based.

Example 60

The dynamic emphasis given to the plagal cadence here suggests a valediction. Schubert had responded to the emotional overtones of the plagal cadence as no other composer, exploring its infinitely varied expressive possibilities in countless songs and piano pieces, and using it to underpin his most characteristic themes; so that it becomes, in works like the Unfinished Symphony, and the 'Reliquie' C major piano sonata, almost a main subject in itself. Now he seems to be taking a reluctant, affectionate farewell. And the effect is heightened by the sense of tonal indeterminacy that colours the whole movement. At the beginning, the meandering unison line suggests, if anything, the key of F minor, and certainly we are aware, at the cadence, of the strong pull of D flat major against F minor. At the double bar Schubert switches to the relative minor, B flat, but once again the attraction of the tonic proves too strong. Nothing daunted, the unison strings sound E natural, *pp*, and we have a sudden glimpse of E minor; then D natural, and after a little more wandering in the tonal wilderness we come to what seems like a full-close in D minor. But it proves to be nothing of the sort. Schubert reveals his C sharp as a D flat, and, sliding the other voices down a semitone, slips enharmonically back to D flat major. The unity of style and content is complete. In this movement, Schubert's love of ambiguity is used to suggest an ambivalent attitude towards the musical language itself.

What gives this work a special place in the affections of Schubert-lovers is its intensely personal quality. It is as though, given some premonition of the approaching end, he set out to write down, not for contemporary taste but for posterity, what he knew he had to say. It has an air of serenity, of reconciliation, and a homogeneity which mark it off from other works; for the trio's wistful detachment is not so far removed from the rapt contemplation of the Adagio–about which nothing has been said, and perhaps nothing needs to be said, except that if one was obliged to choose one movement as evidence of Schubert's greatness it would have to be this one–or from the ambling sociable high spirits of the finale. We do not know why he embarked on a string quintet at this particular time. He may perhaps have heard, from Schindler, of Beethoven's interest in the form. We know that he showed his veneration for the great man's work even on his deathbed, by asking to hear the C sharp minor quartet (op. 131). Did he set out to embody his own vision of the last things in a work which might stand beside that? We can only conjecture. Some of the events of this last year do have a strangely premonitory ring about them. Heinrich Anschütz, who spoke the funeral oration over Beethoven's dead body, told how he met Schubert in the street shortly before his death, and they fell to talking about the state of operatic taste. Schubert confessed himself out of patience with Italian 'tootling', and added: 'Don't talk to me about music. Sometimes it seems to me as though I no longer belong to this world.' It sounds like a throw-away comment, invested with special significance by hindsight. But it could have meant more. To the Schubertians death was a common companion, and to Schubert himself, who shared in the romantic's love affair with death as well as in the stoicism of the time, the prospect of it would not have seemed unwelcome.

If these thoughts were in his mind, however, the records of these summer months leave us no hint of them. Life followed the familiar pattern; reading parties (at which Schober duly impressed the circle with his readings from *Faust*), followed by visits to the 'Moonshine' or the 'Partridge'; a party at Währing given by the Hönigs, and another at the end of the month to bid farewell to the Hartmann brothers, who were returning to Linz having completed their studies. There are no more laconic records of gay goings-on at the café and the pub after the end of August; ironically, there are to be no more such parties to record. There is some irony, also, in the fact that while Schubert was absorbed in the composition of his last great chamber work, the Viennese press gave a gleeful welcome to Seidl's 'Four Refrain Songs', which had been composed some two years earlier, but appear only now. The publisher's blurb indicated clearly enough the ingredients in the work which he hoped would commend it. 'The public has long cherished the wish to have, for once, a composition of a merry comic nature from the pen of this song composer of genius. This wish has been gratified in a surprising manner by Herr Schubert in the present four songs. . . .' But this seems to be a piece of over-selling. Two of the songs are in Seidl's vein of arch humour, but the best of them, *Bei dir allein*, is a straight love song, set in Schubert's *Frühlingssehnsucht* manner.

At the end of August Schubert felt unwell, complaining of sickness and loss of appetite. It seemed to be no more than one of his periodic gastric attacks, and his friends paid little attention; but on the advice of his doctor he decided to move out to the Wieden suburb, where his brother Ferdinand had recently taken over a new house. There he set to work on the final version of his three piano sonatas, which were completed on 26 September. There is no evidence that the move to the Wieden was intended as anything more than a temporary change of air. Schubert left his manuscripts and belongings behind at Schober's; and his indisposition, whatever it was, did not interfere with his work, with his social obligations, or with his plans. On 5 September he attended the first night of Bauernfeld's comedy, *Die Brautwerber*, along with the rest of the circle. The play came off after four performances. Bauernfeld, convinced that it was a complete failure, could not face his friends in the pub after the performance, and wandered disconsolate through the streets till midnight; so it was now Schubert's turn, when he called at Bauernfeld's lodgings in the morning, to urge that a *succès d'estime* is nothing to feel depressed about.[1] Also in the audience that night was Jenger, who took the opportunity for a word with Schubert about the possibility of a visit to Graz. On the 6th he writes to Frau Pachler once again, explaining that he had not been able to find Schubert because of his move. 'Last night I spoke to him at last at the Burg Theatre, and I am now able to tell you, dear lady, that friend Tubby expects an improvement in his finances shortly, and confidently reckons, as this has happened, to avail himself immediately of your kind invitation, and to arrive at Graz with a new operetta.'[2]

[1] *Memoirs* (pp. 237–8), *op. cit.*
[2] *Documentary Biography* (No. 1147), *op. cit.*

This suggests that Schubert may have toyed with the idea of a performance of *Der Hochzeitsbraten* at Graz, for *Der Graf von Gleichen*, though by no means abandoned, was still only at the early planning stage. As for the expected financial improvement, this depended, we can assume, upon his receiving payment for the two works he had sent to Schott in May. This failed to materialise, however, and by the end of September a note of desperation begins to sound in his letters. To Jenger, who had evidently tried to find ways of raising money from the publishers, he writes: 'The second part of the "Winter Journey" I have already handed to Haslinger. Nothing will come of the journey to Graz this year, as money and weather are wholly unfavourable.' Then on 2 October, two months after his last impatient note to Probst, he writes again:

'Sir, I beg to inquire when the Trio is to appear at last. Can it be that you do not know the opus number yet? It is op. 100. I await its appearance with longing. I have composed, among other things, 3 Sonatas for piano solo, which I should like to dedicate to Hummel. Moreover, I have set several songs by Heine of Hamburg, which pleased extraordinarily here, and finally turned out a Quintet for 2 violins, 1 viola, and 2 violoncellos. The Sonatas I have played with much success in several places, but the Quintet will be tried out only during the coming days. If perchance any of these compositions would suit you, let me know.'[1]

This follows the pattern of earlier letters in offering a list of available works, not necessarily in order of composition. It is doubtful whether any conclusions can be drawn from it in regard to the provenance of individual works, though the word 'finally' does suggest that the Quintet was the most recent of them. Probst's reply came within a few days,

---

[1] *Documentary Biography* (No. 1152), *op. cit.*

apologising for the delay in the preparation of the Trio, and promising it 'spick and span with the next consignment to Diabelli'. But on the new works he is less forthcoming, expresses interest only in the songs, and asks particularly for 'anything understandable *à 4 mains*, rather like your variations on the miller's song from "Marie".' Even now, within a few weeks of his death, no one seems prepared to take Schubert seriously except as a composer of songs and piano duets.

Least of all Schott of Mainz, to whom Schubert wrote, also on 2 October, to inquire what news there was of the four Impromptus and the *Mondenschein* part-song sent in May. The reply must have reached him in the first days of November, at the onset of his fatal illness. Schott, having taken the advice of his Paris office, rejects the Impromptus as 'too difficult for trifles', and asks for something less difficult 'and yet brilliant in an easier key'. The part-song he is willing to accept, but at 30 florins not 60; and as though to make it clear that he is fully aware of the strength of his own bargaining position, he encloses a draft for 30 florins.[1] Thus all the high hopes with which the negotiations had started were finally dashed. Even the E flat major Trio, which was to make a deep impression when it did at last appear, was only announced in December, so it seems most unlikely that Schubert ever saw it in print. The disappointment left him depressed and hopeless. He did not send the Heine songs to Probst; he made no move to follow up Brüggemann's invitation. When in October a long and friendly letter arrived from Anton Schindler in Pesth, suggesting that he should give a public concert there, urging him to recruit a few influential sponsors without delay, and inviting him to visit Pesth meanwhile for the *première* of Lachner's new opera,

[1] *Documentary Biography* (Nos. 1151, 1155), *op. cit.*

there was no response. Either he did not feel able to meet the modest expense involved, or perhaps, after so many and so bitter disappointments, the very will to continue the struggle had been weakened. Some time in October he made arrangements to go to Simon Sechter for lessons in fugue, and most of that month he spent on the long and elaborate offertory hymn *Intende Voci* (with words from the fifth Psalm) and other liturgical efforts.

As a final gesture of compliance with the needs of the hour, he composed, also in October, the long-awaited concert piece for Anna Milder. The *Shepherd on the Rock* is tailor-made for the customer. From the first, the famous prima donna had taken it for granted in her correspondence with Schubert that his part was to provide a vehicle for the exercise of her artistry; and indeed, given the state of musical taste in Berlin and Schubert's need of recognition, there was some justification for her point of view. But in 1825 he had resisted Milder's request for a long brilliant piece 'which can be sung in a variety of measures, so that several emotions can be represented'.[1] Now he provides just that, as though resigned to Milder's view that all the public wants is 'treats for the ear'. The verses are put together, presumably by Milder herself, from two separate and unrelated sources, and the three sections, outer ones in B flat major with a quieter G minor section in the middle, are designed to provide the brilliant climax specified in the brief. Rarely venturing outside the confines of tonic, dominant, and sub-dominant, the piece is a kind of melodic revel in classical tonality for piano, clarinet, and coloratura soprano, a sort of Schubertian jam session. But it is without depth of feeling or inner conviction.

On the last day of October Schubert was taken ill while

[1] *Documentary Biography* (No. 538), *op. cit.*

dining at 'The Red Cross' with friends. The symptoms were similar to those he had often suffered, sickness, nausea, diarrhoea; and there was no way of knowing that this was not, in fact, another bout of an endemic typhoid infection such as had attacked him in August 1826 and October 1827, but the onset of a fatal dissolution. For he continued to go about his daily tasks, though complaining of lassitude and weakness. He dined with the Fröhlich sisters. On Sunday 2 November he went with Ferdinand to hear the latter's new mass at Hernals parish church, and after the service the two brothers went for a three-hour walk. Two days later he was at Simon Sechter's with Josef Lanz for his first lesson in fugue. For at least a week after the unfortunate indisposition at 'The Red Cross' his friends could see no cause for alarm in his condition or his mood. On the contrary, Karl Schönstein describes a supper party held at this time, at which Schubert seemed in excellent spirits.[1] 'He was very cheerful, indeed almost unrestrained in his gaiety, a mood which might well have been induced by the large amount of wine he drank that evening, of which he was no despiser at any time.' Not only did his manner seem quite normal, but even his complaints suggested that his illness was no different from the temporary attacks he had frequently had before. Schönstein goes on to mention his irrational fear of being poisoned, and it is not the only hint we have that to some of his friends Schubert seemed to have a touch of the hypochondriac.

In one of the concluding chapters of *Buddenbrooks*, Thomas Mann gives an illuminating account of the stages of typhoid fever which is so apt to Schubert's case that one wonders whether Mann could have had the composer consciously

[1] Schönstein says this took place 'about ten days before his death'. But it is more likely a little earlier. See *Memoirs* (p. 101), *op. cit.*

in mind. Recognising the difficulty of diagnosis, especially when the early symptoms—'depression, weariness, lack of appetite, headache, and unquiet sleep, are nearly all present while the patient is still going about in his usual health', Mann goes on to stress the ambiguous nature of the disease. There is one thing about which the doctor is in the dark. 'Up to the third week, up to the very crisis of the disease, he cannot possibly tell whether this illness, which he calls typhoid, is an unfortunate accident, the disagreeable consequence of an infection which might perhaps have been avoided, and which can be combated with the resources of medical science; or whether it is, quite simply, a form of dissolution, the garment, as it were, of death. And then, whether death choose to assume this form or another is all the same—against him there is no remedy.'

Schubert's complaint was officially diagnosed as *typhus abdominalis*, also the cause of his mother's death in 1812, but the word *typhus* was then used to describe a wide variety of disorders. His illness followed the familiar three-week course of typhoid fever; a first week when the patient, apart from a feeling of lassitude and depression, seems fairly normal, a rapid deterioration during the second week, and the onset of delirium in the third week, when the crisis comes. In Schubert's case these stages can be easily identified. For a week after the expedition to Hernals with Ferdinand he seems to have gone about his business much as usual. At the end of the week, however, about 9 November, there was a marked turn for the worse. Schubert himself, in the last letter he wrote, documented the sudden change in his condition. Writing to Schober on 12 November, he said:

'I am ill. I have eaten nothing for eleven days and drunk nothing and I totter feebly and shakily from my chair to bed and back again. Rinna is treating me. If I take anything I bring it up again at once.'[1]

He goes on to ask Schober to send him some Fenimore Cooper to read, 'so as to assist me in this desperate situation by means of literature'. Whether Schober responded to this appeal we do not know. It is clear, however, that he made no move to visit his friend during his last illness, influenced perhaps by fear of infection, perhaps by a self-righteous recollection that Schubert had not been to visit him during his illness two years earlier.[2] Whatever the reason, the other Schubertians felt no such inhibition.

Some time before he finally took to his bed, an event occurred in which life seems to take on the symbolic pattern of drama, so that the observer finds it difficult to escape the feeling that the composer's end was, to a degree, *voulu*. It is recorded, at second hand, by Ludwig Nohl in 1858: but it comes from Karl Holz, who played at Schubert's public concert, and took part in the first performance of the Octet and the A minor Quartet, so there seems no reason to doubt it. Holz said that shortly before his death Schubert expressed a wish to hear Beethoven's C sharp minor Quartet (opus 131), and that he (Holz) arranged a special performance which so delighted Schubert that his friends feared the excitement may have aggravated his condition. The work had been published in 1827, but not publicly performed. The situation cannot fail to stir the imagination—the young composer, whose own prophetic vision had so recently taken form and shape in the string quintet—listening with a sharpened sense of his own destiny, to those intimations of immortality that seem to be embodied in the most mystical of Beethoven's compositions. There is a risk of reading too much into an event that may have

[1] *Documentary Biography* (No. 1158), *op. cit.*   [2] *Idem.* (No. 663).

taken place some time before Schubert's death.[1] But at the least it is consistent with all the other evidence which points to his preoccupation with Beethoven's work in the last year of his life; at the least we may be permitted to speculate on the fact that shortly before he died Schubert listened to those prophetic sounds, in the confident hope that his own might one day be set beside them.

In the final phase, which began on 14 November, Schubert's illness drew to a rapid conclusion. Delirious attacks alternated with conscious spells in which he continued to work—correcting the proofs of the second part of *Winterreise*—and to talk to his friends. When Franz Lachner came to see him on Monday 17 November he was lying with his face to the wall in a delirious fever. Bauernfeld also visited him on that day. In the afternoon, during a lucid interval, they talked of *Der Graf von Gleichen* and the possibility of starting work on a new opera. Bauernfeld left feeling hopeful of his friend's recovery, but by evening there was a relapse into deep fever.

The following day, in a moment of comparative clarity, he called his brother to him, complaining, as he had done before, that he was being kept in a strange room. 'Though only half-conscious, he said to me: "I implore you to transfer me to my room, not to leave me here, in this corner under the earth; do I then deserve no place above the earth?"' Ferdinand tried to reassure him, insisting that he was where he had been all along, in his own bed. 'And Franz said: "No, it is not true: Beethoven does not lie here".' Ferdinand wrote this down two days after his brother's death; it is our last penetrating

---

[1] O. E. Deutsch (*Memoirs*, p. 300) dates this private recital 14 November, relying doubtless on Holz's statement that 'in five days Schubert was dead'. But Schubert was certainly bedridden by 14 November, and Holz's statement is capable of a different construction.

glimpse of the secret aspirations that revolved in his fevered mind as he found himself face to face with death.

'When the fever is at its height,' writes Thomas Mann, 'life calls to the patient: calls out to him as he wanders in his distant dream. . . . If he shudders when he hears life's voice, if the memory of that vanished scene and the sound of that lusty summons make him shake his head, make him put out his hand to ward off as he flies forward in the way of escape that has opened to him—then it is clear that the patient will die.'

When the doctor called on 18 November he did his best to reassure Schubert, and held out the hope of recovery. But he seemed resigned to death, and replied slowly and intently: 'Here, here is my end.'

Since Schubert died in his brother's house in the Wieden suburb, the funeral service was held at the nearby parish church of St. Joseph, Margareten. The intention was for the body to be interred there also, as would have been normal; but early on the morning of the funeral (21 November) the arrangements were changed at Ferdinand's suggestion, and it was carried to Währing to rest beside Beethoven. For even in the moment of death, Schubert's friends seem intuitively to have begun to grasp the significance of events in which they had played such an uncomprehending part; the final act had given a new perspective to the whole drama. 'He has died in his greatness,' wrote Schwind from Munich—he had been absent from Vienna throughout the illness of his friend; 'the more I realize now what he was like, the more I see what he has suffered'. 'I wish I lay there, in his place,' wrote Bauernfeld in his diary. 'For he leaves the world with fame!' These spontaneous expressions of grief are more illuminating than the versified formal tributes which came in plenty from

Schober, Bauernfeld, Mayrhofer, and others. But they too were an attempt to celebrate a man whose achievement, they dimly felt, had outrun their mundane perceptions. The true scale of that achievement they had no means as yet of even guessing. But looking back, from the vantage point of their present discontents—for the lack of professional recognition added to their grief made this a dispiriting time for the Schubertians—the days of their more carefree companionship took on the sharp outlines of a dream; and the personality of the little man whose friendship they had known assumed a charismatic quality. Even in the moment of his death, the Schubert myth was born.

IX

RETROSPECT

*I return once more to the fact that the
first requirement for the portrayal of
Schubert's artistic development is the production of a chronologically arranged
catalogue of his works. But this undertaking will be very arduous. . . . The
order of the opus numbers provides no clue
at all; for publication was governed
equally by chance and caprice.*

Leopold von Sonnleithner,
5 March 1858

O f all the material collected by Ferdinand Luib in 1857
and 1858 for the biography of Schubert which he planned but never wrote, Sonnleithner's contributions are the
most illuminating and the most authoritative. He alone, of
the composer's friends and contemporaries, combined a
sense of scholarship with a fully sophisticated musical taste;
and the important part he played, as man of affairs and as an
official of the Vienna Music Society, at various critical
phases of Schubert's life, give his account of his friend's
character and career a judicious balance which we do not
find elsehwere in these records. From him we have the best
description of Schubert's own manner in performance (and
an acute appraisal of Vogl's status as a singer and interpreter);
as a member of one of the most musical families of *Biedermeier*
Vienna he was able to fill in the social and artistic background
to Schubert's career; and he it was, not surprisingly, who

highlighted the most serious difficulty facing the biographer, the absence of any agreement about the sequence and chronology of even his most important compositions. In drawing attention to this problem, Sonnleithner himself did his best to clear up the confusion over the origins of the Great C Major symphony, though his unambiguous statement seems to have been lost sight of in the critical brouhaha that followed upon Grove's 'discovery' of the symphony written in 1825. He also in later years made strenuous attempts to recover the lost *Prometheus* cantata, to which Fuchs first drew public attention in 1842. The chronological catalogue of Schubert's work which Sonnleithner identified in 1858 as the necessary preliminary to any critical assessment of his development has certainly proved an arduous undertaking. It was not achieved, in any complete and authoritative form, until the publication of O. E. Deutsch's *Thematic Catalogue* in 1951; and even now, nearly 150 years after the composer's death, there are questions still to be resolved—so it has been argued in this book—which are crucial to any understanding of his work.

In the main it is the instrumental compositions which have proved most problematic. Because Schubert made his name as a song composer, because his songs were copied and sung in musical families throughout Austria often long before they were published, and because enthusiastic amateurs like Karl Pinterics, Josef Witteczek, Albert Stadler, and Johann Ebner made a point of collecting any Schubert song they could lay their hands on, the original date of his songs is not often in doubt, whatever other editorial problems they may pose. But even Schubert's closest friends knew little of his instrumental work other than the piano duets. There is not a single explicit reference to the B flat piano trio in the whole nine hundred pages of contemporary *Documents*. And when, some months after the composer's death, Spaun looked over some biographical notes prepared by Ferdinand Schubert, he confessed to Bauernfeld that he thought they went into too much detail about the instrumental and church compositions. In this field, he thought, 'we shall never make a Mozart or a Haydn out of him'. This monumental misjudgment is due not so much to lack of perception as to ignorance, and one result of this widespread ignorance of the chamber music was that the instrumental works, when they at length appeared, were all thought to be later than they really were. The assumption was that Schubert only turned to instrumental forms in his maturity, whereas he had been composing string quartets and piano sonatas since the age of fourteen.

It is interesting to turn to the chronological table at the conclusion of H. F. Frost's book on Schubert in the first Great Musicians series, and to see how seriously, even as late as 1881, this tendency to underestimate Schubert's maturity as an instrumental composer invalidates the whole list. Nothing is put too early, but the following, all attributed to Schubert's mature years, are put too late:

1824 String Quartet in E flat op. 125 no. 1 (D.87) *Recte* 1813
      String Quartet in E major op. 125 no. 2
         (D.353)   *Recte* 1816
      Sonata in B flat for piano duet (D.617)   *Recte* 1818
1825 Piano Sonata in A major op. 120 (D.664)
                                          Recte July 1819
1826 String Quartet in D minor (D.810)   *Recte* March 1824

These misconceptions were of course widely accepted at this time; many of them were perpetuated in the Collected Edition. They arise from the general tendency to suppose that

Schubert's creative development was slower than it in fact was, and so to post-date his most important work. Nobody seems ever to have *over*-estimated Schubert's maturity as a composer, or ascribed his work to too early a date.[1] The process has been all one-way, and the argument of this chapter is that it is not yet complete.

The origins of the Great C Major symphony have already been so fully considered that, if the reader has survived the discussion to this point, he will not welcome any restatement of the case. It belongs to the year 1825, and the statement remains valid, so far as Schubert's development as a composer is concerned, even if the symphony was substantially revised in March 1828. A further word ought, however, to be said about the B flat piano trio, because it is the only other major work to which we cannot assign a date with any certainty.

The conventional attribution of the B flat trio to the year 1827 rests on nothing more substantial than that it and the companion piece in E flat carry adjacent opus numbers. It would be as logical to suppose that opus 29—the A minor string quartet written in March 1824—is contemporaneous with opus 30—the B flat duet sonata written at Zseliz in 1818; or that *Suleika II* and *Die Forelle* were written in the same year because they were published as opus 31 and opus 32 respectively. On the other hand, there are ample grounds for doubting that the two piano trios belong to the same year. Why, if that were so, should we hear so much about opus 100 —and the long correspondence with Probst over that work bears witness in every line to Schubert's anxiety and con-

---

[1] Except perhaps Spaun, who does suggest at one point that the F minor duet Fantasia was brought back from Zseliz in 1824. But he was clearly misled by the dedication.

cern—and absolutely nothing about opus 99? The internal evidence is a matter of subjective judgment; it is hardly credible, however, that the B flat trio could be assigned to 1827 on stylistic grounds alone. Its affinities lie with the work of 1824/5; the link with *Des Sängers Habe*, a song written in February 1825, is strong enough to be suggestive, though not conclusive in itself, for these stylistic resemblances in Schubert often stretch over the years. Taken in conjunction with the other evidence discussed in Chapter II, particularly the association of the *Notturno* trio movement with Gastein, the internal evidence is strong enough to justify a conclusion that the B flat trio is considerably earlier than the E flat; it also belongs, in all probability, to 1825.

What light does all this throw on the problem of Schubert's creative development? First of all, it becomes possible for the first time to divide his working life, with some plausibility and conviction, into three periods, each with a consistent character of its own. The year 1820 has long been recognised as a turning point. Josef Sonnleithner himself, in the essay already frequently referred to, dated Schubert's rise to fame from 1 December 1820, when Ritter von Gymnich sang *Erlkönig* at a private concert held in the Sonnleithners' house. What happened, over a period of months culminating in the public charity concert of 7 March 1821, was that a series of performances of his songs made his name suddenly famous. In November 1820 his work was unknown except to a small circle of enthusiastic friends. Six months later he was a public figure. Simultaneously, his work took on a new emotional depth, and a new technical sophistication, heralded in compositions like *Lazarus*, the Quartet movement in C Minor, and the four-part setting of the 23rd Psalm, and exemplified above all after his emergence in public favour in the Goethe

songs of 1821, in the Wanderer Fantasia, and in the Unfinished Symphony. With these works he came into his own.
The great creative period of his middle years began, domin-
ated until the end of 1823 by his operatic hopes, and, when
those failed, by his ambition to rival Beethoven's achievement
in the field of instrumental music and grand symphony. With
equal certainty, the holiday tour of Upper Austria in 1825,
which saw at least the partial fulfilment of his plans, represents
a climax and a turning point, a kind of high summer, the
memory of which he treasured, the exalted mood of which
he could never quite recapture, for the rest of his life. The
remaining years are in a lower key, dogged by misfortune and
insecurity, tinged with doubt and disillusion, and uncertain
in their creative aim.

So much emerges clearly from a patient study of the
evidence. But can we identify with equal confidence three
parallel phases in Schubert's development as a composer?
Or must we give up, in his case, any attempt to reconstruct
the wholeness of man and artist out of which, somehow, the
works were born? The answer to these questions depends
very largely upon the view taken of the chronology of the
Great C Major symphony and the B flat piano trio. No one
has yet succeeded in presenting a convincing answer to the
critical problems posed by the conventional attributions of
those two works to the last year of Schubert's life. Given
that these works belong, however, not to the final, but to his
more optimistic middle years, the pattern makes a great deal
more sense. Let us look at it in more detail, taking first an
aspect of his work—the piano sonatas—in which the chronological problems at least have now been solved.

It will hardly be denied that the sonatas fall very readily
into three groups. In his early years Schubert was content to

work largely within the limits of his eighteenth-century models. The sonatas of 1817 and 1818, which culminated in that miracle of Schubertian grace and lyricism, the A major sonata of July 1819, show a growing expressive power, but they nowhere seek to escape from the stylistic ambience of *Spielmusik*. It is clear, however, from the opening bars of the sonata in A minor (op. 143) of February 1823 that Schubert has left that world behind.

Example 61

Here, and in the three sonatas of 1825, he seeks a compromise between the formal requirements of the sonata and the romantic principle of unity of mood. Often he seems to be reaching out beyond traditional forms in the interests of expressiveness, so that to a contemporary critic the A minor sonata of 1825 (op. 42), for instance, appeared to be more of a fantasy than a sonata.[1] These sonatas are more radical, more experimental in conception than those of 1828; there is more of the dynamic Schubert in them, and less of the dreamer. But however one strikes the balance, it will not be denied that they form a homogeneous group with quite distinct and definable characteristics.

This threefold division also works well in the case of the string quartets and the chamber music, provided only that an early date for the B flat trio is accepted; that same

---

[1] *Documentary Biography* (No. 632), *op. cit.*

dynamic vigour and lyrical intensity that characterises the piano sonatas of 1823 and 1825, and the Great C Major symphony, can be found, *mutatis mutandis*, in the two string quartets of 1824, in the Octet, and in the B flat piano trio. In the E flat trio and the string quintet other more introvert qualities make themselves apparent. Even the songs, so varied and so numerous as almost to defy classification except by author, can be seen, if we take the best examples of the early years, and set them beside those of 1823–5, and those of 1827–8, to follow the same trend towards a more personal, more subjective manner. The six Heine songs will serve well enough to represent the thirty-year-old Schubert; setting personal preferences aside, one might choose the earlier ones on a basis of popularity. Thus:

1814–18	*1823–5*	*1827–8*
Erlkönig	*Die junge Nonne*	*Der Atlas*
Gretchen am Spinnrade	*Auf dem Wasser zu singen*	*Ihr Bild*
Haidenröslein	*Du bist die Ruh*	*Das Fischermädchen*
Die Forelle	*Nacht und Träume*	*Die Stadt*
Der Wanderer	*Der Einsame*	*Am Meer*
An die Musik	*Im Abendrot*	*Der Doppelgänger*

There is progression here of a sort; though all are masterpieces, one is aware of the deepening emotional involvement, and the growingly expressive technical resources, of the master.

Thus it is possible to characterise with confidence the young Schubert's creative style, coming to fulfilment as it did in the years 1818 and 1819 in a series of works of a wonderful

freshness and originality—the 'little' C Major symphony, the
B flat piano duet sonata (D.617), the A major piano sonata of
1819, and the 'Trout' quintet. It is not difficult, either, to
find common characteristics in the great works which
signalled the climax of his middle period—the Great C Major
symphony, the piano sonatas of 1825, the Octet, the 'Grand
Duo' sonata, the two string quartets of 1824, the B flat piano
trio, the A flat major variations for piano duet (op. 35) and
many more. It is only in the last three years of his life that his
style is difficult to define 'horizontally', and that for two
reasons; both because works which properly belong to the
middle years have come to be associated with 1827 and 1828
and because the output of these final years is more uneven in
quality and more diverse in style than ever before.

The character of this final period is determined by Schubert's failure to achieve status and recognition as a composer
of instrumental music, and the financial security which would
enable him to write what he wanted. Instead, he was obliged
to compromise with the rising tide of virtuosity and triviality,
so that much of the output of these years bears the imprint of
popular taste either in its conception (*Der Hochzeitsbraten*) or
in its manner (the four Seidl refrain-songs) or both (the
Fantasia in C major for violin and piano opus 159, or *Der
Hirt auf dem Felsen*). Looked at in this way, Schubert appears
as the first victim of the democratisation of taste. Lacking the
ability of some modern composers to escape the dilemma by
regarding composition as a way of talking to oneself rather
than to other people, in these final years he appears in a kind
of dual role, writing one moment for the publishers and the
next for the invisible audience of posterity, in whose judgment he never lost faith. The juxtaposition of these two per-
sonalities is sometimes incongruous. The two Fantasias,

op. 103 and op. 159, were composed within a month or two of each other, but they inhabit different worlds. The string quintet and the last piano sonatas keep company with academic exercises which embarrass the Schubertian, so unmistakably do they anticipate the banalities of 'harmonium music'. This tension between the aspirations of the composer, and the need to come to terms with the relentless pressure of public taste increased steadily during his last years, and finally broke him down.

The disintegration of the composer's musical personality— perhaps diversification would be a better word—manifests itself in a kind of eclecticism. Schubert often sounds like Beethoven, but never more so than in the C minor piano sonata D.958. His choral compositions often take Haydn for a model, but never more obviously than in August 1828, when he wrote the dedicatory hymn 'Faith, Hope, and Charity'.

Example 62

This curious quality of musical empathy enables him to assume, in the last phase of his life, an astonishing number of creative disguises. As well as Schubert–Haydn and Schubert–

Beethoven, we find Schubert–Handel in *Miriams Siegesgesang*, Schubert–Chopin in the Grazer waltzes:

Example 63

Schubert–Wolf in *Der Doppelgänger*, Schubert–Lehár in the yodelling chorus at the end of *Der Hochzeitsbraten*, and alas, Schubert–Stainer in the Benedictus of the E flat mass:

Example 64

One might, at the risk of seeming captious, go on to identify Schubert–Fux and Schubert–Rossini, but enough has been said to make the point. The phenomenon is not peculiar to Schubert; it is everywhere apparent in other romantically tinged classical composers like Dussek and Hummel; but what makes the comparison disturbing is that it is not typical of composers of the foremost rank. It is usually the Dusseks of the creative world who, lacking a strongly individual character of their own, are most adept at disguising themselves in other men's clothes.

The miracle is that, side by side with the eclectic Schubert, the real one survived, chastened and ennobled by suffering and disappointment, to write the F minor duet Fantasia, the Heine and Rellstab songs, the last sonatas, and the string quintet. He lived to prove the truth of the words he had written in his diary years earlier, that 'pain sharpens the understanding and strengthens the mind; whereas joy seldom troubles about the former and softens the latter or makes it frivolous'. The final vision, however, is quite different in tone and temper from the earlier. Absorbed in the inner life, purged of the extrovert nature-worship which colours the work of his middle years, these compositions of 1828 present, in a distilled form, the essence of Schubert's imaginative vision. It is not to this world that the Great C Major symphony belongs. The symphony speaks of 'joy in widest commonalty spread', of the wanderer's quest. In 1828 the wanderer appears to have come to the end of his journey, and stands, looking inward not outward, absorbed in his own vision.

The fact gives a dramatic appropriateness to his early death, and to his life the satisfying wholeness of a work of art. When we consider that Schubert might well have lived on into the heyday of the romantic period, that he might have heard *Tristan*, and *Les Troyens* (parts of it at any rate) and at least the earlier symphonies of Brahms, this judgment runs the risk of seeming facile. But in one sense the consolation it offers to the Schubertian may not be altogether empty. The early romantics, who imposed upon the clear contours of classical forms their own fierce vision, were rarely able to sustain the full intensity of their imaginative fire for long. Wordsworth lived to be eighty, but the poetry by which he is remembered was all written before he was thirty-five. Keats's productive years were even fewer. Samuel Palmer's apocalyptic vision burst into full flower in 1825, and faded five years later, though he lived on into old age. There is something especially fragile and vulnerable about this first venturing forth of the romantic imagination, of which, in music, Schubert, is the supreme exponent. His music speaks, with a kind of consoling sadness, of a lost world of innocence and joy. The strength of his personal vision sustained him through a working lifetime of fifteen phenomenally productive years, none of them without its tally of masterpieces; and even at the end, plagued as he was by ill-health and disappointment, inspired his most eloquent and poetic music.

INDEX

INDEX

'Red Cross, The', 251
Refrain Songs, Four (Seidl)
Reil, Friedrich, 134
Reisebilder of Heinrich Heine, 188, 189
Rellstab, Ludwig, 189, 209, 215, 222, 223, 224, 268
Réti, Rudolph, 163, 179
Rinna, Ernst, 253
Robertson, Alec, 148
Rochlitz, Johann Friedrich, 128, 185
Romberg, Andreas, 111
Rondeau Brilliant, in B minor, for pianoforte and violin, 110, 115
Rondo in A major for piano duet (1828), 214, 215, 227–8
Rondo in D major (1818), 24n.
Rondo in E minor for piano duet, 29
Roner, Franziska, 187, 220
Rosa, Kunigunde, 14, 15, 112
Rosamunde, 44, 83, 231
Rossini, Gioacchino, 109, 148, 175, 179, 267
Rössler, Eduard, 184
Rückblick, 120, 121
Rückert, Friedrich, 20, 56
Rundell, Mrs., *New System of Domestic Economy*, 37

Salieri, Antonio, 42, 127, 135
Samori, 106
Sänger, Der, 139
Sängers Habe, Des, 65n., 261
Sauer and Leidesdorf of Vienna, 67
'Saul', 204
Schaeffer, Erwin, 120n.
Schechner, Nanette, 57, 58
Schelmann, Albert, 130
Schickh, Johann, 209, 236
Schiller, Friedrich von, 91, 198
Schindler, Anton Felix, 56, 57, 58, 80, 81, 97, 116, 128, 129, 202, 205, 218, 222, 223, 224, 229, 245, 249
Schlachtgesang, 198, 209
Schlosser, Louis, 112n.

Schober, Franz von, 15, 22, 23, 25, 26, 27, 28, 46, 47, 55, 56, 75, 90, 103, 106, 107, 108, 117, 118, 124, 125, 126, 133, 139, 147, 174, 184, 188, 189, 198, 220, 237, 246, 247, 252, 253, 256
Schöne Müllerin, Die, 101, 104, 118, 133, 148, 224
Schöne Welt, wo bist du? (*Die Götter Griechenlands*) D.677, 157
Schönstein, Baron Karl von, 15, 100, 189, 238, 251
Schott, B. and Sons, of Mainz, 29, 35, 63, 191, 192, 197, 198, 212, 213, 221, 248, 249
Schubert, Ferdinand, 32, 62, 63, 67, 73, 75–8, 85, 86, 87, 102, 116, 128, 143, 147, 211, 212, 247, 251, 252, 254, 255, 259
SCHUBERT, Franz:
autograph dates, 195–6
Beethoven, relations with, 126–9
circle, the Schubert, 22–3, 26–8, 45, 141
compositions of 1828, 21
creative method, 165–8
dance music, 149–51
development, 12, 13, 19–22, 23–4, 31–3, 94, 261–9
dotted notes, 135–9
Fantasia in F minor 1828, 178–84
Goethe songs, 31–3, 36
Graz, visit to, 142–9
Handel, influence of, 204–7
Heine songs, 188–90
Impromptus Opus 90, 163–5
income, 34–8
liturgical composition, 215–19
Mass in E flat, 240
method of performing his own songs, 130–1
Miriams Siegesgesang, 203–7
Moments musicaux, Op 94, 160–2
operas, 109, 147–8
personality, 13–15, 99–100, 111–114
public concert, 207–9
Quartet in G major, 1826, 49–53

277

Vogl, Michael, 14, 15, 21, 22, 30, 45, 55, 57, 107, 112, 113, 123, 129, 130, 131, 147, 208, 209, 227, 257
Vogler, Georg Josef (called Abbé), 105–6
Vor Meiner Wiege, 145n.

Wagner, Marie, 113, 131
Währing, suburb of Vienna, 47, 49, 55, 56, 117, 126, 209, 246, 255
Walcher, Ferdinand, 101, 132
Wanderer, Der, 264
Wanderer family, 107
Wanderer Fantasy, The, see Fantasy for pianoforte in C major
Wandern, Das, 224
Wanner, Leonhard, 232
Wasserfluth, 123, 137
Weber, Karl Maria von, 110, 111, 120
'Wedding Roast, The', see *Der Hochzeitsbraten*
Weigl, Josef, 115, 116
Weigl, Thaddäus of Vienna, 29, 67
Weimar, 39, 147, 217
Weinen, Das, 145n.
Weiss, Franz, 208
Widerschein, 215n.
Wieden, suburb of Vienna, 24, 116,

247, 255
Wiener Zeitschrift für Kunst, 132, 209, 236
Wildbach, 144
Wilhelm Meister songs, 31, 177n.
Winter, Peter von, 111
Winterreise, 20, 24, 30, 36, 93, 100, 101, 102, 103, 104, 119, 120–5, 133, 136, 142, 185, 187, 206, 225, 237, 248, 254
Wirtshaus, Das, 121, 122, 124
Witteczek, Josef Wilhelm, 15, 106, 107, 108, 187, 220, 258
Wolf, Hugo, 188, 267
'Wolf Preached at by the Geese, The', 174
Wordsworth, William, 269
Worlitzer, Frederic, 110

Young, Gerard Mackworth, 13

Zauberharfe, Die, 57
Zedlitz, Josef, 188
Zierer, Franz, 58n., 227
Zseliz, 29, 43, 71, 102, 118, 159, 177, 216, 260n.
Zur Eiche, 132
Zurich, 39, 48
Zwerg, Der, 91
Zwillingsbrüder, Die, 57